ANARCHY
AND THE
ENVIRONMENT

ANARCHY
AND THE
ENVIRONMENT

The International Relations of
Common Pool Resources

EDITED BY

J. SAMUEL BARKIN AND GEORGE E. SHAMBAUGH

STATE UNIVERSITY OF NEW YORK PRESS

Published by
State University of New York Press, Albany

For information, address State University of New York Press,
State University Plaza, Albany, NY, 12246

Production by Dale Cotton
Marketing by Dana E. Yanulavich

Library of Congress Cataloging-in-Publication Data
Anarchy and the environment : the international relations of common
    pool resources / edited by J. Samuel Barkin and George E. Shambaugh.
        p.   cm.
    Includes index.
    ISBN 0-7914-4183-0 (hc. : alk. paper).—ISBN 0-7914-4184-9 (pbk.
: alk. paper)
      1. Environmental policy—International cooperation.   I. Barkin,
J. Samuel, 1965–   .   II. Shambaugh, George E., 1963–   .
GE170.A52   1999
363.7'0526—dc21   98-41202
                                   CIP

10 9 8 7 6 5 4 3 2 1

Contents

Tables

Preface

This project evolved from a discussion we had about the state of the study of international environmental politics some five years ago. We were both dissatisfied with this literature, because it seemed to us that it was on the whole largely apolitical. Most attempts at general theorizing about international environmental politics, whether from the regimes literature or the market failure literature, began with the assumption of the "common enemy" of environmental threat, and of a collective action or tragedy of the commons situation that hindered international action to meet that threat. The study of international environmental politics thus became a process of finding the appropriate cooperative or institutional mechanisms to overcome the collective action problem. Like the functionalist literature on political cooperation and integration in the 1950s and 1960s, the issues to be dealt with were inherently transnational, but of a basically technical rather than political nature, and thus best addressed technically rather than politically. The measure of solutions to international environmental problems thus became the efficiency of the mechanism for dealing with overcoming collective action problems, rather than the viability of the political settlement underlying the mechanism.

This is unrealistic; international environmental issues are as heavily politicized as most other kinds of international issues. Ignoring this political element will neither make it go away nor make environmental degradation easier to address effectively. It is clear that all governments do not share similar interests in international environmental management, and they often have significantly different notions of what environmental management means. This volume, then, is part of a larger trend in the literature that is working to put the politics back into the study of international environmental politics. We have chosen to do so through the analytical lens of common pool resources, because this allows us to introduce these differences in interest within the framework of rationalist analysis that encompasses so much of the work done in this field.

We developed the hypotheses that are the focus of the analysis of this volume through a deductive examination of the logic of common pool resources, and the case studies were written to these hypotheses specifically. They were developed both by the volume editors and by the contributors to this volume, working as a group. This process of working through this logic, and examining its explanatory value for specific cases, was aided enormously by two workshops that brought the group together, one in the fall of 1995 and one on the spring of 1996. The first of these workshops, held at Georgetown University in Washington, DC, was funded by the Social Sciences Research Council/John D. and Catherine T. MacArthur Foundation, through their Program on International Peace and Security's research workshop grant program. The second was held in conjunction with the Annual Convention of the International Studies Association (ISA) in San Diego, and was funded by the ISA's Small Workshop Grant program. We owe both of these institutions a debt of gratitude; without these workshops this volume would be much less coherent than it has turned out to be.

Much of this volume was also presented on a panel at the 1996 meetings of the American Political Science Association, in San Francisco. Duncan Snidal was the discussant for the panel, and he commented extensively not only on those chapters presented as papers on the panel, but on the manuscript as a whole. Tom Teitenberg also read and provided highly useful and incisive comments on the whole manuscript. Patricia Weitsman and Jacqui Shambaugh provided invaluable project management advice. Renae Ditmer compiled the index. Finally, we would like to thank our chapter authors, who contributed both with their own work and to the process of developing the theoretical structure of the volume as a whole; without their input this volume would not have been possible.

Abbreviations

ICCAT	International Convention for the Conservation of Atlantic Tunas
IWC	International Whaling Commission
LCDP	Large Combustion Plant Directive
LRTAP	Long Range Transboundary Air Pollution
MMPA	United States' Marine Mammal Protection Act
NAFO	Northwest Atlantic Fisheries Organization
NGO	Non-governmental Organization
ODS	Ozone-depleting Substances
OECD	Organization for Economic Cooperation and Development
OEWG	Open-Ended Working Group
PG	Public Good
RAN	Resource Adjacent Nations
UNCLOS	United Nations Convention on the Law of the Sea
UNDP	United Nations Development Programme
UNEP	United Nations Environment Programme
UV	Ultraviolet Radiation

1 Hypotheses on the International Politics of Common Pool Resources

J. SAMUEL BARKIN

AND

GEORGE E. SHAMBAUGH

Introduction

On March 9, 1995, ships of the Canadian Coast Guard fired warning shots at and then boarded and impounded a Spanish fishing vessel on the high seas, outside of Canada's 200-mile exclusive economic zone (EEZ). Technically an act of war, this conflict represented one of the most direct military confrontations among North Atlantic allies in almost half a century. In one sense this confrontation was nothing new; there have been major disputes among countries over access to resources throughout history, the Gulf War being only the most extreme recent example. In other senses, though, it was new. It happened between two postindustrial countries with highly interdependent economies. It concerned an environmental resource, turbot,[1] about which both countries had signed a treaty and actively participated in an international management institution. And finally, the state generating hostilities, Canada, was more concerned with preserving the resource than exploiting it in the short term.

These three novel aspects to the Turbot War, as it is known in Canada, suggest that the management of international environmental goods may be generating increasing levels of political conflict. The resource in question, turbot, is not vital to the national economies of either Canada or Spain, as petroleum might be. And traditional national security considerations were not an issue. Yet two erstwhile allies got to the point of active hostilities over differing interpretations of how to best manage the resource, despite existing institutional arrangements designed to prevent that sort of situation. In other words, this example suggests that, as we approach the twenty-first century, disagreements over the management and conservation of our natural environment can lead to active conflict among countries with no other significant disputes, even when international institutions exist to manage and prevent such conflict.[2]

At the same time, international environmental agreements and institutions are proliferating. States continue to negotiate toward these agreements and institutions at an increasing rate. If such negotiations are to be successful, and if the institutions are to be effective, negotiators and designers of institutions must recognize the nature of international environmental issues. These issues have been considered in a number of ways in the international relations literature, from functional problems in need of technical resolution, to collective action problems, to traditional power politics situations. The way in which one evaluates the issue helps to determine how one approaches negotiating agreements and designing institutions. If international environmental issues are considered in a misleading way or modeled inappropriately, the negotiations and institutions are not likely to lead to effective solutions. To use again the example with which we began, the Northwest Atlantic Fisheries Organization (NAFO) was created on the premise that all signatories were primarily interested in maintaining the fish stock, and wished to distribute the costs and benefits of this maintenance fairly. This assumption proved incorrect; some of the signatories (such as Canada) were more interested in conservation for conservation's sake than others (such as Spain). The result was an institution that succeeded neither in maintaining the fish stock, nor in managing conflict over distribution of the resource.

This volume argues that the logic of common pool resources (CPRs) is the most appropriate and productive way to understand international environmental conflict. Evaluating environmental problems using a common pool resource framework is important in three particular ways. First, it highlights how the political dynamics of bargaining, problem recognition, and resource maintenance change as resource limits are recognized, and environmental goods formerly thought to be unlimited are recognized to be finite. Second, by highlighting the limited capacity of environmental goods to absorb uncontrolled consumption, the common pool resource approach forces policy makers and environmental scholars to confront the distributional issues associated with the maintenance and management of these goods. The CPR approach thus emphasizes the political rivalry associated with the maintenance and consumption of goods that can make the issue of relative gains critical in environmental negotiations. Third, by focusing on environmental goods that are rival, but from which no one can be effectively excluded, the common pool resource approach highlights a unique set of collective action and enforcement problems in international politics. This book analyzes these problems and uses them as a means to evaluate and expand on common hypotheses regarding the effect of the shadow of the future on current behavior, the role of the free rider in management regimes, and the role of market power in solving collective action and enforcement problems in international environmental management.

This chapter defines CPRs and discusses some of the ways in which they generate bargaining dynamics distinct from those found with purely technical issues or collective action problems more generally. The second chapter develops a typology of environmental issues that elaborates on this theme. The following chapters then look at these dynamics in the context of specific international environmental issues about which negotiations occurred and around which international institutions were created. Their findings highlight some of the insights that the CPR approach offers regarding questions of bargaining strategy and sources of leverage actors can exercise during international environmental negotiations, as well as the problems and solutions it suggests for securing the compliance of free riders and maintaining international environmental accords.

Common Pool Resources

We begin with a definition of our basic concept, the common pool resource. Two economic parameters within which goods, including environmental goods, can be located are rivalness and excludability. Rivalness means that consumption by one beneficiary directly subtracts from the ability of other potential beneficiaries to consume the good.[3] Conversely, a good is nonrival if the benefit one beneficiary receives from the good does not affect the amount of benefit other potential beneficiaries might receive. For example, petroleum is rival; if one person burns a gallon of gasoline, it is no longer available for others to use. A radio broadcast, on the other hand, is nonrival; the amount one person listens to a particular station does not subtract from the number of other people who can listen to it. Rivalness is usually seen as an intrinsic property of the good.

Excludability refers to the ability of one beneficiary to exclude others from access to the good. Nonexcludability thus means that once the good is available to anyone, no one else can be excluded from benefiting from it. Unlike the characteristic of rivalness, excludability is usually seen as not entirely intrinsic to the good, but contingent on social arrangements, particularly property rights. For example, software copyright laws make computer software in the United States an excludable good; the manufacturer can legally exclude someone from using a piece of software unless they have paid for it. In countries where intellectual property rights are more lax, software is a less excludable commodity. The partial dependence of the level of excludability of a good on property rights and other social conventions means that the characteristic of excludability can often be changed through political action, whereas the characteristic of rivalness cannot.

Goods can display varying degrees of rivalness and excludability. Chapter 2 will examine what happens when we acknowledge partial rivalness. But for the moment take these two parameters as dichotomous, meaning that goods are either rival or nonrival, excludable or nonexcludable. This yields a matrix containing four distinct types of goods, which will be referred to here as public goods, common pool resources, toll goods, and private goods (Table 1:1). Private goods are those we usually think of in terms of ownership. Examples

Table 1:1
TYPES OF GOODS

| | | **Excludable** | |
		Yes	**No**
Rival	**Yes**	Private goods	Common pool resources
	No	Toll goods	Public goods

range from automobiles to sandwiches, and include anything that we can possess exclusively, and that we can use up. Public goods are at the opposite end of the spectrum. They are goods that, if anyone can gain access to, everyone must be able to gain access to, and which we each can use without compromising the extent to which others can use them. National Public Radio and sunny days are two otherwise rather different goods that share the characteristics of publicness. Toll goods (sometimes referred to as club goods) are those to which access can be controlled, but which do not get used up. A free trade agreement or cable television can be thought of as toll goods. Nonsignatories or nonsubscribers can be denied the benefits of membership, but for those allowed in the good is not diminished (and can in some cases be reinforced) by increasing use.

Common pool resources are goods that display the characteristic of non-excludability, but are rival. If it is available at all, no one can be excluded from access to a common pool resource, but the amount that one party consumes of the resource affects the amount that others can consume of it. A classic example of this is an oil field that straddles national borders. All countries on top of the field can pump oil from it; short of the use of military force, none can be excluded from doing so. Yet unlike a public good, the oil field is rival; the amount of oil pumped by one country reduces the amount of oil left in the ground that will be available to other countries. While collaborative, efficient extraction of the oil is possible, the limited or unknown size of oil fields, combined with the tendency of oil in a field to migrate toward producing wells, has led to very fast, inefficient, and wasteful efforts by competitive drillers to extract as much oil as fast as possible. The amount of waste can be substantial.[4] This problem is often exacerbated by the "rule of capture," which stipulates that subsurface minerals belong to the party on whose land they are extracted. A wide variety of national legislation was enacted in attempts to address this problem in the United States since the 1930s.[5] Unrestrained oil production in the 1920s and 1930s in the United States resulted in an estimated recovery rate of 20–25 percent, while an estimated 85–90 percent would have been possible with managed drilling.[6] Whoever pumps fastest gets the most and is the winner, even if vast amounts of oil are wasted or lost as a result.

The same sort of dynamic can occur with renewable resources. The parallel between the situation discussed above and international maritime resources, for example, is quite marked. Fishing grounds on the high seas and straddling fish stocks are good illustrations. No one can be excluded from access to fishing on the high seas, but overfishing by one national fleet can deplete both the existing stocks and the ability of those stocks to replenish themselves. This will affect the amount that other national fleets can catch, both currently and potentially well into the future.

These four types of goods generate substantially different incentives for management. The main problem that arises in public goods issues is their supply. Since no one can be excluded from consuming a public good, there is an individual incentive to avail oneself of the good without paying for its provision, leading to a problem of undersupply. Common pool resources share this characteristic problem of supply, and also generate problems in the consumption of the good not shared by either pure public or private goods. With public goods, there is an incentive to undersupply, but no incentive to overconsume since consumption is nonrival. With private goods there is also no incentive to overconsume, since nothing is inherently gained by hoarding against oneself.[7] With common pool resources, however, there is an incentive both to undersupply and to overconsume. By overconsuming, one can arrogate a greater proportion of the common pool resource. Even if this means that the total amount of the resource is reduced, one's own consumption can be increased.

The combination of nonexcludability and rivalness in consumption means that there is a stronger individual incentive to exploit common pool resources than there is with either pure public or private goods. Management regimes are also more difficult to coordinate and enforce. Common pool resource issues thus entail different sorts of problems and different sorts of solutions than those demanded by issues relating to other types of goods. It thus matters how one models international environmental issues; it changes both how one sees the problem, and the sort of solution that one seeks. So it is worth first discussing why it is appropriate to model these issues as common pool resources.

International Environmental Issues

The proposition that many environmental issues can be usefully modeled as CPRs is not a new one. Much of the literature on domestic resource management in both political science and economics has focused on CPRs,[8] and there has even been some application of this type of analysis to international environmental issues.[9] This volume advances a much stronger proposition, though; that all political issues of international environmental management, that is, all international environmental issues that generate international political conflict, show some characteristics of common pool resources. More particularly, it is specifically these characteristics that generate the conflict. To make this argument, it is useful to begin by disaggregating international environmental issues into two general types, *appropriation* issues and *provision* issues.[10]

Appropriation refers specifically to the use of the good itself. More technically, with appropriation the relationship between the supply of the good and the level of inputs required to produce or maintain that supply is assumed to be given. Provision refers to the resource facility, in other words the creation, maintenance, or improvement of the environment within which the good is located, and which is required for the good to retain its value. "In other words, in appropriation problems, the *flow* aspect of the CPR is what is problematic. In provision problems, the *resource facility or resource stock* of the CPR is problematic."[11] To use the seminal example of a commons issue, the allocation of grazing rights in a common field is an appropriation issue, while preventing the degradation of the field through pollution or encroachment by other uses is a provision issue.[12] Differentiating between appropriation and provision issues, it should be noted, is contingent on the specific definition of the good in question, in other words, on what the focus of the environmental issue is. For example, if wetland fowl are the environmental good in question, then maintaining a healthy wetland is a provision issue. If the wetlands themselves are the good in question, either as parkland or as a pollution sink, then maintaining the wetland is an appropriation issue.

Crucially, though, the provision and the appropriation aspects of a given issue need not display the characteristics of the same type of good. The provision of a good can have CPR characteristics even when the appropriation of that good displays public goods characteristics. International environmental disputes all display the characteristics of CPRs either in their appropriation or their provision. The two most common sources of environmental disputes, and arguably the two comprehensive sources, resource and pollution issues, demonstrate this point. Disputed international resources, like oil fields and fishing grounds, are common pool issues. These issues involve goods that are rival; if they were not rival, there would be no source of dispute. Nonrival resources, such as stratospheric ozone, do not generate conflict in their use. And if the resources are not to be found nonexcludably among more than one country, then they would not be international. More specifically, though, it is the appropriation of these goods that has CPR characteristics.

International pollution problems also involve significant common-pool resource aspects, but in their provision rather than their appropriation. For example, fresh air is often cited as an example of a public good. This is clearly true of its appropriation, but in a way misplaces rather than clarifies the issues surrounding the politics of fresh air issues. The ability to consume a good like fresh air is not the problem; rather, the problem is the generation of pollution that hinders this consumption. It is the provision of fresh air, in other words the maintenance of the resource stock by restraining the use of the environment as a pollution sink, rather than the appropriation of clean air for breathing, that becomes the issue to be negotiated internationally. The uses and abuses of pollution sinks present a common-pool resource problem. As with a public good, no one can be excluded from polluting the air. Unlike a public good, however, supply is not indivisible, since the ability of an environment to absorb pollution is not unlimited. Before those limits are recognized, the political issues involved are likely to be minimal, given the lack of adverse perceived effects from polluting. After a point, as the health and welfare effects of pollution multiply, the existing level of pollution will hinder the ability of others to pollute without adverse effects. Recognition of these effects leads to the kind of political confrontation characteristic of common pool resources. Political disputes surrounding the control of air pollution can thus be better characterized as common pool resource issues than as public goods issues. The same logic can be applied more generally to other international pollution issues, from water pollution to ozone-depleting chemicals to greenhouse gasses.

To this point we have formally defined CPRs, but the discussion of international environmental issues has referred to goods with CPR characteristics. Formally speaking, a pure CPR is a good that is entirely nonexcludable but completely rival. This construction, though, is an ideal type. There are many goods that are not pure CPRs by this definition, but still create the sort of political dynamics one would expect from a CPR. These goods need not be perfectly rival and nonexcludable. As long as they are largely nonexcludable and display a significant degree of rivalness, they can still generate these dynamics.

From the point of view of political analysis, the key difference between CPRs on the one hand and both public and private goods on the other is subtractability of benefit. With private goods, the owner of a good gains a set benefit from a particular good, independent of the actions of others. Since the good is fully excludable, other potential beneficiaries cannot gain access to it. Therefore, they cannot directly subtract from the ability of the owner of the good to gain benefit from it.[13] Similarly, with public goods one actor's level of benefit depends on the degree to which the good has been provided in the first place, but not on the consumptive activities of others. Once a public good has been provided to a given degree, any consumer can benefit from it up to that degree, without affecting the benefit that other consumers can derive. In other words, the level of benefit from a public good, once provided, is fixed, and is not affected by the behavior of others.

With CPRs, though, this level of benefit is variable. Given a certain amount of the good provided, the level of benefit that one actor can derive depends very much on the behavior of others. More specifically, consumption by one actor subtracts from the level of benefit available to other actors. This creates rivalry over the distribution of benefit. Moreover, it means that large actors cannot provide reliably for their own benefit. Large actors, or groups of large actors, can provide public goods on their own. Noncooperation by others cannot reduce the level of benefit these actors derive from the good once provided. As a corollary, the smaller the group, or the more unequal the size of the participants in a group, the more efficiently it will be able to provide public goods.[14] The same is not true of CPRs, though. As long as noncooperative actors can subtract from the level of benefit of a good, rather than simply withhold contribution to it, it no longer makes sense for large actors, or small groups, to provide it. In order for it to be worthwhile for any actor to participate in the provision of a CPR, they must be able to insure against active noncooperation; they can no longer simply ignore it. A good, then, shows the characteristics of a CPR when, despite the size of the group or of the largest actors within it, noncooperative actors can no longer be ignored.

It is this dynamic—overconsumption by some that diminishes benefits available to others—that characterizes international environmental conflict, and which will be elaborated on in the hypotheses below. This dynamic is not active in all international environmental issues, but it is always a latent problem. In latent CPR problems cooperation in the short term need not be problematic, and political conflict need not arise. It is when resource limits are recognized and consumption ceases to be seen as nonrival that the use and management of international environmental resources become political issues. Thus the fact that an international environmental issue has become politically contentious suggests that a common pool resource dynamic is at work. It should be stressed at this point that we are not arguing that the logic of common pool resources can capture all of the dynamics of international environmental politics. The conclusion to this volume will discuss in some detail how the CPR argument fits with and complements other approaches to the study of the management of the global environment. At the same time, these dynamics cannot be fully understood without acknowledging the CPR element.

Hypotheses

The argument developed in the previous section suggests that the logic of common pool resources is necessary to fully understand negotiations among states concerning international environmental issues, where such issues are politically contentious. This does not at all mean that a common pool resources approach is the only reasonable approach to understanding international environmental politics. It is useful in studying interactions among states on these issues, given state interests. Other approaches are necessary to understand state interests themselves—their domestic sources and how they can be changed, the dynamics of nonstate actor involvement in international environmental issues, and the creation of scientific and technical consensus on sources, degrees of threat, and solutions to environmental degradation, to name three among many areas of study within the broad rubric of international environmental politics. Yet understanding the political dynamics of state interaction in the broad subset of international environmental issues for which individual state interests differ remains crucial to successfully creating and enforcing mechanisms for dealing with these issues.

As suggested above, there is an existing extensive literature on common pool resources. There is also an extensive literature on international cooperation. Unfortunately, these two bodies of literature do not always address each other as directly as they might. The literature on common pool resources often focuses on situations that do not reflect the circumstances of international relations. Efforts to address the specific and formal characteristics of common pool resources have tended to focus on domestic settings, looking primarily at resources that lie entirely within national jurisdictions.[15] The literature in international relations that discusses formal cooperation among states has, similarly, rarely looked at the dynamics of common pool resources specifically. This literature has often characterized international cooperation as a collective action problem or as a prisoners' dilemma game.[16] Common pool resource situations can be reasonably characterized in either of these ways. However, so can a variety of other situations. The prisoners' dilemma game, for example, has often been used to describe public goods situations, and can describe toll goods situations as well. Collective action problems similarly describe a broad range of issue types. Thus the literature on formal international cooperation is useful in describing situations that can include common pool resource issues. The greater precision gained from addressing the dynamics of common pool resource situations specifically, however, can be of great value in understanding in a more detailed and nuanced way the incentives facing states negotiating about international environmental problems.

This volume is designed to do just that, by deducing and describing a set of hypotheses on the effects of common pool resource issue structures on cooperation in managing international environmental problems. These hypotheses all reflect the nature of two key characteristics of international politics, anarchy and oligarchy; anarchy in the sense that there is no higher authority to enforce agreements, and oligarchy in the sense that there are certain countries that are big enough to significantly affect international outcomes on their own. These two characteristics differentiate the dynamics of interstate negotiations on common pool resource issues from, for example, interpersonal negotiations, where there are often enough parties involved that the actions of individuals average out, and where there is usually some form of higher authority to enforce agreements. The hypotheses are divided into three general sections, which discuss the issues of time horizons, free riders, and market power, respectively. Time horizons are always a factor in international environmental issues, and as such provide the most general set of hypotheses. Free ridership implies a preexisting set of standards against which behavior can be judged, delimiting the domain of the second set of hypotheses to situation where these standards exist. And finally, the market power hypotheses apply in the narrowest set of cases, those in which countries with sufficiently large markets are willing to use them to promote environmental cooperation.

All three of these sets of hypotheses are relevant to the creation of institutions for managing the international environment. Knowledge of overuse of a common pool resource increases the significance of relative gains, diminishes the shadow of the future, and makes international environmental issues more prone to conflict. Collective action-based analyses tend to stress the "public enemy" nature of environmental negotiation. They assume that the basic purpose of all participants is to combat environmental problems, and look at ways in which institutions can be created that overcome obstacles to dealing with environmental harm. But in CPR situations, with the increased salience of consumption issues, distributional conflicts are likely to be more pronounced. This is particularly true in an international setting because of its anarchical nature, creating particular enforcement problems, and its oligopolistic structure, with several states big enough to make a real difference to international environmental outcomes on their own. Realist analyses would suggest that, given the greater potential for relative gain in CPR situations as compared with other collective action situations, state action with respect to international environmental management will likely focus on relative gains, on the distribution of costs and benefits among states.[17] In order to make such management more successful, this focus needs to be taken into account at the outset of negotiations on any particular environmental issue.

Time Horizons and the Likelihood of Cooperation

Environmental problems are often modeled as Prisoners' Dilemma games. In this case, lengthening the shadow that the future casts on current decision-making is one of the dominant strategies game theory offers to encourage cooperation.[18] The length of an actor's shadow of the future captures the extent to which that actor's decisions are influenced by the expectation of beneficial future interaction within a specific issue-area. If an actor values the future benefits of an environmental good almost as much as its present benefits, then it does not make sense for a state to cheat on an agreement for gains in the short term at the expense of potentially far greater gains in the long term.[19]

The effects of the shadow of the future are much more complex and problematic in CPR negotiations than with collective action problems more generally. The initial prediction drawn from the rational cooperation literature in international relations, that lengthening the shadow of the future for all parties will increase the likelihood of cooperation, should hold for CPRs as well as in other collective action situations. The dynamics of the negotiation process change radically, though, when the assumption of equal shadows of the future and parallel changes in those shadows is relaxed. Recognition of the limits of a CPR does not stop cooperation from taking place, but it can shift the outcome of those negotiations toward the preferences of the actor with the relatively shorter shadow of the future. In negotiations over public goods, countries can do no more than withhold participation in the supply of a good. In negotiations over CPRs, though, countries with shorter shadows of the future can also credibly threaten to consume the good at a far greater rate than countries with longer shadows would prefer. A principal characteristic of common pool resource problems is that the resources in question are limited to some degree. Consumption in the present, therefore, affects the ability to consume in the future. This logic is fairly straightforward with nonrenewable resources. The amount consumed in the present reduces the amount left to consume in the future. It is also true of renewable resources; if they are over-consumed in the present, they will not renew themselves at a rate sufficient to replenish their stocks and allow for continued consumption at current levels.

Threatening to overconsume a renewable common pool resource is a threat to reduce the base from which the rate of renewable future consumption is determined.

A threat to overconsume[20] is most credible when it comes from the country perceived to have the shorter shadow of the future for the resource in question. That is, the country that places a higher value on present relative to future gains. In contrast, the country with the longer shadow of the future places a higher value on future relative to present gains. It is less costly for the country with a shorter shadow of the future to overconsume in the present because it places a relatively lower value on potential future gains than it is for the country with the longer shadow that places a higher value on the potential future gains. This cost differential only increases over time: the longer the overconsumption lasts, the more it will cost the country with the longer shadow relative to the country with the shorter shadow. Therefore, by threatening to delay an agreement and overconsume, the country with the shorter shadow of the future can threaten to generate costs for other countries that it will not have to bear. The fact that nonagreement will be more expensive for one country will place the other country in a stronger bargaining position.

We would thus expect this dynamic to be particularly acute with common pool resources because the overconsumption can reduce the total gain to be had in the future. A threat to continue holding out in negotiations while overconsuming is equivalent to a threat to reduce the total future benefit available. Since future benefits are valued more highly by the country with the longer shadow of the future, it is in its interest to achieve agreement quickly and thereby preserve the future value of the resource. In this sense, the country with the longer shadow of the future has a strong incentive to behave in a concessionary way with respect to the country with the shorter shadow of the future to secure an agreement as quickly as possible. In other words, the country with the shorter shadow of the future should have bargaining power relative to the country with the longer shadow. This argument leads to our first hypothesis:

H1a: If consumers recognize different shadows of the future, or if potential agreements affect these shadows differently, then the consumer(s) with the shorter shadow of the future should have greater bargaining power than those with longer shadows.

Because the resource is limited, the longer overconsumption lasts, the more it will cost the country with the longer shadow relative to the country with the shorter shadow. Since future benefits are valued more highly by the country with the longer shadow, it will have a stronger incentive to reach an agreement as quickly as possible.

H1b: Over time, an actor with a shorter shadow of the future should increase its bargaining leverage over an actor with a longer shadow if it threatens to delay an agreement or to overconsume at any point during the negotiations.

The final hypothesis in this first group relates to a common assumption underlying many liberal approaches to international environmental management, that all states share some interest in preserving their environment. The corollary of this assumption is that all states should be willing to contribute in some way to this management. If a state's shadow of the future is short enough, though, this need not necessarily be the case. If a CPR consumer's shadow of the future is short enough, in other words if that actor has little enough concern for the future existence of a particular environmental good, then the present value of overconsumption of that good may be greater than the value of future consumption foregone. In such cases it makes sense for the consumer to overconsume the good to the point of extinction. This can make a threat to destroy the good credible, which in turn can generate considerable bargaining power. Since a country with a sufficiently short shadow of the future might then be able to credibly threaten to reduce the future availability of the good to zero, it might also then credibly hold the environmental good in question for ransom. In this situation, any settlement that countries with longer shadows of the future reach that acts to preserve the environmental good is an improvement.

H1c: A country with a short enough shadow of the future can wield a credible threat to destroy a CPR, and thus may be able to extract concessions from other potential CPR beneficiaries up to the total future value of the resource.

Common Pool Resources and the Role of the Free Rider

It is commonly accepted in the literature on collective action problems that a key source of the problem is "free riders." These are actors that accept the benefits provided by collective action, without contributing to the costs of providing it. Free riders are understood here to be those countries that either do not conform to an existing international standard of behavior with respect to an environmental issue, or fail to fulfill the obligations of existing or proposed treaties on such an issue. In public goods situations, free riders fail to contribute to the costs of providing a resource. With CPRs actors can free ride either by failing to contribute to the provision of a good, or by overconsuming that good, thus decreasing the amount that other actors can consume. Overconsumption in this context refers to consumption that is greater than that allowed by an existing internationally accepted baseline for consumption of an environmental amenity. Since all but the largest actors have an incentive to free ride, the costs of collective action—either the costs of provision or the costs of foregone consumption—can be difficult to collect. This in turns tends to lead to the underprovision or overconsumption of the good that the group is collectively acting to manage. In a pure public good situation, free riders are a nuisance, given that their presence may inhibit the optimal supply of a public good; however, once the public good has been established or supplied, their presence does not affect anyone else. Since consumption of the good itself is nonrival, distribution issues regarding the consumption of the good are unimportant.[21]

If the good is a CPR, then distributional issues involving access to the resource, the amount and timing of consumption, and the general distribution of the benefits and costs of exploitation become central concerns for all participants. Since consumption of the good is rival, consumption by any actor directly reduces the amount of a good others have access to. The ability to inflict costs on others by diminishing the amount of a good available to them changes the free rider from a nuisance to an important political actor. The costs that free riders can impose in CPR situations can potentially be much larger than the costs of free riding to the provision of public goods. In a public good (PG) situation, the cost cannot be greater than the actors own potential contribution to institutional management. In CPR situations the cost is not only this lost contribution, but also the total amount that the free rider chooses to overconsume. In the extreme case, when a free rider can make a credible threat to destroy a resource, these costs can approach the total value of the environmental good. The free rider should then be able use this potential for creating costs as bargaining leverage. In fact, we would expect that free riders should be able to extract concessions up to, but not beyond, the point where the value of these concessions is equal to the benefits others would receive from joint management relative to competitive exploitation of a CPR.

H2a: Once resource limits are recognized, free riders should be able to gain concessions in environmental negotiations that approach the costs (economic, social, and political) that they can impose by overconsuming the CPR.

The severity of the effects of free-rider problems is related to the relative size of the largest actor or actors. The larger an actor relative to the whole group, the more it will lose from underprovision or overconsumption of a collective good relative to its savings from free riding. If the largest actor is big enough, it then becomes rational for that actor to manage the good on its own, whether or not others contribute.[22] In international relations theory such an actor, a state large enough that it undertakes to provide systemic management on its own, is often called hegemonic. This literature defines two kinds of hegemons, benevolent and coercive.[23] Benevolent hegemons are those that underwrite the costs of providing collective goods on their own, without enforcing cooperation on others. Coercive hegemons are those that undertake to enforce cooperation, through coercion of other states if necessary.

With public goods, hegemons can compensate for free riders by simply making up for their contribution to the supply of the good. This makes benevolent hegemony a viable mechanism in PG situations. With common pool resources, if the hegemon fails to secure the compliance of all free riders with environmental management agreements, it may be unable to compensate for free riders if they threaten to overconsume the CPR. As a result, benevolent hegemonic solutions to collective actions problems are likely to be ineffective in CPR situations.

H2b: Benevolent hegemonic solutions in environmental negotiations will not necessarily facilitate collective management of environmental problems because the hegemon cannot guarantee that the CPR will be maintained.

Although benevolent hegemonic solutions to international environmental issues understood as common pool resource problems may be infrequent, there is actually more scope for coercive hegemonic solutions in CPR situations than in PG situations. In PG situations, a hegemon should be willing to impose a solution when the contribution withheld by a free rider is greater than the costs of extracting that contribution through threats or negative sanctions. In CPR situations, a hegemon should be willing to impose a solution coercively when the costs of overconsumption by a free rider are greater than the costs of enforcing cooperation. Since the costs of overconsumption can be far greater than the costs of contributions withheld, coercive hegemonic solutions are more likely to be viable in CPR than in PG situations.

H2c: Since free riders can undermine benevolent hegemonic solutions in CPR situations, coercive hegemony will be the preferred form of unilateral management of CPRs.

Finally, the level of excludability of a CPR should affect the propensity to free ride. If a CPR is perfectly nonexcludable, then the maximum cost that a free rider will bear from its overconsumption can be no greater than proportional to its size. If a good is rival and perfectly excludable, then it is a private good, and free riding makes no sense as all the costs created by free riding are born internally. With private goods, a free rider is cheating only on itself. As the degree of excludability increases, the incentives to free ride should decrease, until at some point the incentive disappears entirely. As an example, imagine an oil field that lies under several countries. If oil migrates freely from any part of the field to any other part, then it is perfectly nonexcludable, and the incentive for each country to free ride is highest. If for some reason the oil does not migrate between countries at all, then the oil field is actually a private good, with each country able to exclude the others from that portion of the oil under its territory. In this case, there is no incentive to free ride. As the propensity of the oil to migrate toward the countries that are pumping fastest decreases, the incentive for the countries on top of the oil field to free ride on joint management agreements should decrease as well, as more of the costs of free riding are internalized. Similarly, the greater the propensity of a type of pollution to stay within the country that generated it, the weaker the incentive should be for that country to free ride on international efforts to manage that type of pollution.

H2d: The more the cost of free riding is internalized by the actor in question, the weaker its incentive to free ride.

Market Power

Given the ability of countries with short shadows of the future to alter the outcome of CPR negotiations to their benefit, and their willingness to consume the majority of the resource if the outcome of negotiations does not reflect their interests, the ability of other actors to influence the bargaining process can be extremely important. One way is through the use of market power. Countries with large enough markets for the environmental good in question should be able to use those markets to influence the value of the good, and therefore the incentive structures facing other states.

Much of the literature on CPRs treats the value of the resource as constant and the preferences of CPR exploiters as fixed. Yet the current and future value of common pool resources need not necessarily remain constant, and changes in their value can have a dramatic effect on resource management. While long shadows of the future facilitate joint management efforts, high elasticity of demand for a CPR tends to increase the incentives for individual exploitation and diminished the likelihood that cooperative agreements will be reached.[24] High elasticity of demand means that small decreases in the price of a good will lead to large increases in the quantity demanded. If this is the case, increasing the quantity supplied by overexploiting a CPR in the short term will have little effect on the price per unit of the good. Total income to the exploiter will therefore increase almost proportionally to the amount of the CPR consumed. The resource discussed at the beginning of this chapter provides a good example. On the one hand, turbot tends to be sought after more because it is relatively cheap than because it is particularly tasty. As such, a slight decrease in price, giving it an extra increment of price advantage over other similar species of fish, should increase demand quite a bit. The corollary of this is that a large increase in the amount of turbot supplied to the international market can be cleared by reducing its price only slightly. It thus makes sense for a fleet intent on maximizing profits in the short term to fish as much turbot as possible. Diamonds, on the other hand, have a lower elasticity of demand. This means that large increases in amounts supplied will lower the market price significantly. Profits in the diamond industry are best maximized through restricting rather than expanding the quantity sent to market.

Therefore, anything that can alter the value of the resource or decrease the elasticity of demand for it should increase the likelihood of cooperation. Actors that can decrease the elasticity of demand for a common pool resource should as a result be able to influence the outcome of international environmental negotiations. An example of a change in elasticity of demand for an environmental good might be a change in the primary use of a forest from a source of wood to a source of tourism revenue.[25] If, as is likely, tourism in the forest has a lower elasticity of demand than logging, the incentives for competitive exploitation will diminish.

H3a: If an actor can decrease the elasticity of demand for a CPR or increase the potential future value of the resource, then it should decrease the incentive for competitive exploitation and increase the likelihood of CPR management.

Common pool resources are nonexcludable. This means that the end users of CPRs should have multiple possible sources of supply. Except in a few circumstances, there are likely to be multiple fishers or oil companies from which to buy fish or oil. As a result, CPR exploiters must compete with each other and can usually exercise only minimal control over the price they charge for their goods. Consumers, however, may be able to influence the price and value of the goods in question. The greater proportion of the good a consumer purchases, and the fewer alternate consumers there are, the more that consumer should be able to influence the price or value of the good. A consumer that purchases a sufficient proportion of the good to affect the price at which it is bought or sold should be able to exercise a large amount of market power in negotiations over the exploitation of a common pool resource. If a large consumer decides not to purchase the consumptive benefits of a CPR from a supplier, the value of the CPR to that supplier should diminish. As a result, we would expect a 'market hegemon' to be able to affect the value of CPR extraction, and thereby alter CPR negotiations and management by threatening to decrease the value of CPR exploitation to others. For example, the United States is the world's largest consumer of shrimp. The United States decided in 1991 that only shrimp caught in a certain way so as to protect sea turtles would be allowed into the country. This dramatically lowered the market value of shrimp caught in turtle-unfriendly ways, and had the effect of changing the behavior of most of the Western Hemisphere's shrimpers.[26]

H3b: Large consumers, or countries with large consumer markets, should be able to gain bargaining power by using their markets to alter the value of CPR extraction for others. This leverage should increase as the number of alternate markets decreases and as more consumers join the process.

Research Design

The cases in this volume test these three sets of hypotheses on the political dynamics of CPR management by analyzing a range of issues within the general heading of international environmental politics. The issues that these studies look at are ones in which actual management institutions have been negotiated. This allows us to look at CPR dynamics where negotiations may involve actual and substantial redistribution of resources. These cases cover a range of issues from fisheries management to the control of airborne pollutants. They all focus on the negotiation and success of actual authoritative mechanisms for managing international environmental problems.

Before these case studies are presented, Ronald Mitchell's chapter complements this introduction theoretically by looking at different ways in which environmental resources can be valuated, and by discussing the ways in which international environmental problems differ from their domestic equivalents. He expands the notion of an environmental resource, capturing the idea that people can conceive of natural systems as providing benefits simply through their existence, as well as or instead of through their consumption. He then discussed the effects this distinction might have on the dynamics of international environmental politics, and the ways in which these effects are to be differentiated from their effects on domestic environmental politics. This introduction and Mitchell's chapter thus provide the theoretical framework that the case studies address.

Elizabeth DeSombre analyzes the international politics of the management of tuna fisheries. She looks at two different international agreements established to regulate tuna fishing, one in the Pacific and one in the Atlantic Ocean. She then examines attempts to regulate tuna fishing techniques in order to prevent the incidental killing of dolphins, and addresses the puzzling question of why attempts to manage the tuna stock to preserve catch levels, which benefits tuna fishers in the long run, have largely failed, whereas attempts to manage tuna fishing techniques to preserve dolphins, which provides no direct benefit to tuna fishers, have been notably more successful. Christopher Joyner's chapter on the management of marine living resources in the Southern Oceans complements DeSombre's analysis by discussing a regime that attempts to manage marine resources by region rather than by species. He examines the Convention on the Conservation of Antarctic Marine Living Resources (CCAMLR), and analyzes the shifts in incentives that promoted the increased effectiveness of the regime in the late 1980s and early 1990s. He also questions the long-term prospects of the regime, and asks what future changes would undermine its recent effectiveness.

David Downie's chapter examines the negotiations to curtail the production of ozone-depleting substances. He looks at these negotiations from a

CPR perspective, asking what effects differentials in lengths of shadows of the future had on the resulting agreements, and how the ability of free riders to destroy the ozone, combined with their willingness to absorb risk or harm, affected their bargaining strength in multilateral management negotiations. Furthermore he suggests that the ability of a free rider to overproduce ozone-depleting substances means that the underlying CPR problem cannot be fully solved. As a result, ozone management must be flexible in order to respond to changes in perceptions, interests, and bargaining dynamics in response to changes in actual and perceived patterns of resource valuation and consumption. The ultimate solution rests with altering the incentive structure of actors, as is being attempted through phase-out schedules and the Multilateral Fund in the Montreal Protocol. Barbara Connolly's chapter examines the issue of acid rain in Europe. This case traces the evolution of individual states' knowledge and perception of how they are affected by acid rain, and asks how this change affected states' interpretations of the sort of problem that acid rain generated for them. She also asks how a group of comparatively small Nordic states managed to secure the compliance of the larger European countries with international regimes to limit acid rain.

Richard Matthew explores the factors that predict whether common pool resource disputes will end in cooperative management agreements or armed conflict. His chapter situates this volume within the broader debate about environmental security. In particular, he analyzes the impact of free riders and differing shadows of the future on the potential for conflict in CPR management. Finally, we conclude by reviewing the success of the hypotheses presented in this introduction in explaining the dynamics of international environmental politics, and by situating the discussion of the politics of common pool resources in the broader framework of the larger literature on international environmental politics.

Table 1:2
HYPOTHESES

Shadow of the Future

H1a: If consumers recognize different shadows of the future, or if potential agreements affect these shadows differently, then the consumer(s) with the shorter shadow of the future should have greater bargaining power than those with longer shadows.

H1b: Over time, an actor with a shorter shadow of the future should increase its bargaining leverage over an actor with a longer shadow if it threatens to delay an agreement or to overconsume at any point during the negotiations.

H1c: A country with a short enough shadow of the future can wield a credible threat to destroy a CPR, and thus may be able to extract concessions from other potential CPR beneficiaries up to the total future value of the resource.

Role of the Free Rider

H2a: Once resource limits are recognized, free riders should be able to gain concessions in environmental negotiations that approach the costs (economic, social, and political) that they can impose by overconsuming the CPR.

H2b: Benevolent hegemonic solutions in environmental negotiations will not necessarily facilitate collective management of environmental problems because the hegemon cannot guarantee that the CPR will be maintained.

H2c: Since free riders can undermine benevolent hegemonic solutions in CPR situations, coercive hegemony will be the preferred form of unilateral management of CPRs.

H2d: The more the cost of free riding is internalized by the actor in question, the weaker its incentive to free ride.

Market Power

H3a: If an actor can decrease the elasticity of demand for a CPR or increase the potential future value of the resource, then it should decrease the incentive for competitive exploitation and increase the likelihood of CPR management.

H3b: Large consumers, or countries with large consumer markets, should be able to gain bargaining power by using their markets to alter the value of CPR extraction for others. This leverage should increase as the number of alternate markets decreases and as more consumers join the process.

Notes

1. Technically called Greenland halibut, turbot is a species of fish that straddles the Canadian EEZ in the North Atlantic.

2. There is an established literature on environmental sources of international conflict. See, e.g., Thomas Homer-Dixon, "Environmental Scarcities and Violent Conflict: Evidence from Cases," *International Security*, vol. 19 (1994), pp. 5–40, and Norman Myers, *Ultimate Security: The Environmental Basis of Political Stability* (New York: W. W. Norton, 1993).

3. There are a number of different terms used for this characteristic, including rivalness, jointness of supply, and subtractability. These terms are all used interchangably in the literature.

4. Friedel Bolle, "On the Oligopolistic Extraction of Non-renewable Common-pool Resources," *Economica*, vol. 53 (1986), pp. 519–27.

5. James L. Smith, "The Common Pool, Bargaining, and the Failure of Capture," *Economic Inquiry*, vol. 25 (1987), pp. 631–33.

6. The existence and rate of oil extraction also affects other wells on an oil field by lowering amount of oil and reducing the pressure for the field as a whole, making the remaining oil more difficult and costly to extract. Gary Libecap and Steven Wiggens, "Contractual Responses to the Common Pool: Pro-rationing of Crude Oil Production," *The American Economic Review*, vol. 74 (1984), p. 88.

7. This is why privatization is often seen as a potential solution to common pool resource problems. Privatization essentially means creating a legal mechanism for making a good excludable. A CPR that is made excludable becomes a private good. Once this privatization has occurred, the incentive to overcomsume, in other words to hoard, disappears because one is subtracting from one's own future consumption, not the future consumption of others.

8. Some examples of this literature, from the fields of economics and of political science, include Bolle, "On the Oligopolistic Extraction of non-renewable Common-pool Resources"; Daniel W. Bromley, *Environment and Economy: Property Rights and Public Policy* (Oxford: Blackwell, 1991); Garret Hardin, "The Tragedy of the Commons," *Science*, vol. 162 (1968), pp. 1243–48; Libecap and Wiggens, "Contractual Responses to the Common Pool: Pro-rationing of Crude Oil Production"; Elinor Ostrom, *Governing the Commons: The Evolution of Institutions for Collective Action* (Cambridge: Cambridge University Press, 1990); Martin F. Price, "Temperate Mountain Forests: Common-Pool Resources with Changing, Multiple Outputs for Changing Communities," *Natural Resources Journal*, vol. 30 (1990), pp. 685–707; Smith, "The Common Pool, Bargaining, and the Failure of Capture"; Glenn Stevenson, *Common Property Economics: A General Theory and Land Use Applications* (Cambridge: Cambridge University Press, 1991); Richard Sweeney, Robert Tollison, and Thomas Willett, "Market Failure, The Common Pool Problem, and Ocean

Resource Exploitation," *The Journal of Law and Economics*, vol. 12 (1974), no. 1, pp. 179–92; and Michael Taylor, "The Economics and Politics of Property Rights and Common Pool Resources," *Natural Resources Journal*, vol. 32 (1992), pp. 633–48.

9. For an example of an attempt to address both domestic and international issues within the context of CPRs, see Robert O. Keohane and Elinor Ostrom, eds., *Local Commons and Global Interdependence: Heterogeneity and Cooperation in Two Domains* (London: Sage Publications, 1995). They also argue that almost all goods have some CPR aspect to them, an argument very similar to the one made here. Keohane and Ostrom, pp. 14–15.

10. This distinction follows that suggested by Elinor Ostrom, Ron Gardner, and James Walker in *Rules, Games, and Common Pool Resources* (Ann Arbor: University of Michigan Press, 1994).

11. Ibid., p. 9.

12. Hardin, "Tragedy of the Commons."

13. This refers to the actual use, rather than the sale, of the good. Other potential beneficiaries can affect the market price of the good if the market for that good is less than perfectly competitive.

14. Mancur Olson, *The Logic of Collective Action: Public Goods and the Theory of Groups* (Cambridge, MA: Harvard University Press, 1965), pp. 22–36.

15. In political science, the best single example is likely Ostrom, *Governing the Commons.*

16. See, for example, Kenneth A. Oye, ed., *Cooperation Under Anarchy* (Princeton: Princeton University Press, 1986), Robert Axelrod, *The Evolution of Cooperation* (New York: Basic Books, 1984), and Robert O. Keohane, *After Hegemony: Cooperation and Discord in the World Political Economy* (Princeton: Princeton University Press, 1984).

17. In one of the few explicitly Realist analyses of an international environmental issue, Stephen Krasner found just this, and concluded the logical corrolary, that relative national power was a key determinant of outcomes. Krasner, "Global Communications and National Power: Life on the Pareto Frontier," *World Politics*, vol. 43 (1991), pp. 336–66. Realists derive their emphasis on relative gains from the need to maximize national power, whereas the emphasis here comes from the inherently zero-sum (and in some cases negative-sum) nature of common pool resource extraction. Despite the different sources of this emphasis, though, the focus on relative gains generates similar political dynamics.

18. The shadow of the future refers to a phenomenon roughly similar the discount rate, as economists use that term. To avoid confusion, we will stick with "shadow of the future" terminology. It should be kept in mind here that lengthening a shadow of the future is equivalent to decreasing a discount rate, and a short shadow of the future is equivalent to a high discount rate.

19. This hypotheses is developed in more detail by Kenneth Oye in Oye, ed. *Cooperation Under Anarchy*, pp. 16–18.

20. Overconsumption in this context refers to consumption at a rate greater than the rate that countries with longer shadows of the future are willing to accept. It should be noted that this usage changes slightly in the next set of hypotheses.

21. For an example of oligopolistic cooperation to provide public goods in which distribution issues regarding consumption are assumed to be negligible, see Duncan Snidal, "The Limits of hegemonic Stability Theory," *International Organization*, vol. 39 (1985).

22. This is shown mathematically in Olson, ch. 1.

23. For a review of this literature, see David A. Lake, "Leadership, Hegemony, and the International Economy: Naked Emperor or Tattered Monarch with Potential?" *International Studies Quarterly*, vol. 37 (1993), pp. 459–89.

24. Thomas, J. (1992) "Cartel Stability in an Exhaustible Resource Model," *Economica*, vol. 59, p. 279–93.

25. This example follows the discussion in Price, "Temperate Mountain Forests: Common-Pool Resources with Changing, Multiple Outputs for Changing Communities."

26. Elizabeth R. DeSombre, *Domestic Sources of International Environmental Policy: Industry, Environmentalists, and U.S. Power* (Cambridge, MA: Ph.D. Thesis, Harvard University, 1996), pp. 219–25.

2 International Environmental Common Pool Resources: More Common than Domestic but More Difficult to Manage

RONALD B. MITCHELL

Introduction

This volume's introduction argues that "all international environmental issues that generate international political conflict, show some characteristics of common pool resources." This chapter builds on this argument to develop a framework for understanding the factors that make common pool resource (CPR) dynamics more likely at the international level but make collective management at the international level less likely and less successful. Why are the appropriation and provision problems that bedevil domestic environmental management exacerbated when more than one nation is involved? This chapter argues that nations face greater difficulties in resolving international environmental problems than equivalent domestic ones because the problems are greater and their solutions more elusive. International environmental amenities face greater appropriation problems than corresponding domestic ones because the types of demand placed on the amenity are likely to be more rival, the aggregate level of demand is likely to be higher, and institutional mechanisms to constrain demand are less likely to be available. These amenities face greater provision problems because the incentives and capacity to create and maintain international institutions that could ensure their provision are weaker than in the domestic context.

Definitions

I refer to "environmental amenities" rather than environmental "goods" or "resources" to capture the notion that humans increasingly conceive of natural systems as providing existence (e.g., biodiversity) and nonconsumptive (e.g., scenic views) benefits as well as traditional consumptive benefits (e.g., lumber or fish).[1] Any given amenity has different "aspects" or "characteristics," and it is these characteristics, rather than the amenity itself, that are the source of its value to humans.[2] In analyzing the politics of different environmental problems, we may mislead ourselves by classifying a given amenity as a public good or a CPR since that amenity may be a public good in one aspect and a CPR in another. As Robert O. Keohane and Elinor Ostrom note, "The public goods–CPR distinction is more appropriately used to classify specific aspects of a physical resource rather than to characterize the physical resource as a whole."[3]

Discussing environmental problems in terms of "appropriators consuming environmental resources" causes us to ignore the broader range of environmental problems that involve costs imposed on those who value an amenity's nonconsumptive or existence benefits. Indeed, various ecophilosophies see the human habit of treating nature as a resource as the precise cause of many environmental problems.[4] To capture consumptive, nonconsumptive, and existence benefits in a single term, I refer to all actors who derive value from an environmental amenity as "beneficiaries" rather than as users or consumers. This chapter addresses the problems that arise from the processes by which humans derive benefits from an existing environmental amenity as well as those that arise from the processes by which humans re-create and maintain those amenities. The former "appropriation" problems involve static, time-independent, allocations of benefits while the latter "provision" problems involve dynamic, time-dependent, problems of ensuring a qualitatively and quantitatively healthy future stock of the amenity.[5]

Environmental Amenities and Their Appropriation

Any environmental amenity may provide three types of benefits to human society.[6] It may provide humans with the "consumptive benefits" of using the divisible units of the amenity's resource flow, the "nonconsumptive benefits" of access to the amenity's total stock, or the "existence benefits" from knowledge of the amenity's existence.[7] A public forest, for example, "may be valued for timber production, for a variety of environmental services [such as hiking], or merely for its existence value" as wilderness.[8] Consumptive benefits depend on the quantity and quality of the resource flow from an environmental amenity. Nonconsumptive and existence benefits depend on the quantity and quality of the resource stock.

Prior to the creation of a social institution to regulate or exclude appropriators, the existence and type of appropriation problems plaguing an environmental amenity depend on two factors: the type of benefits people derive from the amenity and the level of demand for those benefits. The former determines the potential type of conflict that may arise, the latter whether that conflict actually does arise. Whenever people value an amenity for its consumptive benefits, the potential for quantity rivalry or overappropriation exists; whenever they value it for its nonconsumptive benefits, the potential for quality rivalry or congestion and crowding exists; and whenever they value it for its existence benefits, no potential for rivalry exists. A potential rivalry will develop into an actual rivalry, that is, a CPR issue will become a CPR problem, whenever the demand for certain benefits from an amenity approaches or exceeds the ability of that amenity to supply the benefits derived from that amenity, that is, its carrying capacity. As demand approaches carrying capacity, a group of consumptive beneficiaries face the threat of overappropriation while a group of nonconsumptive beneficiaries face the threat of crowding or congestion. In contrast, a group of existence beneficiaries do not face any similar threat because, no matter how many beneficiaries there are, the nature of their demands on the amenity are such that the amenity has an essentially infinite carrying capacity. Put differently, consumptive beneficiaries impose negative externalities on other consumptive beneficiaries and nonconsumptive beneficiaries do likewise, while existence beneficiaries do not impose such externalities.

Often, people derive value from an environmental amenity by consuming some portion of the flow of resource units from that amenity.[9] Such beneficiaries are using the amenity as a rival good. The level of consumptive benefits actually derived depends on the quality and quantity of the flow. Consumptive benefits, by definition, preclude others from deriving benefits from the same resource unit. One beneficiary's consumption reduces the resource units available to other consumptive beneficiaries. Although any unit of a rival good that I consume becomes unavailable to anyone else, if aggregate demand remains sufficiently below the capacity of the amenity to supply resource units (the consumptive carrying capacity), no problem arises. An adequate flow of resource units ensures that other beneficiaries continue to have access to resource units sufficient for their demand and that they do not need to expend additional resources to gain access to those resource units. However, as aggregate consumptive demand approaches the amenity's consumptive carrying capacity, each additional resource unit consumed reduces the resource units available to other consumptive users. Each appropriator begins to impose a negative externality on other actual or potential consumptive beneficiaries. All activities involving consumptive benefits have the potential for such quantity rivalry.[10] Amenities that face the possibility of such overappropriation or quantity rivalry among competing consumptive beneficiaries can be conceived of as CPRs, with open-access fisheries providing the traditional example in which each fisher appropriates some number of fish that are no longer available to others.[11]

An amenity may also, however, face problems of quality rivalry or "congestion" that differ from the common conception of CPRs as caused by quantity rivalry among consumptive beneficiaries. Nonconsumptive uses depend on the quality and quantity of the whole stock of the amenity rather than the quality and quantity of the units flowing from that stock.[12] Nonconsumptive users do not preclude others from engaging in similar nonconsumptive use. Because such users do not consume units of the amenity, the quantity of the amenity remains uninfluenced by demand. Indeed, at low aggregate levels of demand, nonconsumptive beneficiaries may not even reduce the quality of the amenity. However, when nonconsumptive demand approaches the nonconsumptive carrying capacity of the amenity, the benefits each nonconsumptive user derives decrease. Instead of overappropriation, crowding results. All nonconsumptive beneficiaries still have the same access to the benefits of the amenity but the quality of the amenity and hence of those benefits declines. Indeed, pollution problems (as demonstrated by the cases in this volume) often exhibit congestion-type dynamics, exhibiting quality rivalry problems with quite different incentive structures than quantity rivalry problems. Rather than the symmetry of classic CPR dynamics, degraders of an amenity's quality need not be victims of that degradation: polluters often impose negative externalities on others without experiencing any of those effects themselves. In such situations, incentives and capacity to remedy the problem are delinked: the nonbeneficiary polluter has the capacity to remedy the problem but would receive no endogenous benefits by doing so, while the beneficiaries of lessened pollution, not being polluters themselves, lack the capacity to remedy the problem other than through side payments.

The threat of crowding or congestion to a nonconsumptive beneficiary comes from other nonconsumptive beneficiaries.[13] For example, when too many hikers frequent Yosemite National Park, the Park does not have fewer "units of wilderness," but rather has less of the quality of wilderness. A hiker can still hike for the same number of days but the quality of that experience is decreased. Long before allowing one more hiker into the park requires the removal of an existing hiker from the park (quantity rivalry), the quality of wilderness has been lost. Quality rivalry can be considered as a distinct form of rivalry. Alternatively, it can be considered as a form of partial rivalry, located along a spectrum between purely rival goods for which "an agent's consumption of a unit of a good fully eliminates any benefits that others can obtain from that unit" and purely nonrival goods for which, when an agent derives value from the amenity, the ability of all other potential beneficiaries remains completely undiminished.[14]

Purely nonrival goods exist when people derive exclusively existence benefits from an amenity. The existence benefits derived are a function of the quality and quantity of the amenity stock. However, deriving such "inherently nonrival" benefits does not degrade the quality or quantity of the resource system or its flow.[15] For truly nonrival beneficiaries, the derivation of existence benefits imposes no externality on other existence beneficiaries, regardless of the level of demand for such existence benefits. With respect to existence beneficiaries, the carrying capacity of the amenity is essentially infinite and no risk exists of quantity or quality rivalry. Those people who derive pleasure from knowing that certain species have been preserved even though they never plan to make consumptive (hunting) or nonconsumptive (watching) use of those species will not have less pleasure if additional *existence* beneficiaries know about the preservation of those species. Allowing new or existing actors to derive additional existence benefits from the amenity entails no marginal costs to those already deriving benefits, and does not induce crowding or overappropriation.[16] In short, new beneficiaries leave "as much and as good" for all other beneficiaries.[17]

To summarize, consumptive, nonconsumptive, and existence beneficiaries face the potential for quantity rivalry, quality rivalry, and no rivalry, respectively. Potential rivalries become actual when the demand for the benefits of the amenity approach the amenity's carrying capacity. A particular environmental amenity will lie along a spectrum of rivalry, ranging from no rivalry to complete rivalry.[18] Appropriation problems never arise for existence beneficiaries. Nor do they arise for consumptive and nonconsumptive beneficiaries so long as the amenity's carrying capacity sufficiently exceeds demand. Whether inherently nonrival or empirically nonrival, these amenities can be properly characterized as public goods so long as no potential beneficiaries are currently excluded.[19] When demand approaches the carrying capacity, however, potential rivalries become actual. Each actor deriving additional benefits from an amenity reduces the quantity or quality of the benefits available to those already deriving similar benefits from that amenity.[20] Although crowding is absent in the winter, during the summer the number of hikers can reduce, even to zero, the pleasure of hiking in Yosemite National Park as each additional hiker reduces the quality of the Park's "wilderness." Similarly, relatively low levels of initial demand make a previously unexploited fish stock a public good in which the first harvests from the stock do "not reduce the quantity available to others since the remaining fish have an increased opportunity to grow until maturity. . . . As more and more harvesting occurs, however, rivalry increases and fisheries become CPRs."[21]

Thus, we can identify the characteristics of any given amenity from which no actors have yet been excluded into three "ideal types." "Public goods" refer to those environmental amenities valued for their existence benefits regardless of the level of demand as well as those valued for their consumptive and nonconsumptive benefits so long as aggregate demand is low enough to avoid actual rivalry. "Congestion CPR problems" involve those amenities in which the aggregate demand for nonconsumptive benefits approaches the

Table 2:1
RIVAL/NONRIVAL DEMAND

	Consumptive Benefits	Nonconsumptive Benefits	Existence Benefits
Rival: Demand Exceeds Carrying Capacity	Overappropriation problem (quantity rivalry)	Congestion problem (quality rivalry)	Public good
Nonrival: Demand Does Not Exceed Carrying Capacity	Public good	Public good	Public good

nonconsumptive carrying capacity, creating quality rivalry. "Overappropriation CPR problems" involve those amenities in which the aggregate demand for consumptive benefits approaches the consumptive carrying capacity of the amenity, creating quantity rivalry.

Why the International Setting Creates More Difficult Appropriation Problems

CPRs are traditionally characterized by the fact that they face overappropriation or congestion problems as well as underprovision problems. This and the next section explore the reasons why the dynamics characteristic of international relations tend to increase the likelihood of both overappropriation and underprovision. Why should we expect CPR overappropriation problems and CPR congestion problems to be more common at the international level? How does the international context make rivalry, and hence overappropriation, more likely, all other things being equal, than it would be at the domestic level?

To investigate how international dynamics contribute to overappropriation, first consider appropriation of an amenity during a period for which the carrying capacity is fixed.[22] The foregoing section argued that overappropriation or congestion will become more likely the greater the share of total demand placed on the amenity by consumptive or nonconsumptive, rather than existence, beneficiaries. In addition, overappropriation or congestion become more likely the greater the total demand on the amenity. International environmental amenities are more likely to experience overappropriation or congestion because both the type and level of demands on an amenity are likely to be greater than at the domestic level.

Any environmental amenity is likely to face a wider range of types of demand under conditions of globally common access than under conditions of national access. The diversity in social, cultural, and economic preferences across countries means that, even if citizens of one country value a particular environmental amenity only as a source of existence benefits (or do not value it at all), citizens of other countries may value the amenity for its consumptive or nonconsumptive benefits. Consider the sea urchin population of the west coast of the United States. When considered simply as a domestic environmental amenity, to the extent Americans value this amenity at all, they do so only for its existence value, that is, as one of many species that they would like to preserve. However, with the opening of global free trade, the Japanese preference for sea urchin meat as a food (known as umi) has placed a consumptive demand on the resource. That demand has been sufficient to produce overappropriation of the sea urchin resource that, in turn, has required governmental regulation of American sea urchin divers. Even very high American demand for the existence benefits of a healthy sea urchin stock would not produce rivalness among Americans because of the inherently nonrival nature of existence benefits. However, the differential preferences introduced when the American sea urchin stock becomes a global, rather than national, amenity places new types of demand on that amenity making overappropriation more likely. Although allowing global access (even if through American divers serving the Japanese market) to a previously national amenity increases the level of demand, the change in the type of demand alone would increase the possibility of appropriation problems. Increasing the number of nations and cultures placing demands on an amenity increases the likelihood that some of that demand will involve consumptive or nonconsumptive benefits, introducing the possibility for quantity or quality rivalry and, hence, overappropriation or congestion.

The different types of demands on an amenity introduced by the greater heterogeneity of cultural values across nations also increase the aggregate amount of demand. In many cases, one nation's demand on an amenity would not, by itself, create an overappropriation or congestion problem. Transforming that resource from a national to a global amenity can create such problems, however, because the combination of that nation's demand with other nations' nonconsumptive or consumptive uses may exceed the amenity's carrying capacity. For example, the aggregate demands on the stock of elephants, tigers, and other endangered species reflects the aggregation of both domestic beneficiaries using the species stock as a source of food, and foreign beneficiaries using the species stock as a source of luxury goods, medicines, or other resources. Similarly, the aggregate demand on a tropical forest reflects the combination of domestic beneficiaries using the forest for firewood and foreign beneficiaries using the forest for lumber. Thus, even when a single beneficiary group's demand does not exceed the amenity's carrying capacity, the aggregation across groups of different types of beneficiaries often can induce CPR overappropriation dynamics. Overappropriation dynamics, therefore, will be more common the greater both the number and the heterogeneity of preferences of the countries with access to the amenity.

Finally, international environmental amenities are subject to greater overall demand as well as a greater likelihood of the rivalry-inducing demands of consumptive and nonconsumptive beneficiaries. Demand on an international amenity is more likely to exceed carrying capacity, and hence entrain overappropriation problems, simply because more actors will seek to avail themselves of the amenity. Even when transnational preferences are homogenous, that is, for example, if the amenity provides only consumptive benefits, aggregate demand will increase as more humans have access to it.

This discussion raises the importance of exclusion and other mechanisms for limiting demand, and hence averting or mitigating overappropriation or congestion problems. Many governments treat amenities providing consumptive and nonconsumptive benefits for which demand does not exceed carrying capacity (see Table 2:1 above) as public goods, refraining from limiting access or excluding appropriation by their citizens. From an international perspective, however, most such amenities are more accurately viewed as "toll goods" (currently nonrival but excluded). National borders serve as the means to exclude foreign nationals from access to the amenity. Amenities which are, or are treated as if they are, transnational or international lack even this basic mechanism of exclusion to limit demand. In cases where the amenity is inherently nonrival because it provides existence benefits, borders do not provide an effective means of exclusion.

As Barkin and Shambaugh note in the introduction to this volume, "excludability is usually seen as not entirely intrinsic to the good, but contingent on social arrangements." Put differently, exclusion is a function of both the amenity in question and the rules adopted to regulate access to that amenity. This suggests three classes of amenities. For "nonexcludable" amenities, inherent characteristics of the amenity make creation of social arrangements to control access either technologically impossible or prohibitively expensive. Economists have traditionally viewed lighthouses as such an amenity, since beneficiaries can neither be excluded nor readily charged.[23] Social arrangements separate the remaining excludable amenities into "excluded" amenities and "nonexcluded" amenities. International imperatives pose greater obstacles to the establishment of institutional arrangements to limit demand on the amenity than do domestic imperatives. Therefore, nonexcluded amenities will compose a larger fraction of excludable amenities internationally than domestically.

Successful resolution of CPR problems at the domestic level usually requires either governmental intervention or a strong sense of community with frequent interaction among interested actors.[24] Governments can, and sometimes do, exclude access to excludable amenities to reduce demand and keep the actual level of rivalry below that at which CPR dynamics develop. Access can be excluded by establishing property rights, imposing taxes, or other policies. For example, some governments establish enforceable licenses for fisheries within their exclusive economic zones. Pigouvian taxes and other forms of pollution charges have gained increasing support in the literature as more discriminating mechanisms for reducing overappropriation.[25] Incentives, the ability to pay, and self-selection rather than fiat determine who has access to the environmental amenity. Charging for access solves appropriation problems by leading those deriving the least benefits from the amenity (or with the fewest economic resources) to reduce their appropriation levels.

Norms and practice make these domestic solutions to overappropriation uncommon internationally. The absence of centralized regulatory control and enforcement and the obstacles to decentralized control and enforcement through collective action at the international level make it more likely that actors will not, in fact, be excluded from excludable amenities. Even when actors have clear incentives to cooperate, the anarchy of international relations makes formation of appropriate international institutions or regimes difficult. The international realm is divided into the sovereign territory of states, where the state itself has exclusive jurisdiction to dictate the rules of access, and the international commons of the high seas, Antarctica, and the atmosphere where access is determined collectively. Although exclusion is possible, experience in international fisheries and deep seabed minerals illustrates the obstacles to international collective action.[26] Though charges or taxes might also be possible, states have proved unwilling to establish the supranational institutions to which those charges or taxes would be paid. In short, the preconditions for resolution of international CPR problems by effective constraints on demand are less frequent internationally, if they exist at all. This inability to constrain demand internationally will make unredressed CPR problems more likely.[27]

The international arena produces fewer incentives to create constraints on demand as well as less ability to provide them. Rivalry among different nations or nationals of different nations over a given amenity is likely to be more intense than rivalry among nationals of a single nation. Certainly competition among the beneficiaries of an environmental amenity, whether whalers, fishers, or polluters, can be intense even within the domestic context. Even if we admit that relative gains concerns about market share (as well as absolute gains concerns about profits) play an important role in competition among firms domestically, realist theory suggests that these relative gains concerns are even more prevalent among states internationally. States that view economic activities that extract resources from, or pollute, an environmental amenity as linked to their national survival will be inclined to increase their demands on the amenity to harm other countries as much as to benefit themselves. The relative gains concerns of states therefore will make the demands placed on an international environmental amenity systematically greater than those placed on an otherwise-similar domestic environmental amenity.

Finally, even when states are not specifically concerned with relative gains and conversion of economic resources into military might, rivalries can be intensified by levels of pride and patriotism that do not enter into domestic demands on an amenity. The Turbot War and the Anglo-Icelandic Cod War provide two illustrations of how the rivalry over fish stocks and other environmental amenities have greater potential for rivalry when two or more nations are involved.

Environmental Amenities and Their Provision

The preceding discussion has assumed that an environmental amenity already existed at a given quantity and quality to highlight the difficulties that can arise strictly in relation to appropriation of an existing environmental amenity. Indeed, analysis based on such an assumption is accurate and sufficient for those environmental amenities whose future health does not depend on current human activities. For some environmental amenities, such as total available land, number of satellite slots, or electromagnetic bandwidth, human activity in time period T has little if any influence on the quality or quantity of the environmental resource available in time period $T+1$. Consumptive use of such resources makes them unavailable to other current users but they become immediately re-available as soon as the first actor's consumptive use ends. Such problems may pose grave appropriation problems but pose no underprovision problems. However, the future quantitative and qualitative health of most environmental amenities does depend on present human activities. Indeed, it is precisely because CPRs face both overappropriation/crowding problems and underprovision problems that they prove particularly difficult to resolve.[28] This section discusses the different causes for underprovision to provide the foundation for the subsequent section's analysis of why underprovision is likely to be more prevalent at the international level than at the domestic level.

Underprovision of environmental amenities may be driven by three quite different dynamics: demand-side underprovision, beneficiary supply-side underprovision, and nonbeneficiary supply-side underprovision. Demand-side underprovision involves cases in which the future carrying capacity of an environmental amenity depends on the level of current demand on that amenity. In such problems, actors that derive current benefits from an amenity also wish to derive future benefits from that same amenity, but influence the amenity's future ability to provide those benefits by the very behavior by which they derive current benefits. For the fixed stocks of nonrenewable resources, such as fossil fuels or minerals, each unit consumed by a current beneficiary is neither any longer available to other current consumptive users (the appropriation problem) nor to any future consumptive users (the provision problem). Current use will also reduce the future stocks of renewable resources whenever the current appropriation rate exceeds the amenity's natural renewal or replenishment rate. Whether dealing with living resources, like forests, or nonliving resources, like water for irrigation, current appropriation influences the likelihood of future underprovision. The common failure of open access fisheries to constrain current demand to ensure the future flow of fish from the stock constitutes a "demand-side provision problem."[29]

"Supply-side provision problems" also plague CPR problems.[30] These can take the form of either beneficiary supply-side provision problems or nonbeneficiary supply-side provision problems. In the former, actors that derive current benefits from an amenity wish to derive future benefits from that same amenity but cannot influence the amenity's future ability to provide those benefits except through behaviors independent of the behavior by which they derive current benefits. Thus, they must contribute resources today, not just constrain demand, to ensure the amenity is available in the future. In what is essentially a combination of a collective action problem and an investment problem, actors must contribute current resources to a collective effort to provide for the future of the amenity. Those who expect future benefits from an amenity may need to undertake activities to ensure its provision that are unrelated to the activity by which they will benefit from that amenity. The failure of hikers to help finance trail maintenance or of the nations of the world (as beneficiaries of a stable global climate) to cut back on their emissions of carbon dioxide illustrate such "beneficiary supply-side provision problems."

However, the future health of many environmental amenities requires action by nonbeneficiaries rather than beneficiaries. A clean environment often requires polluters to stop polluting even though they may place no value on the cleaner environment that doing so creates. For example, the waste-disposal companies that must alter their disposal techniques to protect the marine environment may not view themselves as benefiting from the healthier ocean they help provide. Such nonbeneficiaries will not help supply the CPR unless some pressure *external to the CPR problem* is brought to bear on them.

Underprovision results whenever any of these three sources—beneficiary demand-side provision, beneficiary supply-side provision, or nonbeneficiary supply-side provision—are inadequate to meet future demand for the amenity. Each source of underprovision presents quite different obstacles to resolution, however. Specifically, an amenity whose future health or carrying capacity depends on beneficiary demand-side provision will face incentive but not capacity problems; those in which future health depends on beneficiary supply-side provision problems face incentive and capacity problems; and those in which future health depends on nonbeneficiary supply-side provision face extremely strong incentive problems and may also face capacity problems.

Consider the classic tragedy of the commons: the future carrying capacity of the commons depends on the cowherds reducing the number of cows they currently graze on the commons. We can characterize many overappropriation problems in this way: those who must exercise current restraint on demand are the ones who will benefit if they are collectively able to do so. Future underprovision arises not because of an incapacity for current restraint (the cowherds are capable of grazing fewer cows), but because of the disincentives to exercising such restraint posed by the temptation to shirk or free-ride oneself and the fear that others will shirk or free-ride. The problems of such interactions have been extensively explored in the commons and prisoners' dilemma literature. Despite the many obstacles to resolution posed by such beneficiary demand-side provision problems, the actors who must contribute to future provision of the amenity will benefit if the amenity is adequately provided and so have some, if inadequate, incentives to contribute to its provision, and also have the capacity to contribute to the future provision of the amenity by the restraint of their current demand on it. Beneficiary demand-side provision problems are a major source of underprovision for many CPR problems.

Beneficiaries, being both perpetrators and victims of their own excessive demand, have positive incentives to contribute to such collective action, even if these may not outweigh countervailing incentives to defect from such action. Educational strategies can sometimes overcome these dilemmas simply by providing information that clarifies to perpetrators that they are also victims, a process that seems to explain much of why states have reduced sulfur emissions in Europe.[31] Axelrodian Tit-for-Tat strategies have the virtuous feature that current self-restraint simultaneously contributes to the future health of the amenity by directly reducing demand on the amenity and serves as a contingent threat to revert to overappropriative behavior if others do not also reduce their demand on the amenity. Since future amenity health depends on current demand, beneficiaries have the ability to contribute to future amenity health simply by restraining current demand. There is also an inherent, if not always compelling, logic linking restraint of one's current demand on the flow of benefits from a resource to ensure the future flow of benefits from that resource.

Beneficiary supply-side provision problems face similar disincentives exacerbated by the possibility of an incapacity to provide for the health of the environmental amenity. Whether contributing to the future stock of an amenity by restraining their demand or by providing other resources to facilitate replenishment of that amenity, beneficiaries face the same incentive problems of being concerned about possible shirking by others and being tempted to shirk themselves. However, if the behavior by which actors derive benefits from the amenity is unrelated to the behavior by which they ensure the future health of the amenity, the obstacles to successfully remedying the CPR problem will be even greater. First, negotiating rules on how much different beneficiaries should contribute usually proves more difficult than negotiating how much they should restrain demand, even if the latter is rarely simple. Determining the relative benefits each participant is deriving and hence how much they should contribute to the future health of the amenity proves far more difficult than requiring all beneficiaries to reduce their demand by a fixed percent. Compare the relative ease with which the beneficiary demand-side provision problems of acid precipitation or CFC emission reductions have been negotiated with the difficulties in negotiating the beneficiary supply-side provision requirements to provide funds for reductions by developing countries. Second, more actors are more likely to lack the capacity and resources to contribute or, at least, plausibly to argue that they lack such capacity and resources. The restraint required by demand-side provision does not involve such problems. Beneficiary supply-side provision problems are common for both CPRs and for public goods that are nonrival in character. Both beneficiary supply-side provision problems and demand-side provision problems do, however, have the ability to induce beneficiaries to contribute, through positive action or restraint, to the provision of an environmental amenity by excluding shirkers from the benefits of the amenity once provided.

Nonbeneficiary supply-side provision problems face the greatest obstacles to resolution. Such situations can best be characterized as pure negative externalities: the future health of the amenity often depends on the behavior of actors who do not perceive themselves as receiving any direct benefit from the current or future existence of that amenity. In such cases, the perpetrator is not also victim. The loggers who must change their behavior to preserve habitat for certain species may not see any benefit to doing so. The oil companies that must incur costs to prevent oil spills may not value the cleaner ocean that results. This interposes a distributional element that makes political resolution particularly difficult. Perpetrators that truly do not perceive themselves as victims have no incentives whatsoever to contribute to future provision of the amenity that their behavior is depleting. Unlike the shirkers or free-riders who cause beneficiary demand-side and beneficiary supply-side provision problems, nonbeneficiaries do not perceive themselves as benefiting even if the amenity is provided.

In such arenas, even adopting the longer time horizons implied by longer shadows of the future (see chapter 1) will not induce perpetrators to restrain their demands on the amenity. Clarifying the "costs" of an actor's behavior will not produce incentives to reduce that behavior, if the actor is not the one bearing those costs and does not care about those who are. Likewise, strategies of retaliatory noncompliance (Axelrodian Tit-for-Tat) will have no impact on their behavior. Compare fishing to oil pollution. In a fishery (a beneficiary demand-side provision problem), a company can, at least logically, credibly threaten to recommence unrestrained fishing to induce other companies to maintain their commitments to a regime: because of its desire to derive future benefits from a healthy fish stock, the fishing company is a victim of the current behavior of itself and other fishing companies. In oil transportation (a nonbeneficiary supply-side provision problem), threats by one oil transporter to recommence ocean pollution will not influence other oil transporters: an oil transporter is not the victim of its own or others' current behavior and so cannot threaten or be threatened by strategies involving changes in the level of that behavior.[32]

Why the International Setting Creates More Difficult Provision Problems

Like appropriation problems, features of the international context exacerbate the provision problems common to CPRs. Why should we expect underprovision to be more common internationally than domestically? Several reasons present themselves. Whether underprovision results from demand-side problems or supply-side problems, the international context poses the same obstacles that face appropriation problems: low demand for resolution and a low ability to provide resolutions. States face as strong incentives to free-ride on provision of an amenity from which they benefit as they do to free-ride on consumption of that amenity once provided. International anarchy, interstate rivalry, relative gains concerns, and the other factors discussed above reinforce each state's dominant strategy of not contributing to the future health of the amenity. States that will benefit from the amenity face two potential futures: if other states do not contribute, the amenity will not be provided and therefore making a contribution requires the state to incur a present cost with no future benefit; if other states' contributions do provide the future amenity, the noncontributing state can still derive future benefits without incurring those present costs. In the international context, even if the state might realize an absolute gain by contributing (that is, future benefits would exceed present costs), the fears of relative losses increase the dominance of the shirking option. States that must contribute to the health of an amenity but do not benefit from its provision (nonbeneficiary supply-side providers), such as an upstream or upwind polluter, will have no incentives to refrain from activities that are economically advantageous to them.

At the domestic level, governments often serve to aggregate preferences across perpetrators and victims. Although individuals always benefit by externalizing costs, victims of externalized costs who are citizens of a single state can pressure governments to force perpetrators to internalize those costs. Indeed, a common role of government is to eliminate privately optimal, but socially suboptimal, externalities. Governments, at least representative ones, can aggregate preferences across perpetrators and victims of environmental externalities so that they can identify when social costs of an externality exceed social benefits, and can induce the necessary behavioral changes by perpetrators. Governments can mediate conflicts between actors with heterogeneous interests and incentives. Unlike in the international sphere, governments can force actors who have no interest in resolving a problem to contribute to its resolution nonetheless.

In contrast, international institutions are considerably weaker for aggregating such preferences and for inducing necessary behavioral changes, where they exist at all. The provision of international solutions to force the internalization of externalizing behaviors that are nationally optimal but internationally suboptimal is notoriously wanting. Governments can, and may have incentives to, force individuals who derive no benefits from a given amenity nonetheless to contribute to its provision. In contrast, global governance systems lack the incentives, the ability, or both, to force nations to contribute to the provision of an environmental amenity.

Nonbeneficiary supply-side provision problems pose the clearest distinction between the domestic and international spheres. A firm that pollutes a river through the discharge of its chemical wastes imposes an externality on downstream farmers who use the river for irrigation. As Coase would predict,[33] the farmers may have adequate resources and incentives to offer the firm side payments to reduce or eliminate the pollution. However, when such Coasian bargains are impossible or involve excessive transaction costs, governments have often legislated pollution control because they view the benefits to the farmers of pollution reduction as greater than the costs to the firm. Externality victims that lack the economic or coercive resources needed to induce perpetrators to contribute to an environmental amenity can use political resources to bring their government's economic or coercive resources to bear on the perpetrator. The "polluter pays principle" provides an important normative and legal justification that reinforces a victim's economic disincentives for footing the bill for environmental cleanup. Nonetheless, Coasian resolutions to international externalities can and do take place, as evident in Dutch payments to France to reduce Rhine River pollution.[34] However, such bargains only occur when victim states have adequate resources. Unlike their domestic counterparts, victim states that are too weak to induce perpetrators to contribute to provision of an environmental amenity have no institutional recourse. Domestically, underprovision of an amenity will be remedied whenever the victim either has more power than the perpetrator or can access the power of the state and the state has more power than the perpetrator. Internationally, only the former possibility exists.

Even in issue areas where regimes or other international institutions exist, remedies to induce shirkers to contribute to the provision of an amenity tend to be less available. Policies for exclusion or charges to restrict access and demand to remedy overappropriation can also remedy underprovision. Exclusion can redress demand-side underprovision by decreasing current demand to a level that ensures future health of the amenity. In addition, exclusion can remedy beneficiary supply-side underprovision by threatening to exclude beneficiaries from access to the amenity unless they contribute. In essence, if possible and properly implemented, exclusionary policies can provide solutions to allocation problems, demand-side provision problems, and beneficiary supply-side provision problems. Indeed, property rights, and the enforcement of them as a means of exclusion, have been regularly referred to as the panacea for many environmental problems, from pollution to wildlife loss and everything in between.[35] McGinnis and Ostrom's[36] first design principle for robust CPR institutions is a requirement for "clearly defined boundaries" that distinguish between those with, and those without, rights to withdraw resource units from a CPR.

For nonrival amenities, exclusion and charges deter "provision free-riding" or "shirking."[37] Although nonrival amenities do not face even the possibility of overappropriation, effective threats to exclude or charge for usage can induce potential beneficiaries of such an amenity to contribute to its provision.[38] In such cases, the goal is not to reduce the aggregate benefits people derive from the amenity, but to ensure that beneficiaries contribute sufficiently to provide a socially beneficial amenity. Indeed, once a policy has induced contributions adequate to provide the socially optimal level of a nonrival amenity, potential beneficiaries should not be excluded from deriving benefits from that amenity, since those benefits impose no externalities on other actors.

A rival amenity in which overuse poses both a current overappropriation or congestion problem and a future underprovision problem requires exclusion policies that restrict demand sufficiently to redress both problems. However, an exclusion policy that remedies current overuse may be drastically inadequate to remedy future underprovision, since the latter depends on natural replenishment rates as well as overappropriation. For example, enforceable national whaling quotas adequate to remedy the overcapitalization (i.e., overappropriation) problem of the whaling fleets of the 1960s would not necessarily have been low enough to remedy the demand-side underprovision problem of declining whale populations.

Charges often provide a means of remedying supply-side provision problems even when exclusion and other forms of access control are not possible. As Coase's classic description illustrates, governments remedied the problem of underprovision of lighthouses (a beneficiary supply-side provision problem) by inventing ways to charge most ships benefiting from the light enough to provide the amenity, even when exclusion from the light's benefits was not possible.[39] Charges can help remedy beneficiary supply-side provision problems by leading current beneficiaries of the amenity to provide the resources needed to provide for the future stock of the amenity. However, charges will not work with nonbeneficiary supply-side provision problems because non-beneficiaries, by definition, derive no value from the amenity and so will be unwilling to pay any amount for its use. When underprovision arises because of the shirking of *nonbeneficiaries*, exclusion simply does not address the underlying source of the underprovision problem. Strategies of selective incentives may provide a mechanism for resolving this problem, by linking "private benefits or inducements to the provision of the collective good. Such private benefits would motivate any member (of any size) to contribute, inasmuch as the private benefits can only be obtained by assisting provision. Although collective benefits are nonexcludable, the private benefits are excludable."[40] Unfortunately, recent empirical work suggests that selective incentives or "bribes" do not work when aid recipients' preferences diverge from aid donors'.[41]

Although a compelling logic exists for only requiring beneficiaries of an amenity to contribute to its provision, governments often force nonbeneficiaries to contribute to provision of an amenity because of the practical problems and costs of selectively identifying and charging beneficiaries. Governments can tax or charge even those who do not benefit from the amenity provided. In contrast, no similar arrangements of governance exist at the international level. When states can benefit most by not contributing to a particular amenity (e.g., by not restraining a polluting activity), no higher-level actor can force them to contribute to its provision.

In cases of supply-side underprovision, the natural replenishment rate rather than current appropriation rates are major determinants of future amenity health and carrying capacity. In such cases, policies need not remedy current overexploitation or congestion so long as they generate adequate contributions to ensure future provision of the amenity. For example, one can avoid restraining a polluter in any way, but charge all actors equally (and at levels unrelated to the benefits they derive from the lack of pollution) for some form of cleanup technology. Wetland replacement programs often seek to avoid restricting development while ensuring the future health of wetlands. General revenue taxes are often applied to pollution cleanups or wildlife rescue efforts, even when the source of the pollution remains unaddressed. The ability to force people to contribute to provision of a good need not involve exclusion, especially if the possibility for central enforcement exists.[42] Indeed, such policies are often the only available remedy to nonbeneficiary supply-side provision problems. When those harmed by an externality have no direct power vis-à-vis the perpetrators of that externality, as is the case in many nonbeneficiary supply-side provision problems, the internalizing of that externality may require some form of governmental power to force private actors who influence but do not benefit from an environmental amenity to contribute to provision of that amenity.

Benefits to nonbeneficiary suppliers of an environmental amenity, by definition, are not the natural and noncontingent benefits provided by the amenity itself but rather the manipulated and contingent benefits of rewards that the beneficiaries promise to provide to those who contribute or avoiding the sanctions they threaten to impose for those who do not contribute. Where underprovision arises because of a failure to restrain activities that harm the amenity (like pollution) rather than because of a failure to induce contributions to the amenity (like cleanup campaigns), governments often use force to coerce restraint. The threat or imposition of sanctions can induce polluters to contribute to provision of a cleaner environment. However, huge obstacles exist to centralized or decentralized sanctioning in the international sphere, a fact evidenced in the rarity of such efforts.[43] Collective action problems plague the provision of contingent benefits as well, as evidenced in the small magnitude of most financial mechanisms to date and the frequency with which governments have failed to meet even these limited financial commitments. In this context, promises and threats are likely to lack credibility with the nonbeneficiary and therefore not induce the desired behavioral change.

Much of the international relations literature to date has seen fostering reciprocity within a system of collective regulation as the solution to underprovision of a CPR.[44] Enhancing transparency and reciprocity allows actors to engage in retaliatory Tit-for-Tat strategies that, in iterated interactions, can resolve the externality.[45] Such strategies only exist, however, when actors are symmetrically positioned as both perpetrators and victims. Only those who are victims of another's externality have incentives to retaliate, and only those who are perpetrators of an externality that harms the other have the capacity to retaliate. Indeed, classic Tit-for-Tat assumes similarly-situated consumptive users can and do respond to consumptive defection through consumptive defection of their own. Whalers have the potential to overcome their collective action problem by threatening resumption of whaling to induce other whalers to cooperate. However, this simplified model of interaction misconstrues the dynamics of many environmental problems. Victims of pollution, for example, are frequently not polluters themselves. They must bring to bear sanctions other than their ability to pollute in order to force polluters to desist. Whale-watchers and whale-lovers cannot pose, through their actions, potent retaliatory threats to whale-hunters' interests. If they have sufficient power, they may be able to threaten exogenous sanctions but they cannot alter their use of the resource as a means of inducing restraint by whale-hunters. Internationally, recourse to a source of power above that of the victim is simply not the option it is domestically. In short, underprovision problems are simultaneously more likely and more difficult to resolve internationally.

Conclusions

Features characteristic of international relations cause a given environmental amenity to face a greater likelihood of appropriation and provision problems than if the same problem was confined within a single nation's borders. Overappropriation and congestion problems arise when the demands placed on an amenity exceed its carrying capacity. International factors simultaneously increase the demands on an amenity and decrease the availability of mechanisms to restrict that demand. Cultural, economic, social and political differences cause the diversity of demands placed on an environmental amenity to be greater across nations than within a nation. In addition, simply allowing more people access to an amenity increases the demands placed on it. Thus, for any particular level of an amenity, the greater demands placed on it at the international level cause aggregate demand all too often to exceed the carrying capacity of the amenity, with the resultant overappropriation of consumptive amenities or congestion of nonconsumptive amenities.

At the same time, remedies to appropriation problems are less attractive and less possible internationally. In an international system characterized by anarchy, relative gains concerns, and inherent rivalry, governments find it difficult to accept international versions of the same policies they often use domestically to reduce demand and control overappropriation. In the rare cases in which states agree to limit access to an amenity through property rights, charges, or other policies, collective action dynamics undercut and imperil the enforcement of such agreements.

The incentives and ability to remedy the second important aspect of common pool resources, namely underprovision, are also weaker at the international level. Whether involving excessive demand that reduces the future health of the amenity, insufficient contributions to the health of that amenity from beneficiaries, or insufficient contributions to that amenity's health from nonbeneficiaries, international dynamics exacerbate underprovision problems. Governments often have the incentives and capacity to internalize the externalities that one subset of national actors imposes on another. Governments often aggregate preferences, costs, and benefits across individuals and can force perpetrators of an externality to desist if the social benefits exceed the social costs of doing so. Domestically, weak actors can use the state to force powerful actors to stop imposing externalities on them. No corresponding institution exists internationally to aggregate preferences, costs, and benefits across states or to force a state perpetrating such an externality to desist. Weak states can rarely use international regimes or institutions to force powerful states to stop imposing externalities on them.

An extensive literature has demonstrated the difficulties of remedying common pool resource problems at the domestic level. This volume suggests that, however formidable the problems and scarce the solutions to CPR problems domestically, the international environmental sphere is likely to pose even more formidable problems and make solutions even more difficult to find.

Notes

This chapter has benefited from helpful suggestions from Sammy Barkin, George Shambaugh, Barb Connolly, Beth DeSombre, and the other contributors to this volume.

1. Robert Cameron Mitchell and Richard T. Carson, *Using Surveys to Value Public Goods: The Contingent Valuation Method* (Washington: Resources for the Future, 1989); A. Myrick Freeman, *The Measurement of Environmental and Resource Values: Theory and Methods* (Washington: Resources for the Future, 1993), pp. 2–6; Peter S. Burton, "Land Use Externalities: Mechanism Design for the Allocation of Environmental Resources," *Journal of Environmental Economics and Management* vol. 30 (1996), p. 174.

2. Fred Foldvary, *Public Goods and Private Communities: The Market Provision of Social Services* (Brookfield, VT: Edward Elgar Publishing Company, 1994), p. 11.

3. Robert O. Keohane and Elinor Ostrom, "Introduction," in *Local Commons and Global Interdependence*, eds., Robert O. Keohane and Elinor Ostrom (Boulder: Sage, 1995), p. 14.

4. See, for example, Arne Naess, "The Shallow and the Deep, Long-Range Ecology Movement: A Summary," *Inquiry* vol. 16 (1972), pp. 95–100; Bill Devall, "The Deep Ecology Movement," *Natural Resources Journal* vol. 20 (1980), pp. 299–313; and the selections in Irene Diamond and Gloria Feman Orenstein, eds., *Reweaving the World: The Emergence of Ecofeminism* (San Francisco: Sierra Club Books, 1990).

5. Duncan Snidal, "Public Goods, Property Rights, and Political Organizations," *International Studies Quarterly* vol. 23 (1979), p. 549; Elinor Ostrom, *Governing the Commons: The Evolution of Institutions for Collective Action* (Cambridge, England: Cambridge University Press, 1990), pp. 46–48.

6. Mitchell and Carson, *Using Surveys to Value Public Goods*, pp. 64–65.

7. Richard Cornes and Todd Sandler, *The Theory of Externalities, Public Goods, and Club Goods* (Cambridge, England: Cambridge University Press, 1986), p. 241.

8. Burton, "Land Use Externalities," p. 174.

9. This discussion of appropriation, provision, resource units, and resource systems draws extensively on the excellent treatment of the subject in Ostrom, *Governing the Commons*.

10. Foldvary, *Public Goods and Private Communities*, p. 13.

11. Thomas H. Tietenberg, *Environmental and Natural Resource Economics*, 2nd ed. (Glenview, IL: Scott, Foresman, 1988), ch. 12.

12. Todd Sandler, *Collective Action: Theory and Applications* (Ann Arbor: University of Michigan Press, 1992), p. 74.

13. Crowding occurs when "a marginal user increases the resources required to maintain the quality of the public good." Foldvary, *Public Goods and Private Communities*, p. 13, note 4.

14. Cornes and Sandler, *The Theory of Externalities, Public Goods, and Club Goods*, p. 6.

15. Foldvary, *Public Goods and Private Communities*, p. 13.

16. Ibid., p. 13; Duncan Snidal, "Public Goods, Property Rights, and Political Organizations," p. 535.

17. David Reisman, *Theories of Collective Action: Downs, Olson and Hirsch* (New York: St. Martin's, 1990), p. 200; Cornes and Sandler, *The Theory of Externalities, Public Goods, and Club Goods*, p. 160. Although some have argued that intrinsic values "should be excluded from benefit measurements" of environmental amenities because they are in fundamental normative opposition to any form of economic analysis, humans certainly willingly pay to receive such benefits (see Mitchell and Carson, *Using Surveys to Value Public Goods*, p. 65). Although such preferences may be economically nonrational or irrational, considerable evidence suggests that people actually do derive existence value from environmental amenities (Reisman, p. 147).

18. "A true dilemma exists only when demand for use of a commons exceeds some threshold beyond which one user interferes with the availability of the commons for other users or, in the extreme case, total use begins to exceed the commons' carrying capacity. . . . Only as the supply becomes constricted relative to demand does the potential for individual actions to generate externalities exist." David Goetze, "Comparing Prisoners' Dilemma, Commons Dilemma, and Public Goods Provision Designs in Laboratory Experiments," *Journal of Conflict Resolution* vol. 38 (1994), p. 82.

19. Foldvary, *Public Goods and Private Communities*, p. 13.

20. Ibid.

21. Keohane and Ostrom, "Introduction," in *Local Commons and Global Interdependence*, p. 15; Michael McGinnis and Elinor Ostrom, "Design Principles for Local and Global Commons," unpublished manuscript (Bloomington, IN, 1992), p. 5.

22. The next section relaxes this assumption, examining how carrying capacity in one time period depends on provision and appropriation in previous time periods.

23. Ronald H. Coase, "The Lighthouse in Economics," in *The Theory of Market Failure: A Critical Examination*, eds., Tyler Cowen (Fairfax, VA: George Mason University Press, 1988), p. 258.

24. Ostrom, *Governing the Commons*.

25. Cornes and Sandler, *The Theory of Externalities, Public Goods, and Club Goods*, p. 30; Ernst U. von Weizsacker and Jochen Jesinghus, *Ecological Tax Reform: A Policy Proposal for Sustainable Development* (Atlantic Highlands, NJ: Zed Books, 1992); Thomas A. Barthold, "Issues in the Design of Environmental Excise Taxes," *Journal of Economic Perspectives* vol. 8 (1994), pp. 133–51; Robert Repetto, *Green Fees* (Washington: World Resources Institute, 1992).

26. This logic would predict a greater frequency of overexploitation of international fisheries than of domestic fisheries, even if many domestic fisheries are overexploited.

27. Keohane and Ostrom, "Introduction," in *Local Commons and Global Interdependence*, p. 15.

28. Ostrom, *Governing the Commons*, pp. 46–50.

29. Ibid., p. 49.

30. Ibid.

31. See Barbara Connolly's contribution to this volume, and also Marc A. Levy, "International Cooperation to Combat Acid Rain," *Green Globe Yearbook: An Independent Publication on Environment and Development* (Oxford: Oxford University Press, 1995), pp. 59–68.

32. Ronald B. Mitchell, *Intentional Oil Pollution at Sea: Environmental Policy and Treaty Compliance* (Cambridge, MA: MIT Press, 1994).

33. Ronald Coase, "The Problem of Social Cost," *Journal of Law and Economics* vol. 3 (1960), pp. 1–44.

34. Thomas Bernauer, "Protecting the Rhine River Against Chloride Pollution," in *Institutions for Environmental Aid: Pitfalls and Promise*, eds., Robert O. Keohane and Marc A. Levy (Cambridge, MA: MIT Press, 1996).

35. Andreas A. Papandreou, *Externality and Institutions* (Oxford: Clarendon, 1994), p. 78; Cornes and Sandler, *The Theory of Externalities, Public Goods, and Club Goods*, p. 33; Snidal, "Public Goods, Property Rights, and Political Organizations," p. 545; Robert L. Bish, "Environmental Resource Management: Public or Private?" in *Managing the Commons*, eds., Garrett Hardin and John Baden, (San Francisco: W. H. Freeman, 1977), p. 218; Terry L. Anderson and P. J. Hill, "From Free Grass to Fences: Transforming the Commons of the American West," in *Managing the Commons*, pp. 200–16.

36. McGinnis and Ostrom, "Design Principles for Local and Global Commons."

37. Ostrom, *Governing the Commons.*

38. "Consumers have no incentive to pay to receive the good since they cannot be prevented from consuming it once it has been produced. Nor can they be properly induced to contribute to its production since the incentives point toward a 'free ride' on the contributions of others." Snidal, "Public Goods, Property Rights, and Political Organizations," p. 548.

39. Coase, "The Lighthouse in Economics," p. 77.

40. Sandler, *Collective Action: Theory and Applications*, p. 58.

41. Barbara Connolly and Robert O. Keohane, "Institutions for Environmental Aid: Politics, Lessons, and Opportunities," *Environment* (June 1996).

42. Snidal, "Public Goods, Property Rights, and Political Organizations," p. 551.

43. Gary Clyde Hufbauer and Jeffrey J. Schott, *Economic Sanctions Reconsidered: History and Current Policy* (Washington: Institute for International Economics, 1985); Elizabeth DeSombre, "Baptists and Bootleggers for the Environment: The Origins of United States Unilateral Sanctions," *Journal of Environment and Development* vol. 4 (1995), pp. 53–76.

44. Robert O. Keohane, "Reciprocity in International Relations," *International Organization* vol. 40 (1986), pp. 1–27.

45. Robert Axelrod, *The Evolution of Cooperation* (New York: Basic Books, 1984); Robert Axelrod and Robert O. Keohane, "Achieving Cooperation Under Anarchy: Strategies and Institutions," in *Cooperation Under Anarchy*, ed., Kenneth Oye (Princeton, NJ: Princeton University Press, 1986).

3 Tuna Fishing and Common Pool Resources

ELIZABETH R. DeSOMBRE

Introduction

Conservation and preservation of ocean resources or species cannot be understood within a public goods approach to studying environmental regulations. No matter what one state does it cannot provide the public good of conservation. Regulation of fisheries and fishing in particular must be viewed within the framework of common pool resources: the ocean is as close to a true commons both practically and legally as we can find in international environmental politics. In most senses ocean resources are nonexcludable. States are free to use the resources of the ocean (subject to any agreements they have made), and logistically it is almost impossible to deny anyone access to ocean resources. And, unlike with public goods,[1] use or destruction of ocean resources by one actor affects the availability of those resources to other actors; the resources of the oceans can be "used up." The marine commons has at points come close to the sort of ruin that Hardin predicted would be the inevitable result of freedom in a commons.[2] Attempts to conserve marine living resources have taken a variety of different regulatory approaches that have met with a varying level of success.

Tuna species are some of the most valuable ocean resources for human use.[3] Tuna fishing has been regulated in a variety of ways, for several different reasons, and with varying degrees of success in the last half-century. Two different international agreements exist to regulate tuna in the Atlantic and Pacific oceans, with markedly different approaches and effects. Additionally, access to and conservation of tuna was a driving force behind expansion of Exclusive Economic Zones (EEZs) and were the reason that the United States resisted this expansion. Tuna has also been regulated for a different goal: preservation of dolphins that are caught incidentally to tuna fishing. Because of the long and varied history of tuna regulations, this issue area is a useful one in which to examine whether a CPR approach to understanding international environmental issues can explain the patterns of actions by states and fishers, and whether this approach can suggest alternate regulatory approaches that might better succeed in conserving tuna than those that have been undertaken.

There are several results of tuna regulations that might initially seem puzzling. First, despite the collective incentive to conserve tuna so that fishing by all fishers can continue indefinitely, tuna stocks have become severely depleted. International regulatory efforts to conserve tuna have been attempted but none has managed to change the underlying incentive structure or protect the resource. Attempts at privatization, generally seen as an unproblematic solution to tragedies of the commons, have been unable to prevent depletion of tuna stocks. And although tuna fishers successfully resisted international regulations to conserve tuna stocks which might have helped them in the long run, they have given in to international regulations on the way tuna is caught so as to protect dolphins, when these regulations do not protect the long-term interests of these fishers and have high short-term costs. In addition, unilateral action taken in support of tuna regulations has had a high degree of success in one instance, the protection of dolphins, and much less success in another instance, the conservation of tuna stocks. And lest it be argued that the difference in the aforementioned situation was the degree of hegemony of the state(s) pursuing unilateral goals, the hegemonic actor (the United States) was not able to gain its goals in addressing tuna conservation while it was able to in the case of dolphin protection via tuna regulations. Examining the CPR aspect of regulations on tuna fishing, as well as details of the regulations and the states involved, can help explain these otherwise puzzling results of attempts to regulate tuna fishing.

The hypotheses put forth in chapter 1 contribute toward understanding these potentially puzzling outcomes of regulatory attempts, as well as toward explaining the way in which states have attempted to regulate tuna fishing in general. The potential for free riding is the threat that constantly undermines the potential for actors to work collectively on tuna regulations, especially given the number of actors outside the regulatory system and the difficulty of monitoring and enforcement on the open ocean. It is also a threat that has been used explicitly by those who want to gain concessions from the organizations attempting to regulate tuna fishing. Due to the ability of fishers outside any regulatory regime to subtract from the ability of others to conserve fish stocks, all states with the ability to catch substantial amounts of tuna must be included in a regulatory regime for it to be successful. Threats to withdraw or not to participate can give actors a source of leverage that can be translated into concessions in the regulatory system.

The different degrees to which actors value the resource in the present versus in the future impact the likelihood of successful collective action on tuna fishing, as well as the propensity of the actors to address their concerns outside of multilateral bargaining situations. Those who argue that they are not concerned about the future of the resource can either stay outside an agreement and thereby derail its effectiveness, or gain concessions that make upholding the agreement more difficult for the other participants, and therefore also less likely. And since actors that can present a credible argument that they do not care about the future of the resource can gain concessions in a multilateral setting from those who do, there may be advantages to the actors who value the future of the resource to avoid a multilateral arena for negotiations about regulations.

Hegemony can thus become important in this type of resource issue, even though widespread participation is necessary and states cannot solve commons problems alone. Because the ocean is a true commons, it has been coercive rather than benevolent hegemony that operates in this issue area. Even a coercive hegemon, however, cannot achieve its priorities without overly costly actions in the face of determined free riding. How costly the action may be to any of the actors can depend on the market power that the actors in question can wield in exerting their influence.

The remainder of this chapter is divided into three sections. The first examines the different policies that have been followed in the attempt to regulate tuna catches, the next examines the puzzles presented by the data in light of the hypotheses generated in chapter 1. The chapter concludes by arguing that a greater understanding of the CPR nature of tuna fisheries and of the incentive structures they give to the actors involved could contribute to more successful efforts to preserve tuna fisheries and ocean resources in general.

Tuna Regulations

The main species of commercially fished tuna include yellowfin, skipjack, and albacore, which are found mostly in the Pacific ocean, and bluefin, which is found mostly in the Atlantic ocean. All these populations are highly migratory (although they have specific regions in which they spend greater percentages of their time) and have been fished for centuries. Once human populations grew and fishing technology began to improve by the middle of the twentieth century it became clear that international attempts to conserve these fish stocks would be necessary. These were initially approached regionally and then some states attempted to privatize access to the Pacific tuna stocks. More recently, regulations on tuna have been applied in the Pacific ocean for the purpose of protecting dolphins.

Conservation of Pacific Tuna

The tuna in the Pacific Ocean became vulnerable to overfishing as fishing technology improved over time and as more and more states found it profitable to fish in the Pacific for tuna. The desire to conserve tuna stocks there represents a desire to ensure that there will be a sufficient tuna population to allow for perpetuation of the tuna fishing industry. Fishing states, led by the United States, formed an international organization to address tuna conservation issues in the area before overfishing became a problem, in efforts to prevent the depletion of fish stocks. This organization had some success in slowing the decline of pacific tuna stocks, but no longer meaningfully regulates tuna fishing.

The convention for the establishment of the Inter-American Tropical Tuna Commission (IATTC) was signed May 31, 1949, establishing a commission to collect data and do studies of yellowfin and skipjack tuna in the Eastern Pacific Ocean. The convention was created "to establish a means of cooperation in the gathering and interpretation of factual information to facilitate maintaining, at a level which will permit maximum sustained catches, the populations of yellowfin and skipjack tuna" in the Eastern Pacific.[4] The original parties to the convention were the United States and Costa Rica, with accession open to all states that fish for tuna in the area. Current additional parties to the convention are France, Japan, Nicaragua, Panama, and

Vanuatu. Canada, Ecuador, and Mexico were parties to the agreement at one time, but have since withdrawn. Costa Rica has also withdrawn.

Data collection began immediately on the convention's entry into force in 1950.[5] A decade later the commission began to notice and predict a decline in the population of yellowfin tuna, and recommended regulation of fishing for yellowfin beginning in 1961. The member states agreed to these regulations beginning in 1966.[6] The Commission's Yellowfin Regulatory Area (CYRA) was designated as the area in which catches of yellowfin tuna would be regulated.[7] Regulations took the form of minimum catch lengths for tuna, as well as an overall quota of tuna that could be caught within the CYRA, on a first-come, first-serve basis. When quotas were agreed on, fishers would radio in their catch statistics and the Commission staff would conclude when the season would need to close in order not to exceed the quota. Incidental catches of yellowfin tuna up to 15 percent of overall catch were allowed during the closed season for vessels fishing for other types of tuna.[8]

A quota was implemented for the years 1966 to 1979; from 1980 to 1985 the Commission agreed on a quota, but the member states did not implement it; for 1986 and 1987 the Commission did not recommend a quota; since then, none has been implemented.[9] The main issue that caused the breakdown of the regime was the question of Exclusive Economic Zones and preferential access to tuna for what the organization called Resource Adjacent Nations (RANs). The Latin American states in particular had declared zones of up to 200 miles off their coasts, within which they wanted the right to regulate fishing practices. Tuna fishing as the most lucrative and most foreign-dominated fishing practice was the focus of these attempts.[10] For similar reasons, the United States resisted these efforts.

When Latin American states began to argue that they should be allowed to determine fishing policy near their coasts, the organization responded (in an effort to keep them in the agreement) by including special allocations for RANs in the regulations. But because Canada and the United States in particular wanted to avoid setting the precedent of allowing special access to ocean resources for those whose waters contained more of them, these special allocations were based on economic hardship rather than on resource adjacency, as the RANs would have preferred. Some states pulled out of the Convention over this issue. Eventually, as the demands from RANs grew along with the recalcitrance of the non-RANs, regulatory agreement became impossible within the IATTC. Several agreements have been negotiated to try to circumvent these problems, but none has entered into force.[11]

Conservation of Atlantic Tuna

Bluefin tuna in the Atlantic ocean initially were of marginal importance in international fishing activities. Their large size (representing a big profit per catch), combined with new methods for catching and shipping fish and the depletion of other stocks, however, have made bluefin tuna a more attractive stock for fishing. Despite attempts at regulation, stocks of tuna in the Atlantic ocean have been depleted to such an extent that bluefin tuna is now considered an endangered species.[12]

The International Convention for the Conservation of Atlantic Tunas (ICCAT), signed on May 14, 1966, established a Commission that began its activities in 1969. The Convention was negotiated on the initiative of the United Nations' Food and Agriculture Organization, "to maintain tuna populations at levels which permit the maximum sustainable catch for food and other purposes."[13] The area of concern for the Commission is the Atlantic Ocean and adjacent seas. There are twenty-two states party to the agreement, including the United States, Canada, Japan, France, and a number of developing states.

Regulations adopted by the Commission include minimum catch-size regulations for tropical tuna, bluefin tuna, and swordfish, and some quotas. For purposes of management (and because of a theory that two distinct stocks of bluefin tuna populate the Atlantic ocean) the Commission has divided the ocean at the forty-fifth parallel into East and West regions. The ICCAT has imposed catch quotas for West Atlantic bluefin tuna. Unlike the Inter-American Tropical Tuna Commission, the ICCAT divides the majority of its quota among the major tuna-fishing states in the region: the United States, Canada, and Japan. The population of bluefin tuna was not greatly overfished at the beginning of the ICCAT, but the increasing regulations and declining stocks of tuna in the Pacific led fishers to travel through the Panama Canal to fish in the Atlantic during the closed Pacific seasons, increasing pressure on the Atlantic stocks. Additionally, in the 1980s, the use of new methods to ship bluefin to Japan immediately after catching, and the growth of the US sushi market increased the demand—and the price—for bluefin. ICCAT estimates that the bluefin population declined from approximately 225,000 in 1970 to 22,000 in 1990.[14]

In general, members have disagreed about the need for regulations; claims by Resource-Adjacent Nations for special allocations make regulation more difficult, and differences in scientific opinion are magnified by fears that analysis of scientific data represents the national preferences of the scientists' countries.[15] The organization does not have a history of success: conservationists refer to its acronym as representing the "International Commission to Catch All the Tuna."[16] This situation represents a classic CPR problem in which market failure results from a disjuncture between individual incentives to exploit tuna and a collective incentive to manage it. Because free riders cannot be excluded from fishing, the incentive for any individual fisher to stop fishing, and the ability of the free rider to deplete the fishing stock for everyone else, minimizes the incentive for any individual to stop fishing. Although collective management was attempted in this situation, two problems prevented it from working successfully. First, because of the value of each individual fish caught, fishers who did agree on collective regulation wanted to make sure that the quotas were set high enough that they would be able to profit from their tuna catches, thus leading to inflated fishing quotas. Second, in a classic case of free-riding, a number of fishers flagged their vessels with flags of convenience from states not participating in the international regulatory regime so they would not be subject to international regulations.[17]

Exclusive Economic Zones and Tuna Conservation

The expansion of the area of ocean considered to be under the control of the state adjacent to it, to the 200-mile Exclusive Economic Zone (EEZ) that is now recognized under international law, both derives from and represents a conflict over the regulation of tuna. The desire to control access to resources off their coasts, tuna prominent among them, led Latin American states to declare and enforce 200-mile fishery conservation zones, beginning in the late 1940s and early 1950s. The United States actually inadvertently began the drive for extended coastal jurisdiction by declaring an extended fishery conservation area in 1945, but did not intend it to allow states to exclude others from fishing in such large regions.[18] Chile and Peru declared 200-mile zones in 1947 and Ecuador claimed jurisdiction over a 12-mile zone in the same year.

This expansion, particularly as it relates to tuna regulation, was opposed by some states. Most prominent in opposition was the United States, which, although it technically extended its jurisdiction in 1976 under the Magnuson Fisheries Conservation and Management Act, exempted "highly migratory species," defined as "tuna," from its claim. The United States went so far as to institute economic embargoes on fish or fish products from any state that "as a consequence of a claim of jurisdiction which is not recognized by the United States" does not allow US vessels to fish for tuna within its Exclusive Economic Zone.[19] On the one hand, the United States argued that this policy was for the sake of tuna conservation, which cannot be effectively achieved by anything other than international regulation since tuna are highly migratory. On the other hand, it seems clear that pressure from US tuna fishers, who catch most of their fish in foreign EEZs, contributed to the US policy to accept solely international regulation of tuna.[20] Beginning with the 1982 United Nations Convention on the Law of the Sea, the claiming of EEZs was codified within international law, and the United States ultimately accepted this principle by removing the exception for "highly migratory species" from its EEZ declaration under the Fishery Conservation Amendments of 1990.[21]

Preservation of Dolphins through Tuna Regulations

An additional reason that tuna fishing is regulated is to protect dolphins. For reasons that are not entirely clear, schools of yellowfin tuna in the eastern Pacific Ocean swim under groups of dolphins. Because dolphins surface for air and are then visible to fishers, an efficient method of catching yellowfin tuna is to encircle schools of dolphins with purse-seine nets, thus gathering the tuna that swim under the dolphins. In the process of such activity dolphins are held under water and can drown.

The United States' Marine Mammal Protection Act (MMPA), passed in 1972, aims "to reduce the rate of incidental kill or serious injury [of marine mammals] to insignificant levels approaching zero,"[22] and imposes restrictions on US tuna fishers in support of that goal. This regulation marked a move to valuing the existence benefits of dolphins over the consumptive benefits from tuna (although tuna could still be caught, just in less efficient ways). These existence benefits are generally seen to derive from the fact that dolphins are mammals and may be highly intelligent. There is therefore objection to using them as a resource, the way tuna is used.[23] Due to pressure both from environmental groups concerned about dolphins and from tuna fishers concerned about the competitiveness effects of bearing a costly regulation not imposed on their foreign competitors,[24] the United States worked to apply this regulation internationally. It did this both by pushing regulations in the IATTC[25] and by refusing to import tuna from states that did not adopt comparable dolphin protection measures in their tuna fishing.

Regulations that prohibit the use of purse-seine nets to catch dolphins or regulate the level of incidental dolphin mortality have now been adopted by many states that fish for yellowfin tuna in the Pacific Ocean. These regulations are on tuna fishing, even though the object of concern is preservation of dolphins. This unilateral effort by the United States to change the way tuna fishing is conducted, backed by threats and imposition of economic sanctions, has met with general success in either changing the way that tuna fishers catch tuna, or in driving out of business those who do not go along with the new rules.

CPRs and the Analysis of Tuna Fishing

The puzzles presented by this story of uneven success at regulating tuna and mixed experiences with unilateral efforts to do so can be understood by examining the common pool resource aspects of tuna fisheries. The hypotheses presented by this project can explain what at first seem like unusual strategies or outcomes for attempted tuna fishing regulation. Specifically, the power of free riders, the issues of differing shadows of the future, and the different types of market power threatened and used can illuminate the dynamics that underlie the varying (and generally dismal) success at regulating tuna fishing. Issues of the different types of use that a resource has can influence the way it can successfully be regulated as well; in particular, managing a resource that is valued for its existence has different regulatory implications than managing one that is valued for its consumption.

Free Riders

Within international regulation, the threat of free-riding can give a state a high degree of influence. In the case of Latin American states and tuna, their threat to consume greater amounts of tuna than would be allowed by the agreement (in this case, by privatizing the resource)[26] led them to receive special consideration within the IATTC initially, until the refusal of the organization to grant what these states considered sufficient concessions eventually caused its downfall altogether. The organization initially agreed to reserve portions of the catch for states or vessels with economic difficulties. This policy itself was a compromise, since the United States did not want to set the precedent of allowing coastal states specific rights to the tuna near their coasts, even though that was in practice what was accomplished by these policies. Beginning in 1969 small vessels (originally those with a capacity of less than 300 tons) were allowed to catch a combined total of yellowfin tuna of, at the outset, 4,000 tons per state after the season's closing date.[27] These exceptions led to a situation in which, by 1979, roughly 25 percent of the yellowfin tuna caught was taken outside the quota by special exception.[28] Put another way, in the mid-1970s, US and some Canadian vessels were, in effect, the only ones regulated by the IATTC, since all other states could qualify under one of the exceptions.[29] As stocks declined, quotas grew harder to agree on, and as special exceptions became the rule, the IATTC foresaw its demise and eventually ceased regulating catch levels altogether. At this point, the concessions that would have been required to satisfy the Latin American coastal states were higher than the benefits that the other states would receive from joint management.

In the case of Atlantic tuna, the threats of free-riding came from two different types of states. In the first place, states within the agreement threatened not to continue to participate should the quotas not be high enough for them to earn a sufficient income from catching bluefin. This led to higher quotas than were probably scientifically advisable.[30] Second, there are fishers who operate under flags of convenience so as to be able explicitly to circumvent the international regulations. Some ICCAT members suggest that up to 80 percent of the Atlantic tuna catch is caught by vessels flagged in states that do not belong to the organization.[31] Although these states do not attempt to alter the regulations, they help deplete the stock by free-riding on the multilateral agreements that are working to protect it.

In general, then, free-riding is the mechanism through which any concerns about the potential of multilateral cooperation to manage commons mechanisms are played out. The individual concerns may be due to degrees to which the actors value the future of the resource and the difficulty of enforcement, but the specific way that they are expressed is through the action or threat of free-riding.

Shadows of the Future

The varying shadows of the future of actors subject to or pushing for the different tuna regulations can explain much of what happened with these regulations. The lack of successful tuna conservation measures in general is the clearest type of result we would expect in a common pool resource problem. In fact, the most successful effort at cooperation on this issue came in the early years of the IATTC when it was realized that there was a CPR *issue*, but not yet a *problem*. Early efforts of the IATTC to collect information were met with a high degree of cooperation. Tuna fishers regularly reported their catch levels and areas to the organization with no incentive to give incorrect information, as long as their information was used to provide useful information (to which they had access) about tuna stocks and levels. As soon as catch levels were regulated, however, fishers' reporting of their catch levels would lead to a closed season once the total catch reached a certain number. Each individual fisher therefore gained the incentive to underreport catches so that the season would be extended long enough for that fisher to continue to catch more tuna. Despite a collective interest in protecting tuna stocks, each individual fisher's shadow of the future was shorter than the shadow of the future of the group collectively. Incorrect information was probably reported during the early years of regulation, leading to a decrease in the stock since regulations were based on predictions from faulty evidence.[32] Because it is impractical to count the number of fish in the ocean, information on how many fish there are of a certain type is inferred from information reported about catches and fishing effort. If fishers underreported their catches or the effort required to catch their quotas, in an effort to extend the fishing season, then quotas would be determined based on misinformation. Specific tuna fishers with particular reasons to value current catch over future catch, such as those facing overcapitalization of their fishing vessels, would have an even greater incentive not to report information correctly, or not to comply with closed season regulations, in order to compete effectively.

The same thing is true for bluefin tuna fishing where one fish can represent such a huge profit that the shadow of the future in general of individual fishers is short. In addition, bluefin tuna may be an example of a "step good," where there is not a smooth continuum along which actions move. Since each individual fish is so large and may be worth so much money, the optimal catch rate (for the species to survive) may be expressed in percentage of a single fish, an obviously impossible quota to set. The commons incentives that structure the situation such that each individual fisher cannot be assured of the compliance of others shortens the shadow of the future and leads to an inability to regulate collectively in the absence of extensive monitoring and enforcement. Such monitoring is particularly difficult with fisheries given the size of the ocean and the number of fishing vessels fishing at all times for various species of fish. The shadow of the future in general, then, accounts for failures of successful commons regulations in ocean fisheries.

The problem of shadows of the future has suggested privatization as a solution to commons problems in general. With privatization, individual actors bear all the consequence of their actions (as well as all the benefits), and none of the consequences of the actions of others. They know that resources they take steps to preserve will be around in the future, which has the effect of lengthening the shadow of the future. This factor should be even more important for fisheries than it is for nonrenewable resources, since fish that remain in the ocean will breed and produce more fish for the future. Attempts at privatization of tuna stocks have generally failed to conserve tuna stocks, however, and have interrupted attempts at international cooperation to address the commons problem. Privatization of the ocean is more problematic than simply dividing Hardin's cow pasture since, as Brian Tobin, then Fisheries Minister of Canada pointed out, "fish swim."[33] Although the United States may have pushed for international rather than domestic regulation of tuna stocks for self-interested purposes, it was right that the highly migratory status of tuna make them particularly inappropriate for domestic regulation. Tuna swim long distances, between the EEZs of neighboring states, and out to and across the open ocean. In the case of Latin American creation of EEZs, privatization may have slowed the destruction of the commons because it removed the largest and most efficient fisher—the United States—from the area where tuna spent much of their time. But it was ultimately not a strategy that could succeed in creating long-term conservation.

It is also the case that privatization by individual states will not necessarily address the commons incentives faced by fishers of these states; this situation may instead replicate the tragedy of the commons on a national scale if there is no attempt to assign individual property rights in the fishery to individual fishers. The privatization of regulation of Pacific tuna has failed completely in preserving the stocks, and has precluded any international attempts to do so.

More puzzling is the fact that the United States, the most powerful state at the time and the world's largest tuna market, was unable to determine tuna policy in this area. It certainly tried; the United States imposed economic sanctions on seven states on ten different occasions for preventing US access to their EEZs to fish for tuna.[34] The different shadows of the future of the actors in question combined with the inability to unilaterally solve CPR problems, can explain the US lack of success. The United States wants multilateral cooperation on tuna regulation, but if others refuse, there is nothing one state can do alone to protect the resource. The fact that, short of the use of military force, no state can be forced to join a collective activity to protect a commons gives those who want to act outside a multilateral regulatory system a lot of power.

Even more interesting is the observation that the shadow of the future may influence the willingness of a state to undertake unilateral action in the first place to preserve the CPR. The longer a state's shadow, the more willing it is to act in a way that precludes or avoids international cooperation. If a state values a resource much more in the present than in the future, it gives that state the ability to extract concessions in international bargaining situations. In multilateral situations, therefore, the states that can show that they put a low value on the future existence of the resource are more likely to gain their objectives. States with a long shadow of the future are therefore unlikely to prevail in a multilateral setting against those with a shorter shadow. These states that value the future of the resource highly are therefore more likely to gain their objectives outside of a multilateral setting. That can help explain which states chose to act outside of multilateral fora in each of these instances.

In the case of regulation of tuna within EEZs, Latin American states had long shadows of the future for tuna specifically around their coasts: they wanted to make sure that the tuna they found along their coasts would be there for the foreseeable future, and this future value was threatened by US factory fishing vessels that came near their shores to take "their" tuna. Because Pacific tuna spends large portions of their time near Latin American coastlines these states believed they could manage the stocks individually. In addition, their shadow of the future for this specific tuna stock was lengthened by the fact that they did not have factory fishing vessels that could catch tuna elsewhere, and they therefore placed a high (and long-term) value on the tuna stocks that swam near their shores. This fact led them to work outside the previous multilateral regulatory framework to attempt to protect the resource over the long run. Their long shadow of the future led them to be willing to withstand fairly costly sanctions from their primary tuna market; sanctions that could even lead to a decrease in the amount of foreign aid they received. But the tuna did spend most of its time off their coasts, and they were poorer than their hegemonic northern neighbor and a greater percentage of their total income (and food for domestic consumption) came from tuna fishing. They therefore had an incentive to preserve it in the long run, and therefore were willing to withstand these threats in order to be able to create the ability to control tuna fishing within their EEZs. Unfortunately, for a number of reasons, including the highly migratory nature of tuna and the failure to further privatize to individual rights within EEZs, this plan did not actually serve to conserve tuna.

Conversely, because US concern came from environmentalists who value dolphins for their existence benefits, the United States had a longer shadow of the future than the other states (many of the same states as in the previous example) and therefore wanted to gain worldwide regulation of dolphin mortality in the course of tuna fishing. For the United States, the continued existence of dolphins was the important aspect of these tuna regulations. Dolphins thus were as important in the future as they are now; existence benefits by definition lead actors who favor them to have a long (or technically infinite) shadow of the future. This long shadow can help account for the fact that the United States undertook tuna regulations for the sake of dolphin protection in a unilateral rather than multilateral way. This observation may suggest the counterintuitive hypothesis that existence benefits may more often be gained (or at least sought) through unilateral measures to protect them. Since valuing a resource for its existence benefits always implies a longer shadow of the future than valuing it for its consumptive benefits, those who value a resource for existence benefits will be at a negotiating disadvantage when engaged in regulatory discussions with those who value a resource for its consumptive benefits. They may therefore have more luck working outside a multilateral setting to gain their goals.

The advantages of hegemony, or at least relative power, should be pointed out in this case, however. This case definitely represents the type of coercive hegemony expected in commons situations. It was only through serious unilateral pressure, willingness to withstand the risk of retaliation, and particularly strong market power that the United States was able to succeed at imposing its dolphin-protection predilections on others. While a hegemonic actor with particular characteristics may be able to impose its form of regulation on others and in that manner protect the resources in a commons, the fact remains that actual unilateral provision of a CPR good is impossible. In this example the hegemon was not able to protect the resource unilaterally, but rather use its power to persuade others to protect the resource as well.

Market Power

The fact that the United States is the largest market for tuna should give it influence in setting international policies relating to tuna, especially when its threats against states that do not accede to its regulatory demands in this area have specifically required embargoes on tuna from the recalcitrant states. Why, then, did the United States (with the same degree of market power) succeed in imposing its tuna regulations relating to dolphins when it did not have success in preventing the regulation of tuna within EEZs?

Part of the story almost certainly relates to the fact that in one instance the tuna is regulated as an appropriation problem, and in the other it is regulated as a provision problem. Catching tuna is an appropriation problem if the focus is tuna and the concern is whether there will be a sustainable stock of tuna remaining to reproduce. Catching tuna is a provision problem if the focus is dolphins and catching tuna causes the death of dolphins. Changing perspective on the type of CPR problem the same activity represents includes a different set of actors than would be involved in the environmental problem if the issues were only an appropriation problem for the appropriators. When it became a problem of provision of protected dolphins of concern to those who value the existence of dolphins, the market power of the United States in tuna increased. Actors who did not care about the appropriation of tuna now cared about the provision of dolphins, and were willing to change their tuna consumption for that purpose. Environmental groups set up boycotts of tuna that was not caught in a "dolphin-safe" manner and foreign tuna fishers found themselves having to change their tuna-fishing practices even faster than required by US law to meet the particular demands of the market of those who cared about dolphins for their existence value. In changing the type of environmental problem that was considered to be behind the regulations on tuna, a different set of values, and a different set of actors were engaged.

Another reason that seemingly similar US market power was able to succeed in the case of protecting dolphins and not in the case of maintaining international regulation of Pacific tuna had to do with the types of relative power that market power had to counter, which in turn hinges on the extent to which the solution reached redistributed power. The incentive structure that the market power has to overcome is much lower in the case of dolphin protection than in the case of resisting EEZs. Protecting dolphins in the course of tuna fishing does not redistribute the power of access to resources— if everyone has to catch tuna with the same restrictions there are no benefits for anyone relatively. (In fact, the benefits came initially to US industry from having to convince others to meet the same standards they did.) To the extent that it is more costly for states that did not previously protect dolphins to catch tuna under the new system, that cost is at least shared equally among those who catch tuna. The creation of EEZs and regulation of tuna within them, however, does redistribute access to resources. How much power one has to use in a given situation depends on how hard it is to change the interests that one is trying to change.

Although states resisted US attempts in both cases, the resistance to continuing international tuna conservation measures was much stronger, due to the redistribution of access to resources gained by states that wanted to regulate tuna within EEZs. That, combined with a weaker form of market power since public outcry did not rally against tuna from states that regulated within

EEZs, led the United States to have less influence in that case than in the dolphin-protection case.

Although attempted changes in the elasticity of demand might influence the ability of states to collectively regulate CPRs successfully, such changes were not directly attempted in any of the tuna regulations examined here. One might expect tuna to have a fairly high elasticity of demand, since its main use is as an inexpensive source of protein. Perhaps the fact that the United States so completely dominates the tuna market makes the ability of other states to change that elasticity of demand less likely.

Conclusion

When viewed through a CPR lens, the outcomes of attempted tuna fishing regulations make sense. The mere collective incentive to regulate a commons falls prey to Hardin's "tragedy" and it is therefore not surprising that states have not had success at regulating this commons collectively. The fact that individual discount rates are higher than collective ones explains general failure to protect tuna stocks internationally. The CPR approach can also explain why regulating was more successful when it focused on preserving the existence of dolphins than the consumption of tuna itself.

The inability of privatization to solve this tragedy comes in part from the inextricably common nature of ocean resources and tuna in particular. Although there may be some advantages to privatization, tuna are the wrong species of fish to regulate in that manner since they are so highly migratory. The victory of states that preferred unilateral regulation of fisheries, explained above, was a hollow victory, since it did not actually preserve tuna stocks any more successfully than international regulation had. It should also be pointed out that EEZs did not create true privatization, since it is impossible for individuals to "own" fish that swim in the ocean in the same way they could own cows or parts of a common pasture. Even "owning" part of the ocean is meaningless to some extent when the resources in question swim in and out of that area. The closest thing to true privatization in ocean fisheries is to give individual (usually tradable) quotas to fishers, a strategy that has been applied within EEZs of some countries such as New Zealand and Iceland. These efforts still involve the difficulties of monitoring and enforcement, as well as ensuring that quotas are designed correctly,[35] but they have had some success in regulating fisheries that can be contained within an EEZ. Privatization for tuna fisheries did not work both because it was incompletely implemented and because the highly migratory nature of tuna makes them unlikely candidates for privatization.

The fact that unilateral attempts—by the same hegemonic actor—to force a set of international regulations on tuna fishing failed in one case and succeeded in another can be attributed to the problem of free riders, the existence of different shadows of the future among the actors, and some variations in what would otherwise seem to be the same degree of market power, held by the same actor. Some of these factors come from the fact that these two types of regulations, on the same set of actors, actually represent very different aspects of CPR problems. Regulations to conserve tuna can be seen as appropriation problems while regulations on tuna to protect dolphins are instead provision problems. More important, the first turns on issues of consumptive value attached to tuna, and the second turns on issues of existence value of dolphins, thus leading to different discount rates for the actors involved. And each engages a different set of actors, as well, with different results.

The tuna example, therefore, shows not only the value of examining resource issues in terms of common pool resource problems, but also shows how the aspect of the problem considered changes the set of incentives that influence the outcomes. Fisheries regulations are among the least successful environmental regulations worldwide, and perhaps more attention to the CPR dynamics that exist in addressing them will make their success more likely.

Notes

1. The differences between public goods and CPRs are discussed more fully in chapter 1.

2. Garrett Hardin, "The Tragedy of the Commons," *Science* vol. 162 (1968), pp. 1243–48.

3. "The Tragedy of the Oceans," *Economist* March 19, 1994, p. 24.

4. IATTC Annual Report 1950 and 1951 (La Jolla, CA: IATTC, 1952), p. 3. (All IATTC Annual Reports are published the year following their date, and all by the IATTC in La Jolla, California. These reports will henceforth be cited as "IATTC Annual Report [year].")

5. IATTC Annual Report for the Years 1950 and 1951, p. 17.

6. IATTC Annual Report 1966, p. 8.

7. IATTC Annual Report 1962, p. 15.

8. IATTC Annual Report 1967.

9. IATTC Annual Reports 1966 through 1990.

10. N. Peter Rasmussen, "The Tuna War: Fishery Jurisdiction in International Law," *University of Illinois Law Review* no. 3 (1981), p. 7578.

11. The United States, Costa Rica, Guatemala, Honduras, and Panama negotiated an Interim Agreement in 1983 but it has not come into force; Ecuador, El Salvador, Mexico, Nicaragua, and Peru signed the Lima Convention, establishing the Eastern Pacific Tuna Organization, in 1989; it, likewise, has not come into force.

12. There was an unsuccessful attempt to list bluefin tuna in Appendix I under Convention on International Trade in Endangered Species, which would have prohibited trading in this species. Although this attempt did not succeed, many environmental organizations claim that bluefin tuna are among the most endangered species. See, for example, World Wildlife Fund, "WWF's 1994 Ten Most Endangered List," http://envirolink.org.arrs.endangered.html, May 26, 1996.

13. Alberto Szekely and Barbara Kwiatkowska, "Marine Living Resources," in Peter H. Sand, ed., *The Effectiveness of International Environmental Agreements: A Survey of Existing Legal Instruments* (Cambridge: Grotius Publications, Ltd.), p. 276.

14. *Los Angeles Times*, May 29, 1993, p. A1.

15. John Van Dyke, "Tuna Management in the Pacific: An Analysis of the South Pacific Forum Fisheries Agency," *University of Hawaii Law Review* vol. 3 (1981), p. 28.

16. Ted Williams, "The Last Bluefin Hunt," *Audubon*, July–August 1992, p. 18.

17. Peter Weber, "Protecting Ocean Fisheries and Jobs," http://www.runet.edu/~geog-web/GEOG340/read007.html, March 9, 1996.

18. See Rasmussen, pp. 758, 764.

19. 16 U.S.C. 1825.

20. See Rasmussen, p. 760; also Elizabeth R. DeSombre "Baptists and Bootleggers

for the Environment: The Origins of United States Unilateral Sanctions," *Journal of Environment and Development* vol. 4 (1995), pp. 63–64.

21. P.L. 101–627, Title I, Section 101(b).

22. Section 101(a)(2) of the Marine Mammal Protection Act.

23. Anthony D'Amato and Sudhir K. Chopra, "Whales: Their Emerging Right To Life," *American Journal of International Law* 85 (1991), pp. 21–62.

24. See DeSombre, "Baptists and Bootleggers," pp. 53–75.

25. The IATTC at this point, with its inability to set tuna catch levels, did not have much other regulatory capacity and many of its original members had withdrawn. It did, among other things, set up an observer system to certify that dolphin protection measures were taken by individual fishing vessels.

26. Although privatization would not necessarily lead to overconsumption, it would change the amount of the resource available for others to consume, as discussed below. For that reason it can be considered as a threat of free-riding.

27. Clifford L. Peterson and William H. Bayliff, "Organization, Functions, and Achievements of the Inter-American Tropical Tuna Commission," *Inter-American Tropical Tuna Commission Special Report No. 5* (La Jolla, CA: IATTC, 1985), p. 24. This exception was changed for 1970 through 1975 to vessels with capacity lower than 400 tons, and the allocation was raised to 6,000 tons per state. In 1976 the allocation was allowed for vessels with capacity up to 600 tons, and beginning in 1977 special exceptions to this standard were negotiated for individual states.

28. Joseph and Greenough, p. 120.

29. A. D. Rose, "The Tuna Example: Is there Hope for International Cooperation?" *San Diego Law Review* vol. 11 (1974), p. 788.

30. Van Dyke, p. 28

31. Peter Weber, "Protecting Ocean Fisheries and Jobs," http://www.runet.edu/~geog-web/GEOG340/read007.html, March 9, 1996.

32. James Joseph and Joseph W. Greenough, *International Management of Tuna, Porpoise, and Billfish: Biological, Legal, and Political Aspects* (Seattle: University of Washington Press, 1979).

33. This insight was made in the context of the Canada-Spain "Turbot War" in 1995, though Pierre Trudeau, when Prime Minister of Canada, is said to have made this observation at an earlier point.

34. Elizabeth R. DeSombre, *Domestic Sources of International Environmental Policy: Industry, Environmentalists, and U.S. Power*, Ph.D. Dissertation, Harvard University (April 1996), pp. 247–48.

35. See, for example, Parzival Copes, "A Critical Review of the Individual Quota as a Device in Fisheries Management," *Land Economics* vol. 62 (1986), pp. 278–91.

4 Managing Common-Pool Marine Living Resources: Lessons from the Southern Ocean Experience

CHRISTOPHER C. JOYNER

Introduction

The Southern Ocean, lying beyond the limits of national jurisdiction, constitutes part of the global marine commons. As such, the living resources within that ocean area entail a common pool resource (CPR) of the high seas, susceptible to lawful exploitation by persons from any state possessing the capability to harvest those resources.

Beginning in the early 1970s, however, several fishing states began widespread exploitation of living resources in the southern seas. Concerns arose among other states that unless these multinational exploitation efforts were checked, or at least somewhat regulated, various stocks of common-pool living resources could become severely depleted. Multilateral exploitation of the Southern Ocean thus has presented the international community with a CPR problem and continues to present it with a long-term CPR issue. A CPR problem exists when overconsumption of a limited resource occurs. The management of CPRs is threatened and diminishing fish species in the Southern

Ocean becomes a CPR problem. A common-pool resource issue arises where a potential exists for overconsumption. Excessive exploitation of the Southern Ocean has demonstrated that the renewable resources there are indeed limited and can be depleted by overconsumption. The management of species in the Southern Ocean which potentially may be exploited, but have not yet been harvested beyond their capacity, therefore represents a CPR issue. As a consequence, the international political dynamics of the exploitation and management of living resources of the southern seas will be used to analyze a series of hypotheses regarding CPR problems and CPR issues.

Toward this end, the second section sets out the limits of the Southern Ocean and the CPRs at risk. The costs and incentives for exploitation in south polar waters are evaluated in terms of both their consumptive and existence benefits. On the one hand, the cases suggest that CPRs that are valued for their existence, like fur seals and whales of the Southern Ocean, are relatively easy to manage because actors generally share common interests and have similar shadows of the future for benefit to be gained from the resource. On the other hand, CPRs that are valued primarily for their consumptive benefits, like fin fish and krill of the Southern Ocean, pose greater difficulties for CPR management and long-term CPR issues. These actors are far more likely to have different shadows of the future and are likely to be motivated by exogenous factors that affect their assessment of the net gain to be had by consumption and overconsumption. The second section will evaluate how shifts in the net consumptive benefit of CPRs affects the likelihood of their exploitation and management. It then examines certain implications of these factors for actions and bargaining strategies of those actors who place more value on existence benefits of the CPR. The third section analyzes the evolution of the special fisheries regime in place in terms of the impact and treatment of knowledge about the resources on the actions of those who value consumptive and existence benefits. It concludes by exploring the implications of these differences for the issue of enforcement and the likelihood of long-term management of the CPR issue for living resources in the Southern Ocean.

The Southern Ocean as a Common Pool

Nature of the Area

The Southern Ocean covers about 10 percent of world's oceans and covers approximately 36 million square kilometers. It is comprised of the southern extremities of the Indian, Atlantic and Pacific Oceans, and serves as the hub of the earth's atmospheric and marine currents. The northern boundary of the Southern Ocean is defined by the Antarctic Convergence, a natural oceano-graphic zone meandering around the 50 degrees South Latitude mark. It is here where cold southern surface waters are pushed below the warmer, northern waters moving to the south. The Convergence forms an effective biological barrier: very few species migrate beyond it. It is thus a natural boundary within which to manage the tremendous resources of the Antarctic oceans.

The Antarctic seas biologically are among the most productive on earth. The Southern Ocean teems with abundant quantities of marine living re-sources such as seals, whales, fin fish, squid, and in coastal areas, sea birds (in-cluding penguins). The vital nexus in the Antarctic food chain, however, is a 2-inch long, shrimplike crustacean known as krill. Krill swarms, which thrive on the high productivity of phytoplankton photosynthesis, serve directly as the principal food for numerous species of indigenous marine life, including whales, seals, squid, and penguins.[1]

The Southern Ocean and Environmental Amenities

Both existence and consumptive benefits characterize motivations for ex-ploiting and managing living resources in the Southern Ocean. On the one hand, seals and whales have been accorded the status of existence benefits in the south polar marine environment. Protection and preservation of these re-sources has become predicated more on the knowledge of those living amenities' existence than on their perceived commercial value. On the other hand, fish and krill resources have been treated more in terms of consumptive benefits. Harvesting of fish and krill continues by fishermen from various states. Motivations to conserve fish and krill resources stem from the need of fisher-men to enhance future consumptive benefits, as well as from the desire of con-servationists to preserve stocks for ecological balance. This distinction makes a difference in the likely success of management efforts because it affects the value and shadow of the future each would-be exploiter assigns to the resource.

Resource exploitation in the Southern Ocean resembles the problem of overgrazing used to describe the tragedy of the commons. Fish, krill, seals, and whales are renewable resources that can be sustainably harvested. How-ever, excessive harvesting since 1970 has threatened to exhaust these re-sources, demonstrating that their carrying capacity is limited and presenting would-be consumers with a CPR problem.

Successful management of a CPR problem inevitably rests on overcoming the interests of individual states to maximize their share of the consumptive economic benefits, while maximizing the existence benefits they derive from the resource. In the Southern Ocean agreements have been established to manage the harvesting of seals and whales, as well as fin fish and krill. The balance between consumptive and existence motivations for the management and exploitation in each case can explain some of the variation in the political dynamics and success of these agreements. For example, success has been more straightforward in the case of seals and whales where the existence benefits of the resource play a relatively large role in determining resource exploitation and management. In contrast, the management of CPR problems and issues were more complex for fin fish and krill, where the consumptive benefits outweighed existence benefits as the primary motivation for exploitation and management.

In 1972 a special Convention on the Conservation of Seals[2] was negotiated among a certain group of states. This multilateral instrument, which entered into force in 1978, aims at limiting the vulnerability of Antarctic seals to commercial exploitation through overharvesting and aspires to "promote and achieve the objectives of protection, scientific study, and rational use of Antarctic seals, and to maintain a satisfactory balance within the ecological system."[3] Importantly, since the promulgation of this Seals Convention, no sealing activities have been reported in the Southern Ocean.

With regard to whales, the operative instrument for conserving and protecting their numbers is the 1946 International Whaling Convention,[4] which established the International Whaling Commission (IWC). The IWC agreed in 1982 to a moratorium on taking whales and in 1985 it entered into force.[5] More recently and far more significantly, France in 1992 proposed at the forty-fourth annual meeting of the IWC creation of a whale sanctuary in the Southern Hemisphere. In 1994 the IWC formally voted at its forty-sixth annual meeting to adopt the Southern Ocean Whale Sanctuary.[6] The sanctuary bans commercial whaling in over 8 million square miles of ocean in the Southern Hemisphere and protects the primary feeding grounds for over 90 percent of the world's remaining whales. Given the sanctuary's proper implementation, the tragic history of whaling in the Antarctic, with more than 1.5 million whales having been killed this century, will be brought to a close.[7]

The convergence of interest regarding the existence benefits of whales and fur seals can help to explain the success of the whaling and seal regimes. In both cases, since existence benefits outweighed consumptive benefits, actors had both equivalent and long shadows of the future for seals and whales. As suggested in chapter 1, increasing the shadow of the future by the same amount all around can facilitate finding a solution to a CPR problem. The success of the whaling and seal regimes in the Southern Ocean generally support this proposition.

It is important to note, however, that one exception stands out to the agreements. Japan was the only involved government not to sign on to the IWC Whale Sanctuary. Japan's position holds consistent with its preference for consumptive benefits versus existence benefits from whaling. Because it continues to value consumptive benefits over existence benefits, Japan's shadow of the future for whales was different and likely shorter than those governments that valued existence benefits. That is, while Japan had a vested interest in preserving a whale stock sufficient to continue whaling, it placed relatively less value on the existence of each individual whale for its own sake. In line with hypothesis 1a in chapter 1, if consumers recognize different shadows of the future, or potential agreements affect these shadows differently, then consumers with the shorter shadow of the future will have greater bargaining power than those with the longer. Based on this proposition, Japan should be able to extract bargaining concessions from others that value existence benefits of whales. Even so, Japan has not yet sought to pull this lever. Recent reports indicate that the Japanese "scientific whaling" fleet intended to defy the sanctuary during late 1995 with the aim of harvesting 440 minke whales (up from 330 in 1994).[8] Increased whaling to appease domestic consumer interests is apparently deemed paramount by the Japanese government as compared to using the whaling issue as a bargaining tool in international diplomacy.

The most pervasive and severe threats to living resources in the Antarctic marine ecosystem are harvesting activities to catch fin fish and krill. The primary motivations for exploitation and preservation of these stocks are based on consumptive benefits rather than existence benefits of the resource. As a result, the shadows of the future for exploitation and management of these resources are likely to vary among potential exploiters more than they do for whales and seals. The factors that affect the shadow of the future perceived with respect to the exploitation and preservation of fin fish and krill are also likely to be much more complex and varied than those affecting goods that are thought of primarily in terms of existence benefits. Until the 1980s, fishing operations in Antarctic waters were conducted almost exclusively by fleets from former Eastern bloc states. Large-scale harvesting of fin fish began by the Soviets in 1969–70 around South Georgia, and the next year, around

Kerguelen Island. Poland, the former German Democratic Republic and Bulgaria joined in fishing there in 1977. During the 1980s and 1990s, however, catches fell off rapidly.[9] Japan, too, fished in Antarctic waters, with most of its fishing activities concentrated in the South Atlantic.

Fin fishing has mirrored the procession of whaling in the Southern Ocean, but on a far more collapsed time scale. Each went through stages of discovery, exploitation, and depletion of various stocks in southern waters. Depletion of demersal fish stocks, seen in the harvesting of Patagonian toothfish and the sub-Antarctic lantern fish, began in the latter 1980s and has since persisted.

Krill catches reached their maximum annual take of 500,000 tons in 1981–82.[10] In subsequent years, catch levels fell considerably before stablizing in 1991 to a range between 350,000–400,000 tons.[11] The shift in the exploitation pattern of krill demonstrates an interesting dynamic of market power and the affect of the absolute value of the resource on the likelihood of competitive exploitation versus joint management. Hypothesis 3a argues that high elasticities of demand for CPR resources tend to increase the incentives for competitive exploitation and diminish the likelihood that cooperative agreements will be reached. The case of krill demonstrates the reciprocal event. Much of the decline in the krill catch can be explained by the increasing relative costs (or decreasing net benefit) of processing krill and a resulting shift toward fin fishing. Until a new market increases the demand and value of krill fishing, this is likely to continue. To wit, catch levels reported for krill during the 1997–98 season amounted to only some 81,000 tons.[12]

The Soviets, traditionally the leading fisherman in the Antarctic commons for both fin fish and krill, tended to favor the South Atlantic and accounted for some 85 percent of catches in the region. It seems Japan and the lesser fishing states will maintain the levels because the consumptive benefits from exploitation have remained unchanged. In contrast, declining economic conditions in the former Soviet Republics have dramatically increased the costs of exploitation. Only Russia and Ukraine still fish, although Russia has not outfitted a fishing fleet in Antarctic waters for the past six seasons.[13] This behavior is consistent with the proposition that a deteriorating net value of the consumptive benefit of a CPR decreases the incentive for individual exploitation and decreases the incentive for compliance with joint management regimes. Shifts in the net consumptive benefit of the resource due to shifts in the ability to pay the high costs of processing has helped to solve the 1980s concern about overconsumption of krill, leading to a stabilized consumption rate far below previous levels.

The total krill catch today appears considerably less than the reckoned global sustainable yield. Even so, because krill swarms remain so locally concentrated, usually in foraging areas of breeding predators, precautionary limits on permissible catches have been adopted by concerned states. In the South Atlantic that annual limit is presently 1.5 million tons, with a provision that when the catch reaches 620,000 tons (the highest recorded annual catch), finer limits would be imposed. Precautionary limits were also adopted for Prydz Bay/Enderby Land coast, currently at 390,000 tons.[14]

It is important to remember that, while the CPR problem of krill overconsumption has been effectively managed at least in part, the CPR issue of potential overconsumption remains. Under current demand conditions, the high costs of processing will keep the net consumptive benefits of krill exploitation relatively low. If world demand for krill increases, however, the net consumptive benefits of exploitation will rise as well. Hypothesis 3b in chapter 1 argues that large consumers, or countries with large consumer markets, can gain bargaining power by using their markets to alter the value of CPR extraction for others. The value can either be decreased, due to shifts in consumer demand away from the CPR, or increased by increasing demand for the CPR. The latter scenario presents a number of implications for future management of the CPR issue of the Southern Ocean's living resources.

In the long term, greater concern may be warranted over the future national fishing strategies of certain large Third World countries. While India is a contracting party to CCAMLR, China is not. Yet, were India and China to enter the krill fishery in a serious way, those efforts could impact significantly on krill stocks in the Southern Ocean. With India's growing population of 850 million and that of China's at 1.4 billion, it is not unimaginable that either or both of these Asian giants could turn to Antarctic fish or krill stocks to supplement their national protein needs. Neither India nor China presently has credible fishing fleets capable of harvesting and processing fish or krill in vast quantities in Antarctic waters. Nor has either government indicated a serious inclination to embark on such a national strategy at present. Increased domestic demand for protein could, however, radically shift the net consumptive benefit of large-scale harvests. If this happens, enforcement of the regime will become problematic and the threat of overconsumption by either the Chinese or Indian government will become credible. As a result, the threat of overconsumption by Chinese and Indian fishers will likely give them leverage in negotiations over the enforcement and reformulation of the regime.

The CCAMLR Regime

Resource Knowledge and Enforcement

The growth of commercial fisheries poses significant risks for CPRs in Antarctic seas. How well these renewable resources are able to be used depends on the ability to recognize and deal effectively with a number of complex and often interrelated factors. Perhaps the most important factor is that krill is the foundation species of the Antarctic marine food web—that many species of mammals, birds, fish, and squid in the Antarctic marine commons are dependent on krill, either directly or indirectly, as their primary food source.

A second factor directly spins off from krill's central role in the Antarctic marine ecosystem. Harvesting krill could produce multiple impacts, including any or all of the following: (1) increases in the abundance of competing species and possible replacement of krill as the dominant herbivore in the Antarctic marine food web might occur; (2) conditions that interfere with the recovery of depleted and endangered whale populations might be fostered; (3) depletion of independent populations of seals, birds, fish, and squid might be caused; and of course (4) depletion of krill populations certainly would take place.

Still another salient consideration concerns the availability of pertinent information on the Antarctic ecosystem. Data on the biology and ecology of krill, krill competitors, and krill predators remain inadequate to predict with much confidence what quantities of krill and other species might be taken from the ecosystem without depleting the target species or skewing the numerical or biological relationship among target, dependent, and associated species. Lack of knowledge regarding the sustainability of a resource will have different effects on the likelihood of CPR management and exploitation depending on whether the resource is valued for its consumptive or existence benefits due to the different shadows of the future associated with consumptive versus existence benefits of CPRs (see chapter 2). On the one hand, if the primary motivation for CPR exploitation and management involves existence benefits, as with whales and fur seals, lack of dependable data is likely to make those who worry more cautious, more willing to overmanage the resource, and more susceptible to threats made by those who desire the same goods for consumptive purposes. On the other hand, lack of certain information about a resource is likely to make those who value it for consumptive reasons less willing to alter their behavior until convincing knowledge about overconsumption is available. The following section will evaluate the implications of these factors for the Southern Ocean, in particular the impact of information and the issue of enforcement for the CCAMLR regime.

The Task of Conservation

During the 1970s, a certain group of states became increasingly aware of the risks associated with the exploitation of living CPRs in circumpolar Antarctic waters. These states, collectively known as the Consultative Parties owing to their special association with the 1959 Antarctic Treaty, agreed to negotiate a special agreement among themselves based on an ecosystem approach that would include within its scope resources that were not commercially exploitable.

In 1980 the Convention on the Conservation of Antarctic Marine Living Resources (CCAMLR) was promulgated.[15] The explicit aim of this agreement, which entered into force in 1982, is to control exploitation of living CPRs in the Southern Ocean by creating a regime for managing conservation of those resources.[16] Importantly, CCAMLR is a legally binding international instrument. That is, CCAMLR's provisions are legal mandates; they are not mere hortatory directives. Governments that opt to become party to this agreement are obligated to abide by legal regulations set out in its provisions.

Under CCAMLR the concept of "conservation" means "rational use."[17] But CCAMLR is not only concerned with fishing. The Convention incorporates an "ecosystem approach" for management of common pool resources in the Southern Ocean. That is, if harvesting of any species occurs, then due regard must not only be paid to the impact of that harvesting on the target species, but also on other species and the marine ecosystem as a whole.[18]

The ecosystem approach is the principal innovation supplied by CCAMLR to achieve the critical goal of conservation. The conservation principles articulated in the Convention require that: (1) exploited populations not be allowed to fall below a level close to that which ensures their greatest net annual increase; (2) depleted populations must be restored to such levels; (3) ecological relationships between harvested, dependent, and related species must be maintained; and (4) risks of changes to the marine ecosystem that are not potentially reversible over two or three decades must be minimized.[19] These stringent principles embody the ecosystem approach to living resource conservation and distinguish the Convention from other marine resource management regime.

Management of fishing must not only strive to conserve a targeted species;

it must also take into account the impact of harvesting on those creatures that prey on and compete with the target species. Hence, scientific research on the marine ecosystem becomes essential for sustaining the ecosystem approach, and inevitably, for effecting responsible conservation policies throughout the Antarctic marine commons.

At present, the most depleted fishery is that for *N. rossii* (a codlike species) around South Georgia and the South Shetlands. The reason for the drastic decline and inability of this species of cod to recover remains a mystery. A series of ecological events may have compounded threats to their life cycle. To wit: populations of seals have expanded tremendously in these same regions. Perhaps seals are eating larvae of species, or maybe penguins are eating larvae. These predator conditions, coupled with overharvesting during 1970s, produced such a drastic decline in the *N. rossii* population that they have not yet been able to come back.[20]

A particularly noteworthy CCAMLR conservation regulation was adopted in 1991. Conservation Measure 32/X set precautionary catch limits of 1.5 million tons per year for krill in the Atlantic sectors.[21] The Commission has given high priority to setting additional precautionary catch limits for krill elsewhere in the Convention area and to adopting special conservation measures that ensure that sufficient krill is kept available to meet the needs of predators. While the impact of this measure is not fully quantifiable—and thus not subject to direct attribution—the biomass estimate of krill has recently been revised upward some 3–5 million tons,[22] a significant increase over estimates in previous years.

The krill experience furnished an important step toward achieving precautionary management in an uncertain biological environment. To that end, Conservation Measure 32/X suggests the logic that some preclusive action might be necessary before sufficient scientific data on an environmental situation can be obtained or assessed. That is, the reactive management policies of the 1980s became viewed as insufficient and too capricious. Such reactive policies perhaps might remedy a bad situation, but they were unable to deal adequately with pending threats to the ecosystem. It was more prudent to act now with some conservation policies than to wait for more data and possibly pay an exorbitant environmental price later.

This ecosystemic approach is the principal conservation innovation supplied by CCAMLR. As set by the Convention, three ambitions guide the ecosystem approach: (1) to keep the harvesting of any species on an sustainable basis over the long term; (2) to maintain balanced ecological relationships between harvested, dependent, and related populations—that is, to ensure that depleted populations are restored to sustainable use levels; and (3) to minimize the risk of irreversible changes in the marine ecosystem. Scientific research on the marine ecosystem and its component therefore becomes the critical ingredient in sustaining ecosystem approach.

Jurisdiction of CCAMLR

The jurisdictional reach of CCAMLR for its conservation efforts is impressive. Through its ecosystem approach, the scope of the Convention encompasses all marine living resources within the area roughly bounded by the Antarctic Convergence—which reaches northward to 40 degrees South Latitude. CCAMLR thus differs from the northern ambit of 60 degrees South Latitude used by other ATS instruments.[23]

Defined in broad terms, CCAMLR covers all species of marine living organisms in the Antarctic commons, including seals.[24] The nature of the instrument suggests the obvious. CCAMLR is not meant to apply so much to the area south of the Antarctic Convergence as it does to the marine living resources found within that area. In this respect, CCAMLR differs from other agreements in the Antarctic Treaty System, which focus more on activities in a given area rather than on the resources per se.[25]

Distinctions are set out in CCAMLR between different maritime zones, even some in the area that it circumscribes. Notable here are understandings negotiated within the Convention that acknowledge the rights by France to agree to application of the conservation measures to waters around Kerguelen and Crozet Islands. These understandings recognize France's right to use its own national measures to regulate these zones.[26]

Participation in CCAMLR is open to states, as well as other competent international entities not party to the Antarctic Treaty. While far-sighted in terms of conservation appeal, this opportunity also revealed a recognition by the Consultative Parties of their inability to lawfully regulate fishing activities on the high seas by third countries. Consequently, accession to CCAMLR is permitted by "any State interested in research or harvesting activities on relation to the marine resources to which this Convention applies."[27]

That CCAMLR includes a consensus rule for decisions in the Commission was done to accommodate and protect the position of the claimants. Significantly, however, consensus also coincided with the interests of fishing states in the region—in particular, Japan and the then Soviet Union—who wished to retain their own discretion in the exercise of those activities in the region. This can be explained in terms of their concerns about consumptive as opposed to existence benefits. It also reflects their potential roles as free riders on future accords.

As of early 1999, the Commission has twenty-two members.[28] All states that fish in southern waters are members of the Commission, save for two—Ukraine and Bulgaria. Both of these states are now acceding states to the Convention, and may likely join the Commission later.

On a separate conservation track, the CCAMLR Commission in 1990 endorsed the objectives of General Assembly Resolution 44/225 (1990) concerning large-scale pelagic driftnets, agreeing that such driftnet fishing should not be allowed into the Convention area. If enforced, that prohibition would practically exclude the entire Southern Ocean from large-scale pelagic driftnet fishing by CCAMLR members.[29]

The Commission also agreed that members that have neither accepted nor ratified Annex V of the International Convention for the Prevention of Pollution from Ships (MARPOL 73/78) should take steps to do so and to ensure that their vessels operating within the Convention area are in compliance with provisions of Annex V (especially dispersal of synthetic materials, e.g., ropes and fishing nets).

Beginning in 1991, members contemplating opening a new fishery within the CCAMLR area are supposed to notify the Commission in advance. Information must be provided on the type of fishery, target species, fishing methods, region, biological information on dependent, and associated species.[30] This information will be evaluated by the Scientific Committee to assess potential yields and risks of opening up such a fishery.[31] Recent examples of such fisheries include the United States' crab fishery close to South Georgia and Chile's new fishery for Patagonian toothfish around the South Sandwich Islands.[32]

Enforcement for Compliance

Compliance depends on enforcement. Enforcement of a collective management agreement is possible only if noncompliance can be detected. Inspection monitoring and enforcement are also necessary with respect to compliance. This is needed even if a CPR problem has not yet evolved. Effective collective action relies heavily on voluntary compliance. No institution can operate effectively unless the preponderant majority of those subject to it voluntarily comply with it most of the time. Monitors must constantly audit common pool conditions and member compliance with the agreement. Monitors must be members, or at least accountable to the membership.

Inspection and monitoring produce benefits even when no one is discovered cheating, as they serve as deterrents to those who might cheat. Inspection and monitoring also assure others that the adherence of others apparently is being met.

Governments may be more willing to comply with rules for managing common pool resources under two preeminent conditions. First, compliance will come when governments believe that the goals of collective oversight are being achieved, thus making themselves and the group better off than under an open access regime. Second, compliance is more likely when governments believe that others are also complying with the given collective management rules. Such perceptions make for compliance and reduce the need to rely on coercion for cooperation.

Inspection and monitoring contribute to these conditions by deterring individual governments that might be tempted to break the rules and by assuring each government that others are also abiding by the agreement, thus increasing confidence that full benefits of common management will be realized.

A system for vessel inspection was not put in place until 1989–90. Since 1991, though, inspectors have boarded vessels for a few hours with the authority to observe and inspect catch, nets, fishing gear, harvesting activities. Problems with these CCAMLR inspections have become evident, however. The remoteness of these fishing grounds, difficulties with logistics and high costs associated with maintaining inspection vessels necessitate firm backing of states with strong national interests to make the system effective (e.g., the efforts by France in its claimed Kerguelen fishing zone). Such national commitment is often lacking. In addition, inspectors are not appointed by the Commission. Rather, they are designated by national governments party to CCAMLR to inspect their own vessels. This situation permits monitoring that may be less than independent or impartial. During 1991–92, of eighteen inspections performed, sixteen were done by inspectors on board vessels of their own nationality.[33] During the 1990–91 season, Soviet inspectors carried out some 150 inspections, but reports of these inspections were not submitted to the Commission on the proper CCAMLR reporting forms.[34] Such conditions can foster a free-rider problem.

Implementation of a scheme for international scientific observation was delayed until 1992–93. Nevertheless, its purpose is to gather information on fishing activities in the Convention area, including details on vessel operation, biological data about species caught, and records of incidental mortality. While some concern surfaced that observers might become de facto inspectors, the scheme presently works through bilateral agreements, with observers being nationals of the states that delegate them.

Enforcement of conservation measures obviously remains key to effecting CCAMLR's resource management system. In principle, a conservation measure is agreed on by members, and if no objection is registered within 90 days, it becomes binding on members after 180 days.[35] Since 1988, however, measures taken for the fishery around South Georgia have become binding immediately after adoption in consideration of the severity of depletion of fish stocks there.[36]

At least 117 conservation measures have been approved by the Commission since 1982. Many of them, however, lapsed and intentionally have not been renewed. In 1998 the number of CCAMLR conservation measures in force totals 56.[37]

The conservation measures adopted by the Commission clearly reflect the conservation-oriented function of CCAMLR. For one, directed fin fishing in the Atlantic sector has been prohibited for all species, save for mackerel icefish, Patagonian toothfish and lanternfish, within the subarea of South Georgia.[38] Other measures adopted and implemented include mesh size restrictions for fishermen, the designation of areas closed to fishing, closed seasons for catching particular species and by-catch provisions.[39]

Dispute Settlement

For regime cooperation to be preserved, means for dispute settlement must be available should conflict arise between participating governments. Group members need access to low-cost methods of resolving disputes over the use of common pool resources and interpretation of the rules. Disagreements are bound to arise. Institutions designed to settle disputes must be perceived as adequate, efficient, fair, and impartial. Open communication to discuss disagreements and resolve disputes must be permitted.

Of note, CCAMLR's dispute settlement provisions in Article XXV have been extracted nearly verbatim from Article XI of the Antarctic Treaty. Peaceful settlement of disputes is intended to proceed through a process. First, attempts should be made to settle the dispute bilaterally by consultation and negotiation between the disputants themselves. Failing that, those parties should agree on resolving the dispute by inquiry, mediation, conciliation, arbitration, judicial settlement, or any other peaceful means they decide on.[40] Provision is also made for mandatory settlement of the dispute though the International Court of Justice, or through arbitration. In the latter option,

CCAMLR actually improves on the dispute settlement procedure by providing for an arbitral tribunal in the Annex to the Convention.

While disputes among parties to CCAMLR have been avoided, certain problems have clearly caused tensions between blocs of party states. Since 1984, the Scientific Committee has advocated increasingly strict regulation for fin fishing, which has been greeted each year with greater support by the Commission. Even so, opinion in the Commission often became polarized between fishing and nonfishing states. Fishers viewed fin fish in terms of consumptive benefits, nonfishers viewed fish in terms of nonconsumptive and existence benefits. This creates different incentive structures and different shadows of the future as regards fishing. As a result, arriving at consensus on more rigorous conservation measures became stalled, and progress on adopting conservation measures only came slowly.

On the one hand, fishing governments (mainly Japan and the Soviet Union) argued that scientific advice could only be uncertain since there was a lack of adequate information—information that not coincidentally, could be provided only by the fishing states themselves. As a consequence, and not surprisingly, fishing states contended that conservation measures for the purpose of ensuring existence benefits should not be adopted given this dearth of scientific data, thus allowing for fishing to continue and consumptive benefits to be secured.

On the other hand, other nonfishing CCAMLR members believed that, even absent detailed data, the preferable strategy was to err on the side of caution. It was better to adopt reasonable conservation measures to ensure the potential of long-term existence benefits than to risk the decline of fishery stocks falling below sustainable levels by permitting unregulated taking of consumptive benefits.

The Commission remained frustrated in its deliberations until the late 1980s, as compromise proved elusive between the majority of Commission members advocating conservation measures and the few free-rider fishing nations motivated by short-term economic interests. Even so, it is important to understand that CCAMLR did not preside over the drastic depletion of fishery stocks in the Southern Ocean. That depletion had already occurred. The Commission remained stymied until the late 1980s from acting to halt the decline—and thus facilitate the recovery—of those stocks that had been depleted before CCAMLR had ever entered into force.

Given this history of obstruction, the temptation arises to question whether the principle of consensus decision-making might at times carry too exorbitant a price for all out of respect for the wishes of one, or a few. In this connection, decision-making by consensus demonstrated that cost by effectively paralyzing the Commission for more than half a decade. At the same time, one must be mindful of the actual world of international politics. The fact remains that no decision-making procedure can compel governments to accept policies or conservation measures that are perceived as being contrary to their national interests.

Improvement in the implementation of stronger conservation measures for fish stocks during the 1990s was brought about by several factors. For one, a more constructive dialogue between the Commission and the Scientific Committee had been under way since 1985. This improved relationship accrued from several conditions: better inferences were being obtained from increasing accumulation of biological data from fisheries; additional data were being acquired from fishery-independent analyses; and there was the increasing tendency of the Soviet Union (later Russia and the Ukraine) to be more accommodating in reporting and voting in light of the domestic economic constraints on its distant water fishing fleets, coupled with its desire to obtain more foreign aid from the very states who were nonfishing members of the Commission. In sum, consumption patterns and economic motivations of the fishers changed due to changes in their own domestic economic conditions.

The Availability of Sanctions

Recourse to sanctions should be available to induce members to comply with regime rules and procedures. Some form of sanctions for use against deviant governments must be possible. To remain stable and credible international conservation agreements, particularly those that purport to manage common-pool resource areas, must be enforced. Enforcement can come from internally imposed codes of conduct, or from threats—implicit or explicit—of retaliation. Members who violate the agreement should be assessed graduated sanctions by other members. The degree of sanctions should depend on the gravity and context of the violation. Perhaps not surprisingly, successfully managed common pool resources activities carry low levels of sanctions.

In the case of the CCAMLR, individual states remain responsible for legal enforcement of management measures adopted by the Commission. That is, the primary obligation for imposing conservation measures rests with a member government. Thus, in a real sense CCAMLR relies on voluntary compliance by governments to enforce its rules and regulations on their own nationals. The Convention does not provide for sanctions against a deviant party that either refuses or is unable to implement or enforce conservation measures on its nationals. Consequently, CCAMLR's structure has sometimes been considered as weak for enforcement of the Commission's conservation measures.

Even absent the application of sanctions, CCAMLR can be considered a successful CPR management instrument. Today no fishery in the Southern Ocean has been left uncovered by the Commission's conservation measures. Noteworthy also is that the Commission has adopted particularly strong conservation efforts to dissuade incidental mortality rates.

In assessing CCAMLR, it must be remembered that the Commission was handed a situation in which the total catch of demersal fish approximated some 30,000–40,000 tons a year. By 1980 most stocks had already been depleted to levels less than 30 percent of their estimated original biomass level. Stocks of only two significant species—the mackerel icefish and Patagonian toothfish—had escaped serious depletion. But icefish around South Georgia (in Sector area 48.3) had suffered a major biological collapse, the cause for which remains unknown.[41] The plain fact is that CCAMLR inherited a bad situation regarding the condition of standing stocks in the Convention area. Most stocks since 1980 have recovered, except two, *C. gunnari* and *N. rossii*. Interesting to note here is that no Commission member has indicated a desire to reinstate fishing for these species, probably because neither the potential for profit nor the fish stocks are sufficiently attractive.[42]

It is similarly important to realize that data on fish stocks come from national governments—often those of fishing states—and that those data on stocks can be fudged, or the various species caught can be lumped together for the sake of convenience. Such practices skew scientific reality for the sake of harvesting expediency. Also given that fishing data come from governments, the scientific analysis and monitoring of that data requires financial commitment by those governments. Obtaining those financial resources remains difficult in an era of tightening budgetary constraints on Antarctic scientific activities.

Allegations are sometimes posited that consensus decision-making weakens CCAMLR. Still, one must view the situation in its proper context. Once a measure is approved by consensus in the Commission, there is no going back on the decision by a government. In a majority rule decision-making system, a government can object and declare its unwillingness to be bound by such a decision. The consensus process tends to preclude that opportunity. The objector system is not used in CCAMLR, except in rare instances where technical inabilities might prevent a government from meeting its obligations.

The fact is that no state ever formally objects to proposed measures because that point is not permitted to be reached in the Commission's deliberations. In sum, the Commission plenary serves as the opportunity to negotiate compromise positions, not to force some issue to a divisive vote.

Illegal fishing activities within the Convention Area have become a serious concern for CCAMLR in 1998 in 1998. As global fisheries continue to be depleted, fishermen have pushed into southern seas. During the 1995–96 season, illegal fishing for Patagonian toothfish moved from the waters around South Georgia and the Shag Rocks to the exclusive economic zone surrounding South Edward Island. At least twenty vessels were reported to be fishing straddling stocks in these waters, including ships from Vanuatu, Panama, Portugal, and South Africa.[43] Since 1994, several activities that contravene conservation measures, especially fishing out of season, have also been reported by Chile and Argentina. To their credit, these governments have taken legal actions against a number of their nationals' apprehended vessels, including fines, confiscation of catches, and suspension of fishing permits.[44] Even so, in 1998 unlawful fishing activities still persist in sub-Antarctic waters.

Finally, a major problem that CCAMLR must someday confront concerns the issue of straddling stocks on the high seas. Certain fish species, especially the toothfish around South Georgia and the lanternfish around South Georgia—as well as krill around Kerguelen—straddle the Convention area and swim northward into the high seas, outside the protective jurisdiction of CCAMLR. In those waters, of course, the possibility exists that those whole stocks might be caught, a situation that would no doubt contribute to severe depletion of those species. Concern over straddling stocks in the Antarctic commons will remain important to the Commission, even if a new international fishery agreement for straddling stocks on the high seas is promulgated in the near future.

Regime Self-Regulation

The legitimacy of self-regulation by the collective management group should be internationally recognized. The right of group members to design and operate their own institutions must not be effectively challenged by outside authorities. By the same token, group members must be able to alter institutions and change rules to meet changing ecological, political, and economic conditions.

CCAMLR's main purposes are conservation of all living CPRs in Antarctic waters and maintenance of their ecological relationships. A significant aim of CCAMLR thus becomes to ensure that exploitation of living CPRs not be detrimental to natural predators.[45] This concern prompted the Commission, through its Scientific Committee, to create an Ecosystem Monitoring Program (CEMP). The objectives of CEMP are "to detect and record significant changes in critical components of the ecosystem, to serve as the basis for the conservation of Antarctic Marine Living Resources. The monitoring system should be designed to distinguish between changes due to the harvesting of commercial species and changes due to environmental variability, both physical and biological."[46]

The CEMP is a program purposefully designed to detect significant changes in key components of Southern Ocean ecosystem and to distinguish between changes due to commercial harvesting and those from natural causes. Beginning in 1985, this approach has aimed at making systematic recordings of selected species of seals and seabirds in an attempt to develop schemes for monitoring harvested species and impacts on them by relevant environmental factors.[47]

The main goals of the CEMP mirror conservation objectives set out in Article II of CCAMLR. It is obviously an impossible task to monitor all organisms and their interactions in Antarctic waters to effect these principles. Hence a more feasible option has sought to identify key species and special environmental variables considered as being highly sensitive to changes in food availability (e.g., reproduction cycles, growth conditions, feeding behavior, species abundance, and populations distribution). Information from monitoring these variables, coupled with catch and fishing effort data from the fishery and biological data from catch samples, are being collected and studied to determine the extent to which CCAMLR's conservation principles are being applied to manage fishing activities in circumpolar seas.[48]

The CEMP was designed to monitor food availability to predators, and the food (i.e., prey species) of greatest interest is krill, in particular *Euphausia superba*. As repeatedly noted, krill occupies the critical position in the Antarctic ecosystem, and is the principal food of fish, seabirds, seals, and whales. At the same time krill has become targeted as a commercial fishery in the Antarctic marine commons.

The primary consumer species being monitored are seals, seabirds, and whales. Selection of these species as predator indicators turned on the belief that their numbers might demonstrate substantial change should decreases occur in the availability of krill. Other criteria for choosing these species included krills' importance in the Antarctic marine ecosystem, and already having knowledge of their biological behavior.

Monitoring sites were chosen because of their proximity to known fishing grounds, the presence of predators, and the availability of substantive research on those areas. At present CEMP is focusing on three integrated study regions—around South Georgia, around Prydz Bay, and around the Antarctic Peninsula.

The CEMP remains an ambitious program. The quality of its results depend on the quality of science and the degree of support from participant governments. Clearly, CEMP could add much to the knowledge of Antarctic marine CPRs and enhance opportunities for their conservation. The critical indicator of CEMP's success, however, will be reflected in the extent to which the program's findings influence decision-making within the Commission—a consideration that ultimately depends on how well individual governments appreciate the limitations and validity of those findings. In this connection, it remains imperative that as many member states as possible become involved in and contribute to CEMP.

CCAMLR's Balance Sheet

Management and conservation of living CPRs in Antarctic waters are only as sound as the weakest assumptions from data on the intricacies of the ecosystem. Present knowledge of the dynamics in the Antarctic marine commons is often based on incomplete information. To realize the conservation objectives contained in Article II of CCAMLR, the Scientific Committee of the Commission must be able to predict and assess the direct and indirect effects of harvest levels and strategies on target, dependent, and associated species. The success of conservation efforts will be keyed to management actions that can accomplish several ambitions. These include the ability to: (1) restore and maintain the ecological balance between target, dependent, and related species; (2) foster rapid recovery of depleted whale and fish populations; (3) prevent wasteful use and depletion of dependent and associated populations, as well as target species; and (4) protect breeding areas and other habitats of like biological importance to dependent and related populations, as well as to target populations.

Conservation and management of living CPRs in Antarctic seas is severely complicated by significant gaps in information. More must be learned about the physical features of the Southern Ocean. In particular, more knowledge is needed about the influence of currents, eddies, and gyres on the distribution of nutrients, phytoplankton, krill, and organisms higher in the tropic scale. Better data on pack-ice dynamics could reveal much about nutrient cycling and biological productivity. Little remains known about the physical, biological, and demographic factors that affect the abundance, productivity, and distribution of krill. More research is necessary on the location and feeding habits of whales within the Antarctic commons. Likewise, better information on the distribution, abundance, reproductive cycles, and feeding habits of seals, fish, birds, and squid in the Southern Ocean should be accumulated. The CEMP is intended to close many of these gaps in information and thus contribute to fashioning more prudent conservation policies for the Antarctic marine ecosystem.

Lessons for CPR Management Regimes

A number of lessons can be drawn about the CCAMLR regime and resultant efforts to manage CPRs in the Southern Ocean. For one, international regimes such as CCAMLR can affect economic behavior in fundamental ways. Such intragroup dynamics can shape expectations of members. By affecting the nature and degree of certainty regarding expectations, multilateral regimes cause governments to change their economic behavior. This has been the case of CCAMLR, as governments have integrated conservation measures adopted by the CCAMLR commission into national legislation and foreign policy considerations. In effect, the CCAMLR regime has come about with the recognition by all governments of a similar shadows of the future for CPRs in the Southern Ocean. In particular, this has been the case for fin fish and krill, whose consumptive benefits have fallen for fishers and existence benefits (in terms of greater numbers of fish) have risen for nonfishers.

A second lesson suggests that international economic decisions by individual governments also can be affected by multilateral regimes. Group regimes can shape incentives and constrain behavior of member governments, as in the case of collective conservation measures adopted and implemented by CCAMLR. Regimes also change in response to changing economic conditions, and these changes are passed on to group member governments. Change may occur directly or indirectly. Regimes created by international legal instruments depend on collective actions by state governments. When economic conditions or circumstances change, individual governments alter their behavior, and can also alter the collective action supporting existing regime. The shift by fishing states in CCAMLR from policies of obstructing conservation efforts during the 1980s to policies of cooperation on conservation measures during the 1990s highlights this point.

Thus, consistent with hypothesis 3a in chapter 1, in situations where high elasticities of demand for CPR resources increase individual incentives for competitive exploitation, the likelihood for cooperative agreements can become diminished. Obviously, too, increases in the value of consumptive benefits of resources vis-à-vis existence benefits can break down the likelihood of cooperation in CPR management in a commons area. Neither is the case for the Southern Ocean. Whales and seals retain their value as existence benefits under the CCAMLR regime (except for Japan). Likewise, the perceived consumptive benefits of krill and fin fish have not yet displaced those governments' willingness to participate cooperatively in a management system regulating those CPRs.

A third observation suggests that international agreements for marine resource conservation (such as CCAMLR) mirror economic problems of collective action for managing common pool resources. Under international law, states are sovereign polities. While coercion is not wholly absent from international relations, for the most part states are free to manage their own affairs and pursue their own policies free from external control. There is no supranational regime or world government. If genuine international regulation is to occur, states must arrange that situation for themselves. Put in political economic terms, governments must come to recognize similar shadows of the future for CPRs and pursue initiatives to act cooperatively. In the case of CCAMLR, enforcement of the convention's rights and duties falls to the governments of member states.

A fourth lesson stems from the fact that international law is consensual and functions mainly without coercive constraint. Power in international relations occurs almost exclusively at the level of the state. Some international agencies may possess the authority to devise new international norms for some or most states, but such agencies lack the power to enforce compliance on all governments. It is therefore difficult (and unlawful) for some group of states to enforce a common agreement on other nonconsenting states. Thus, international law is generally limited to what national governments have agreed to be bound to. Governments are rarely bound to provisions to which they have not given consent. As a result, the rules and regulations of CCAMLR, as well as subsequent measures adopted by the Commission, apply only to those governments that have formally given their consent through ratification of the CCAMLR agreement. Other nonparty states remain unbound to those conservation restrictions.

A fifth point turns on the role of each state in forming a collective management arrangement. Regimes ultimately consist of individual actions. Over the long run public support is essential to maintaining success of any political or economic order. In the international arena, pressures for institutional change increase when existing international institutions produce outcomes that diverge from the interests of individual states. Even where such individual states do not constitute a majority, pressures for change will likely, albeit perhaps gradually, have effects on regime dynamics.

In the case of CPRs in the Southern Ocean, since 1990 increases in the value of existence benefits for nonfishing governments—coupled with decreases in the value of consumptive benefits for fishing governments—have converged to promote sufficient incentive to promote and sustain for expanded CPR management under the CCAMLR regime. A number of new conservation measures and the CEMP monitoring system are clear indications of that pattern.

A sixth lesson relates to state support. In a rapidly changing world where global interdependence is the norm and where global communications can quickly inform governments of alternative choices, and in the absence of coercive hegemony, regimes that lack the support of their subjects are unlikely to succeed, or even last for long. The goals of policy makers therefore are to create regimes that are consistent with the motivations of individual actors and that harmonize individual and collective economic interests. Such regimes must combine enough stability to permit individual governments to form expectations and coordinate actions with sufficient flexibility to adapt to changing conditions. This is, of course, the fundamental strategy sustaining the policy-making viability of CCAMLR. The CCAMLR regime does not act with superimposing authority on member governments. It is a consensus regime, and functions because its members perceive it to be in their economic, political, and security interests to make it function.

Uncertainty in managing CPRs points up a seventh observation, namely that individual states develop international institutions to assist them in gathering and processing information and to regularize patterns of interaction. Institutions can reduce the uncertainty of human interaction by providing a degree of order and predictability. The need for new or expanded institutions arises from the complexity of global problems that individual states must solve and the limitations on the governmental ability to gather information and implement action. Creation of the Commission and Scientific Committee for CCAMLR, as well as activation of the CEMP monitoring program, underscore this necessity for acquisition of data.

The importance of regimes tends to grow with the frequency of interstate contact. In a world with a high degree of interaction among individual governments, individual state behavior becomes interdependent. Decisions are influenced by expectations about the behavior of others. Institutional rules evolve to reduce this source of uncertainty by setting norms and procedures that do not need to be rethought or re-created each time they are used. Consequently, as more states engaged in increased resource harvesting in the Southern Ocean, the need for an international management regime such as CCAMLR became more pronounced.

Finally, one can conclude that once individual states perceive that collective action by existing international institutions no longer produces the most desirable outcomes, those states will search for alternatives. It is always possible that individual governments might choose to defect from existing institutions and act autonomously. Some governments could come to calculate that the consumptive benefits of CPRs in a commons exceed the value of the regime, or that respect for existence benefits has fallen below the price of participation. But the penalty or loss of collective benefits associated with defecting might be prohibitive—even if the institutions themselves are inefficient. Rather than defect, however, individual states may attempt to transform the institutional framework from within. The fact is, though, any institutional change involves transaction costs. These costs are likely to escalate with the magnitude of the change required.

In the case of CCAMLR, changes have occurred through the adoption and renewal of additional conservation measures. Importantly, despite tensions between fishing and nonfishing states in the Commission during the 1980s, no state has yet defected from CCAMLR. The reason seems clear: No pressing economic incentives have arisen to encourage such a defection, each member government considers participation in CCAMLR to be beneficial to its national interest, and for governments appreciating existence benefits, the conservation of CPRs in the Southern Ocean has taken on a value all its own.

Notes

1. For more extensive treatment of the Southern Ocean as a common pool area, see Christopher C. Joyner, *Antarctica and the Law of the Sea* (The Hague: Martinus Nijhoff 1992), pp. 1–39 (Biogeography of the Southern Ocean). More generally, see also Christopher C. Joyner, *Governing the Frozen Commons: The Antarctic Regime and Environmental Protection* (Columbia: South Carolina University Press, 1998).

2. Convention on the Conservation of Antarctic Seals, done June 1, 1972, 29 U.S.T. 441, T.I.A.S, No. 8826.

3. Seals Convention, preamble.

4. International Convention for the Regulation of Whaling with Schedule of Whaling Regulations, done in Washington, D.C., Dec. 2, 1946, entered into force Nov. 10, 1948. 62 Stat. 1716, T.I.A.S. 1849, 4 Bevans 248, 161 U.N.T.S. 72.

5. Notwithstanding this agreement, Japan has persisted to take 300 minke whales a year from Antarctic waters for "scientific" purposes. Norway indicated that it would resume commercial whaling in 1993 and planned on taking 800 minke whales that year. Jeremy Cherfas, "Whaling ban stays in place—for now," *New Scientist*, May 22, 1993, p. 5.

6. Significantly, the vote was 23 in favor, to one opposed (Japan). The sanctuary's primary boundary runs from 40 degrees South longitude, then drops down to 60 degrees in the southeast Pacific (at 130° West) and extends around the tip of South America (as far as 50° West), to join the Indian Ocean Whale Sanctuary at 55 degrees South.

7. "Southern Ocean Whale Sanctuary Established by I.W.C.," *The Antarctica Project* vol. 3:3 (Summer 1994), p. 1.

8. "Whale Sanctuary Update," *The Antarctica Project*, vol. 4:4 (November 1995), p. 4.

9. See Karl-Hermann Kock, "Fishing and Conservation in Southern Waters," *Polar Record* vol. 30: 172 (1994), pp. 4–5 [previously published as SC-CAMLR-XII/BG 11 (Hobart: CCAMLR, Sept. 22, 1993)], and the discussion in Darry Powell, "Antarctic Fishing and Its Likely Development," in John Handmer & Martijn Wilder, eds. *Towards a Conservation Strategy for the Australian Antarctic Territory* (Canberra: Centre for Resource and Environmental Studies, Australia National University, 1993), pp. 75–89.

10. Kock, "Fishing and conservation in southern waters," 5. See Figure 6, "Nominal catch of Antarctic Krill," in Ibid., 9.

11. CCAMLR, *Statistical Bulletin*, vol. 5 (1983–92) (Hobart: CAMLR, 1992).

12. CCAMLR, "Report of Working Group on Fish Stock Assessment," Oct. 12–22, 1998 (Table: Catches by species and area for 1997/98).

13. "Busy Agenda at Antarctic Fisheries Meeting," p. 1; Kock, "Fishing and Conservation in Southern Waters," pp. 5–6 and Powell, "Antarctic Fishing," pp. 82–85. In 1994–95 the Ukraine increased its krill catch to 51,000 tons, up from 8,700 tons in 1993–94.

14. Powell, "Antarctic Fishing," p. 82.

15. Convention on the Conservation of Antarctic Marine Living Resources, done at Canberra May 7–20, 1980, entered into force on April 7, 1982. 33 U.S.T. 3476, T.I.A.S., No. 10240, reprinted in John Heap, ed., *Handbook of the Antarctic Treaty System* (Washington, D.C.: U.S. Department of State, April 1994), p. 178.

16. Article II, paragraph 1 of CCAMLR asserts its principal objective to be "the conservation of Antarctic marine living resources."

17. CCAMLR, Article II, paragraph 2.

18. CCAMLR, Article II, paragraph 2.

19. CCAMLR, Article II.

20. Interview with David Agnew, CCAMLR Research Scientist, May 12, 1994, CCAMLR Headquarters, Hobart, Tasmania.

21. CCAMLR, *Report of the Tenth Meeting of the Commission (CCAMLR-X)* (Hobart: CCAMLR, 1991), p. 29.

22. SC-CAMLR, "Report of the Fifth Meeting of the Working Group on Krill," in *Report of the Twelfth Meeting of the Scientific Committee*, annex 4 (Hobart: CAMLR, 1993), p. 130 [Fig. 1].

23. The International Convention on Regulation of Whaling is not restricted to the Southern Ocean, though for the Southern Ocean 40 degrees South is imposed as the northern most boundary permissible for factory ships.

24. As provided for in CCAMLR's Article I, paragraph 2, "the populations of finfish, molluscs, crustaceans and all other species of living organisms, including birds, south of the Antarctic Convergence."

25. Compare Article VI in the Antarctic Treaty with Article I in the Seals Convention.

26. See CCAMLR, Final Act, paragraphs 1–5.

27. CCAMLR, Article XXIX, paragraph 1.

28. Members of the CCAMLR Commission in 1999 include Argentina, Australia, Belgium, Brazil, Chile, European Economic Community, France, Germany, India, Italy, Japan, Republic of Korea, New Zealand, Norway, Poland, Russian Federation, South Africa, Spain, Sweden, Ukraine, United Kingdom, Uruguay, and the United States. States that have acceded to the Convention, but who are not members of the Commission, include Bulgaria, Canada, Finland, Greece, Netherlands, Peru, Ukraine, and Uruguay.

29. See Resolution 7/IX, "Driftnet Fishing in the Convention Area," CCAMLR, 1990 *Report of the Ninth Meeting of the Commission* (CCAMLR-IX), (Hobart: CAMLR, 1990), p. 19.

30. Conservation Measure 31-X, CCAMLR, *Report of the Tenth Meeting of the Commission* (Hobart: CAMLR, 1991), pp. 27–28.

31. See Ibid., paragraph 4, p. 27.

32. CCAMLR, *Report of the Eleventh Meeting of the Commission* (Hobart: CCAMLR, 1992), pp. 19–20.

33. Kock, "Fishing and Conservation in Southern Waters," p. 23.

34. CCAMLR, *Report of the Tenth Meeting of the Commission*, CCAMLR-X (Hobart: CCAMLR, 1991), p. 18.

35. As stipulated by CCAMLR, Article IX.

36. Conservation Measure 7–V, in CCAMLR, *Schedule of Conservation Measures in Force*, 1997/98 (Hobart: CAMLR, 1997), p. 4.

37. Ibid., i–iii (Table of Contents).

38. See Conservation Measure 72/XII and Conservation Measure 73/XII, in ibid., p. 25.

39. See CCAMLR, *Schedule of Conservation Measures in Force, 1997/98*, pp. 12–35.

40. CCAMLR, Article XXV (1).

41. Contributing factors likely may be that this had been the first major fishery to be exploited in 1970, and that the region had been well mapped by whalers earlier in the century. Interview with David Agnew, May 12, 1994, CCAMLR Headquarters, Hobart, Tasmania.

42. Interview with David Agnew, May 12, 1994, CCAMLR Headquarters, Hobart, Tasmania.

43. "The XVth Meeting of the Convention on the Conservation of Antarctic Marine Living Resources (CCAMLR)," *The Antarctica Project* vol. 5:4 (November 1996), pp. 9–10.

44. Ibid., 10. But see also "Illegal Fishing Threatens CCAMLR's Ability to Manage Antarctica's Fisheries," *The Antarctica Project* vol. 5:2 (June 1996), p. 2.

45. See CCAMLR, Article II, paragraph 3 (b).

46. *Report of the Fourth Meeting of the Scientific Committee*, SC-CCAMLR-IV, (1985) para. 7.2, p. 34.

47. J. P. Croxall, "Use of Indices of Predator Status and Performance in CCAMLR Fishery Management," *Selected Scientific Papers*, 1989, SC-CAMLR-VIII/9 (1989), pp. 355–65.

48. CCAMLR, "CCAMLR Ecosystem Monitoring Program," (1991) (pamphlet).

5   The Power to Destroy: Understanding Stratospheric Ozone Politics as a Common-Pool Resource Problem

DAVID LEONARD DOWNIE

Introduction

The Montreal Protocol stands at the center of an innovative and historic environmental regime that confronts one of our most serious environmental threats. Many analysts and policy makers cite the ozone regime's history, structure, and initial success as breakthroughs in environmental cooperation and possible blueprints for other international environmental agreements.[1] The regime has received significant scholarly attention and become a popular case study in discussions of environmental politics.[2] Most of these discussions adopt the language of public goods, placing the challenge and success of the ozone regime within this framework.[3]

However, do the language and logic of public goods problems offer the only, or even the best, framework with which to analyze the ozone regime's development? Would recasting the ozone depletion issue as a common-pool resource problem offer different insights? Would it provide greater appreciation of the obstacles to effective cooperation or improve our understanding of bargaining power within the issue?

This chapter considers these issues through four interrelated questions. (1) Is stratospheric ozone protection a common-pool resource problem? (2) If so, what insights can analysts gain from thinking about the issue within this framework? (3) Which of the hypotheses outlined in this volume's introductory chapter are supported by this case? (4) How should answers to these questions influence the methods and mechanisms used for effective management of CPRs? I begin with a short outline of the ozone regime.

The Ozone Regime

The ozone regime is the set of integrated principles, norms, rules, and procedures actors have created to coordinate and regulate behavior in an attempt to protect stratospheric ozone.[4] The international agreements that delineate the main elements of the regime include the 1985 Vienna Convention for the Protection of the Ozone Layer, 1987 Montreal Protocol on Substances that Deplete the Ozone Layer, and the Amendments, Adjustments and Decisions to the Protocol agreed to during nine Meetings of the Parties: Helsinki, 1989; London, 1990; Nairobi, 1991; Copenhagen, 1992; Bangkok, 1993; Nairobi, 1994; Vienna, 1995; San Jose, 1996; and Montreal, 1997.[5] Of these, the Montreal, London, Copenhagen, and Vienna agreements are the most important.

Also central to the ozone regime are operations of its constituent institutions. The Open-Ended Working Group (OEWG) holds discussions in preparation for the annual Meeting of the Parties. The Scientific, Environmental Effects, and Technology and Economic Assessment Panels provide reports on issues relevant to the negotiations (under instructions from the Parties and OEWG).[6] The Multilateral Fund provides financial assistance to developing countries to aid their transition to ODS alternatives and attract their participation in the regime.[7] The Implementing Agencies, sections within the World Bank, United Nations Development Programme (UNDP), and the United Nations Environment Programme (UNEP), execute work plans approved and funded by the Multilateral Fund's decision-making body, the Executive Committee. The Ozone Secretariat administers the regime for the Parties. The Implementation Committee Under the Non-Compliance Procedure provides a forum for discussing issues of noncompliance and offers recommendations to the Parties.[8]

Stratospheric Ozone and ODS

Stratospheric ozone—the ozone layer—helps shield the earth against ultraviolet radiation (UV) produced by the sun. Very large increases in UV-B levels reaching the earth's surface would produce disastrous consequences and even small increases could be dangerous.[9]

The atmospheric release of certain man-made chemicals, collectively known as ozone depleting substances (ODS), threatens stratospheric ozone. Broad scientific consensus exists that chlorine and bromine released from ODS into the stratosphere are responsible for significant depletion of stratospheric ozone, including the huge, seasonal "ozone hole" over Antarctica and the increasingly severe depletions above northern midlatitudes.[10]

The most prominent ODS are chlorofluorocarbons (CFCs), the otherwise benign and remarkably versatile chemicals used in refrigeration, air conditioning, foam blowing, materials production, aerosol sprays, and industrial solvents.[11] When released, CFCs drift slowly to the stratosphere where they are broken down by ultraviolet radiation. This releases chlorine atoms that act as catalysts in the destruction of ozone. Other ODS include halons, methyl bromide, carbon tetrachloride, methyl chloroform, and HCFCs.[12] For more than fifty years, many of the world's largest and most influential companies produced, or used CFCs in refrigeration, air conditioning, aerosol sprays, foam blowing, materials production, and industrial solvents, including the cleaning of circuit boards and computer chips.

A Brief History of the Ozone Regime

The 1974 discovery that CFCs could threaten stratospheric ozone[13] produced extensive scientific and public policy debates, especially in the United States. Industry vigorously opposed the CFC-ozone link and attempts to regulate CFCs for many years. In the late 1970s, the United States and several other nations established domestic controls on the use of CFCs in aerosol sprays. However, Japan, the European Community, the Soviet bloc, and large developing countries did not and governments enacted no further significant regulation until the late 1980s.[14]

International controls were even more difficult to achieve. Nevertheless, nations have created an impressive regime.[15] The regime's first formal component, the 1985 Vienna Convention, did not established binding controls on CFCs but did acknowledge that a potential problem existed, committed its signatories to work toward establishing a protocol, and specified a clear role for the United Nations Environment Programme (UNEP) to continue promoting and coordinating scientific and regulatory efforts.

The 1987 Montreal Protocol limited the production and use of five CFCs and three halons, halving each party's allowable CFC levels by the year

2000 and freezing halon levels (both from 1986 baselines). Developing countries obtained ten year grace periods in meeting these requirements. The Protocol also included an innovative review process to allow the Parties to strengthen controls in response to new information. This included the OEWG, Scientific, Environmental Effects, and Technology and Economic Assessment Panels, the ability to "adjust" as well as to formally Amend binding regulations, and annual Meetings of the Parties.

The 1990 London Amendment and adjustments mandated that Parties phase out production and use of the original five CFCs and three Halons, ten additional CFCs, and carbon tetrachloride by 2000 and methyl chloroform by 2005.[16] The agreement also established a $180 million, interim (1991–93) Multilateral Fund to attract developing nations to the regime and help them meet regime requirements. The fund was designed to increase to $240 million should China and India join the Protocol, which they did in 1991 and 1992, respectively.

The 1992 Copenhagen agreement again increased control measures, mandating that developed country-Parties phase out halons by 1994; phase out CFCs, methyl chloroform, and carbon tetrachloride by 1996; freeze the production and use of methyl bromide in 1995; and cap the production of HCFCs, a less ozone-depleting CFC alternative, in 1996 and gradually phase out HCFC production by 2030.[17] Developing countries would not be subject to these controls until the Parties reviewed the operation of the regime in 1995. The Parties also made the Multilateral Fund a permanent institution. In 1993, regime delegates agreed to a $510 million budget for Fund-sponsored projects in developing countries during the 1994–96 period.[18]

In December 1995 in Vienna, the Parties brought every major chemical threatening the ozone layer under strict global controls.[19] The 1995 Vienna Adjustment required developed countries to phase out HCFC production by 2030 and methyl bromide by 2010. Developing countries confirmed their commitment to phase out CFC and halon production by 2010 and agreed to eliminate HCFCs by 2040 and to freeze methyl bromide levels by 2002. The 1997 Montreal Amendment and adjustments strengthened controls on methyl bromide, mandating full phase-outs in both developed and developing countries during the next twenty years.

If all Parties fully implement the ODS controls in the current regime then peak ozone depletion should occur early in the 21st century and the ozone layer should fully recover sometime in the middle of the 21st century.[20]

To date, participation in the ozone regime remains high. As of 18 February

1998, 166 states were Parties to the Vienna Convention, 165 to the Montreal Protocol, 120 to the 1990 London amendment, and 77 to the 1992 Copenhagen amendment.[21] Only one significant producer, Russia, has clearly failed to meet mandated production controls.[22] In addition, only Russia and a few other CEITs (countries with economies in transition) have violated consumption controls during this period.[23]

Most significantly, as mandated by the Copenhagen Amendment, CFC production in industrialized countries, except Russia, had been nearly eliminated by the end of 1995.[24] Halon production in developed countries except Russia had been nearly eliminated by the end of 1993.[25] As a result, atmospheric growth rates of several major ozone-depleting substances have slowed.[26]

This does not mean that regime makers have saved the ozone layer. Nations must still fully implement all the agreements. China, India, Russia, and several other countries must prove they intend to meet all their future obligations under the amended Protocol. Alternative chemicals and processes still must be developed for some uses of HCFC, halon, and methyl bromide. Other threats to stratospheric ozone, such as expanded supersonic travel, could arise. Several environmental factors including the impact of possible global climate change (including upper stratospheric cooling), volcanic eruptions, and unforeseen, nonlinear chemical events in response to current and future chlorine loading also could complicate this scenario.[27]

Ozone as a Common Pool Resource

Scholars and practitioners usually characterize protecting the ozone layer as a public goods problem. This characterization is not inaccurate but it is incomplete. As noted by the editors, pure public goods must display two key characteristics: nonrivalness and nonexcludability. A good is nonrival if the consumption or enjoyment of the good/resource by one party does not affect the ability of other parties to enjoy or consume the good/resource. Nonexcludability means that once the good is available to any one party, no one can be excluded from enjoying or consuming the good.

A healthy ozone layer certainly meets these criteria. The benefit or "good" of a healthy ozone layer—protection from increased ultraviolet radiation (UV)—exhibits both nonrivalness and nonexcludability. My "consumption" of UV protection in no way impacts the ability of others to enjoy this good. Similarly, once the ozone layer is protected or restored, no one can be excluded from enjoying UV protection. This logic holds for individuals, corporations, and nation states. Sweden, a leader in pushing for international controls will not be able to exclude Russia, currently in technical violation of the amended Montreal Protocol, from enjoying shelter from UV should the ozone layer be fully restored and protected.

Yet this is not the only way to frame the issue-area. Rather than focusing on the "good" of UV protection provided by the ozone layer, let us focus instead on the threat that ODS pose to this good. Anthropogenic releases of chlorine and bromine into the stratosphere deplete the good of UV protection. Stratospheric ozone is a potentially finite resource, a good that can be used up by ODS emissions.

From this perspective, stratospheric ozone can be considered a common pool resource (CPR). It displays the characteristic of nonexcludability but also of rivalness. No state can be excluded from using the ozone layer, either as a UV shield or as an ODS sink.[28] The characteristic of nonexcludability is satisfied. Yet, ODS production beyond a certain level reduces the amount of ozone in the stratosphere. Sufficient production over time will deplete the good entirely. Thus, the amount of stratospheric ozone consumed by one state's ODS production does impact the amount others can consume. It does affect their ability to enjoy UV protection. The characteristic of nonrivalness is not satisfied.

There is a second, related approach to understanding stratospheric ozone as a CPR. Again, the key is casting the problem not as the ability to consume the good of UV protection but as the ability to enjoy the good of ODS production and release (and thereby consume stratospheric ozone). Here, however, the focus in on the generation of ODS itself as a good, as a CPR.

As with a public good, no one can be excluded from producing ODS and polluting. Unlike a public good, however, the ability of the ozone layer to absorb ODS is not unlimited. Despite their wonderful properties, there is a finite amount of ODS that states can release. After a certain point, existing levels of ODS pollution will hinder the ability of other states to produce and release ODS as the human health and environmental effects of ozone depletion impact their populations. Therefore, ODS production is rival, presenting a common-pool resource problem.

Ozone Politics and Common Pool Resource Dynamics

All three formulations—stratospheric ozone protection as public good, stratospheric ozone as common pool resource, and ODS production as common pool resource—provide insights into different aspects of the issue area. Most discussions consider only the first formulation. However, understanding ozone politics also as a common pool resource problem provides additional insights, including greater clarity concerning the obstacles to effective cooperation.

This is not to say that ozone politics only exhibits the characteristics of CPRs or that the insights provided by understanding ozone as a CPR would be otherwise impossible. Such claims would be silly and their constituent arguments represent a waste of time for both analysts and policy makers. What is most important is gaining maximum insight into the obstacles to, and development of, a successful ozone regime. This section delineates five advantages of adding to the traditional analytical framework by focusing on stratospheric ozone politics as a CPR.

First, it provides a more accurate analytical lens by focusing attention on the central political issue of the ozone problem and its solution, distributional issues in allocating ODS production. These issues also represent the central obstacle to solving the ozone problem.

Distributional issues, winners and losers, are largely unimportant in pure public goods situations but are emphasized in CPRs. Such issues are clearly important to ozone. Although the ozone layer as an ultraviolet screen is a public good, this use of the stratospheric ozone layer is not the central political issue. The key political issue is distributing and limiting the ability to destroy the ozone layer. Ozone negotiators did not debate who would use the ozone layer as a sun screen. Nor did they arrive at the control schedules outlined above simply through enlightened deduction. Rather, regime negotiators debated which ODS would be produced, by whom, and over what period of time.

Thus, the key issue in the ozone debates, immediately apparent in CPR logic, is allocating the use of the resource, in this case for the use of the ozone layer as a sink for ODS. To address the problem of ozone depletion, negotiators have to grapple with how to distribute global ODS production; that is, they must decide which actors will be permitted to produce and use which ODS over what period of time. Each proposal and each agreement can create significant national and corporate winners and losers.

Considering ozone depletion as a CPR focuses attention on this central issue of distribution. Certainly, the importance of ODS creates incentives to free-ride, understood as threatening to create collection action problems. Equally important, however, is that there is a finite amount of ODS that can be produced before the ozone layer is destroyed. In the absence of force, no one can be excluded from producing ODS but one actor's ODS production (and consequential ozone depletion) limits the ability of others to produce (assuming they are not suicidal). Thus, even if all actors generally agree that ODS should be reduced and eventually eliminated, the process of allocating a decreasing and finite amount of ODS production represents a key obstacle to effectively managing the problem.

The second advantage is that CPR logic better exposes the main source of bargaining strength in the ozone debates; an exploitable power to destroy. Noncooperators with large ODS production capacities can threaten not only to withhold contributions to creating the good (which can be compensated for in a pure public good), but also to destroy everyone else's ability to enjoy the good. This creates potent bargaining positions for those with plausible capacity, motive, or ignorance. They can resist action not only until they bear little or no costs, but even until they achieve substantial gains. Formally, they should be able to hold out until the cost of "buying them off" approaches the cost that those who most value the resource would pay for its protection.

Large developing countries such as China and India refrained from joining the ozone regime in a manner that can be interpreted, whether intentional or not, as testing the value developed countries attached to a healthy ozone layer. Indeed, the reluctance of many developing countries to join the regime, combined with a perceived ability to destroy its goal, contributed to their success in securing creation of regulatory grace periods and the Multilateral Fund.

Third, CPR logic also helps expose several derivative sources of bargaining power. Each also can be seen as a potential obstacle to cooperation as they can accentuate distributive bargaining, lessen government concern, and harm the contractual environment.[29] Obviously, public goods theory also allows for the importance of these factors but CPR logic helps to expose their importance and provides a better framework to understand how and why specific bargaining dynamics change as actors recognize resource limits, as ODS production evolves, and as the regime develops. These sources of bargaining power include:

1. Existing Production Capacity. In some public good settings, issue dominance can bring greater responsibility (e.g., absorbing costs of free riders), in ozone it also conferred power. For example, European opposition prevented binding CFC controls in 1985 and weakened the provisions agreed to in Montreal in 1987.[30] At both meetings, the Nordic

countries, Canada, and the United States considered pushing for stronger international controls even if it meant that the European Community (EC) would not join the regime. However, in both cases the coalition decided that any international regulatory system would fail if it did not directly include European production capacity. EC production levels gave them the power to alter the nascent regime.

In addition, as production capacity has changed so has bargaining power. In recent years, the relative bargaining strength of the U.S., Japan, Australia, and Europe appears to have weakened somewhat (as they eliminated CFC production) while that of large developing countries has increased (along with their production capacity).[31]

2. Potential Production Capacity. By the mid-1980s CFCs were reaching the end of the product cycle. China and India with 40 percent of the world's population, fast-growing economies, and tremendous needs for refrigeration, air conditioning, and industrial solvents represented enormous CFC production potential and significant obstacles to an effective regime. Their outright refusal to sign the Montreal and London accords unless they received regulatory relief, financial assistance, and technology transfers threatened the viability of the ozone resource and conferred significant bargaining power.

Explicit or implicit exploitation of the power to destroy the CPR produced significant gains for developing countries. Regime terms now include significant regulatory extensions for developing countries[32] and targeted payments from the Multilateral Fund. This has allowed large developing countries to significantly expand CFC production and to build CFC export markets while also developing high-end HCFC production, use and export capacity.[33]

In India, CFC production rose 419 percent from 1986 through 1993 (to 11,438,800 ODP tons).[34] HCFC production rose 123 percent (to 118,900 ODP tons).[35] Meanwhile, CFC consumption rose 140 percent and HCFC consumption 38 percent.[36] Thus, not only has India increased its production and consumption of CFCs considerably since production was frozen in OECD countries, but also it has used this market opening to develop significant export capacity. In addition, most of the increase in HCFC production, consumption, and export (in India and other developing countries) has been financed through the Multilateral Fund as part of its efforts to reduce CFC production.

Similarly, China's CFC production rose 116 percent from 1986 through 1992 while its consumption rose 95 percent.[37] South Korean CFC production rose a remarkable 589 percent and HCFC production rose 69 percent while consumption rose 130 percent and 35 percent, respectively.[38] Mexican CFC production rose 45 percent and consumption 19 percent from 1986 through 1993.[39] Several other large developing countries also report large increases in CFC consumption from 1986 through 1992, including 119 percent for Indonesian and 97 percent for Thailand.[40]

3. Willingness to Absorb Risk or Harm. Low levels of state concern present a significant obstacle to effective environmental cooperation. It can also confer bargaining power in distributive negotiations in CPR issues such as ozone depletion.

Developing countries often state during environmental meetings, including the ozone negotiations, that economic development and poverty alleviation remain their priority.[41] They are willing to absorb the risk and even harm of ozone depletion in order to use ODS. The more risk they accept, the more leverage they gain in pursuing larger shares of global ODS production or larger side payments to give up those shares. Other actors must give in or risk destruction of the resource. Brinkmanship is not normally associated with either public goods or environmental problems but it can figure prominently in politics of CPRs and played a role in the development of the ozone regime.

4. Ignorance of Problem. Feigned or real ignorance of the problems and its consequences also confers bargaining advantages in ozone and other CPRs. Denying that a particular chemical represents a threat—an argument used until recently with regard to methyl bromide[42]—can create the same leverage as a willingness to absorb risk or harm.

5. Variations in Impact. Rivalness can matter even more when some states experience a resource's depletion more quickly or more severely. Ozone depletion in its extreme form could kill literally millions through skin cancer and disease, cause cataracts, harm food crops, and devastate ecosystems. However, these impacts would not be uniform, especially in their early stages. The ozone layer is thickest over the tropics. Temperature, chemistry, and circulation patterns mean that ozone depletion occurs first and most severely over the higher latitudes of the northern and

southern hemispheres. Fair-skinned people are most susceptible to skin cancer from increased UV. Such facts can produce bargaining leverage for those least affected.

6. Knowledge. Understanding the extent to which humans can load chlorine into the stratosphere without dangerously altering its chemistry could allow well-informed actors to exercise brinkmanship, safe in the knowledge that the distributive position they are demanding is within their acceptable range of atmospheric pollution. Somewhat similarly, lack of knowledge can allow a Party to be pushed into a control regime that exceeds its desire for environmental protection, when compared to economic needs, out of fear that doing otherwise would precipitate ecological disaster.

Technical knowledge of ODS alternatives cuts both ways. On the one hand, those holding it can press for more stringent controls, protecting their benefits from the common pool resource while also creating economic advantages in the global marketplace. This logic could help explain both Dupont and the European Community's (unrelated but similar) reversals on CFC controls.[43] On the other hand, states with a high tolerance for brinkmanship or for the pain of a depleted ozone layer can demand access to new technology as their price for not destroying the CPR. Developing nations, led by China and India, appear to employ this argument regularly.

The ability to convey knowledge concerning the seriousness of the problem and to use that knowledge to frame the negotiations can also be important. Even in a CPR, if destruction of the good carries very high costs, self-interested actors will attempt to keep their use of the resource within acceptable limits. This does not eliminate distributional bargaining, exploitation of various positional advantages, or perverse economic incentives, but it can ease the creation of allocative mechanisms and increase compliance.

A fourth advantage of seeing ozone as a CPR is that it provides a better understanding of the impact of nonparticipants on regime development. In CPRs, nonparticipants do not simply free-ride, adding to the costs of creating the good, but actually threaten the creation and maintenance of the good. If a healthy ozone layer were a pure public good, then it could be provided by a privileged core group. From 1990 onwards, the United States, EC, Australia, and Japan appear to represent such a group. They possessed most of the world ODS production, exhibited sufficiently high levels of concern in agreeing to phase out all CFCs, halons, and HCFCs, and certainly had the economic resources to support free riders. Yet, they could not and still cannot provide the good of ozone protection on their own. They could not tolerate significant free-riding because free riders in this case do not simply increase costs to the core group, they destroy the good the group wishes to create or protect.

Fifth and finally, CPR logic helps prevent blissful assumptions regarding how evaluations of future payoffs will affect cooperation. Some neoliberal institutionalist strategies for increasing the likelihood of cooperation are not as relevant to CPRs as they are to public goods. For example, ozone can be used up. CFCs are profitable and extremely useful. This can create a "use it or lose it" dynamic, especially for developing countries, which while not operating as strongly as it does in water or oil depletion, still creates perverse incentives to manipulate compliance with phase-out schedules. Future iterations are discounted (the resource will be gone) and relative gains become increasingly important. Both raise obstacles to effective cooperation.

Similarly, the nonrival character of a public good argues for long-term regime stability. Once mature, regime terms should ensure the protection and supply of the good. This is not true for CPRs. CPR issues are more prone to conflict and less amenable to solution through institutional mechanisms than public goods issues. Bargaining dynamics and interests in CPRs are likely to change over time, presenting new obstacles to cooperation as actors face new incentives and opportunities to seek distributive gains. This certainly occurred during the development of the ozone regime. Thus, observers cannot assume that the regime's initial success indicates that Parties have provided the "good of UV protection"; or that actors have safeguarded the "common resource of stratospheric ozone"; or even that positive trends will continue.

The Hypotheses and This Case

Ozone's characteristics as a CPR impacted problem recognition, bargaining (including the content of specific proposals), and the robustness of the contractual environment. In this section, I wish only to list the clearest examples (many of which are implicit from the previous section) of how several of these impacts support elements of the hypotheses introduced in chapter 1.

Time Horizon Hypotheses

Hypotheses H1a, H1b, and H1c are all supported by the ozone case. As noted above, lower state concern—whether from a greater willingness to absorb risk, ignorance of the potential danger, or perceived variations in impact—presented an obstacle to effective cooperation and conferred bargaining power in the ozone negotiations.

By arguing that their access to ODS was more important than protecting the ozone layer, at least in the immediate future, large developing countries gained leverage in the negotiations. This allowed them to press for concessions from the United States, EC, Australia, New Zealand, the Nordic states and others with a higher comparative concern for saving the resource (and whose shadows of the future were far longer). As a result, developing countries demanded and won significant regulatory extensions in 1987, 1992, and 1995, creation of the Multilateral Fund in 1990, and increases in the size of the Fund in 1992 and 1996. Indeed, one can see the negotiations on these issues, as well as those on technology transfer, as explicit tests and confirmation of hypothesis H1c. Each negotiation tested the value that OECD countries attach to ozone protection. Credibly short time horizons on the part of the G-77 and China forced OECD countries to "pay" for the creation and maintenance of the regime. However, during each negotiation OECD countries found some developing country demands too economically or politically expensive.[44] The credible threat to destroy, or seriously deplete, the CPR yielded great benefits but only to the point where the demands began to exceed the value placed on a particular level of resource protection.

Finally, changes in the level and perception of CPR depletion altered bargaining dynamics. In the late 1980s doubts concerning the seriousness of the threat to ozone faded and cooperation increased significantly. Now, however, regime controls have reduced pressure on the resource and positional bargaining has increased. Developing countries are increasingly hostile to propositions for new controls and demanding large increases to Multilateral Fund resources,[45] the 1995 Vienna and 1997 Montreal agreements actually slowed the phase-out pace set by previous agreements,[46] Chinese and Indian production of several important ODS is actually increasing,[47] the United States and other states have successfully created a new class of regulatory exemptions for methyl bromide; several Eastern European countries, including Russia, are requesting broad regulatory extensions,[48] and the several key donors have expressed reservations regarding large Fund replenishments.[49]

Free-Rider Hypotheses

The ozone case largely supports hypotheses H2a and H2b. As noted, nonparticipants in the ozone regime do not simply free ride, adding to costs to other Parties, but actually threaten the success of the regime. This provides significant leverage to free riders of sufficient size.

In addition, as postulated in H2a, increasing knowledge of resource limits increased the leverage of free riders. Rapid advances in scientific understanding of the cause and scope of the problem altered the bargaining dynamics. Cooperation among the large, industrialized nations was no longer considered sufficient by proponents of ODS control. Success required firm commitments on the part of large developing countries who had previously chosen not to participate. The new importance of eliminating such free riders helped lead to financial and regulatory concessions by OECD countries.

The ozone case does not support hypothesis H2c, although this may be a function of particular issue area characteristics rather than a theoretical inadequacy. Despite the clear fact that "overconsumption by a free rider in [this] CPR situation [was] much higher than the costs of a non-contribution in a PG situation," an imposed solution or coercive hegemony did not occur and appears to be impossible. Short of physically destroying CFC plants in Brazil, China, India, Indonesia, and other large developing countries, no clear coercive options exist. Regime trade sanctions against non-Parties apply only to ODS related products and would have little impact on such large internal markets. Perhaps for this reason, or perhaps because other potential, coercive issue-linkages were deemed too expensive, actors focused on purchasing participation and compliance via the Fund, and regulatory extensions. Fear of losing access to CFCs via trade sanctions may have drawn some developing countries to the ozone regime but once domestic production reached sufficient levels in the 1990s, other factors provided the incentives to remain in the regime.

Hypothesis H2c also may be less applicable because no hegemony existed during the creation and expansion of the ozone regime.[50] The United States was first among equals in total military and economic power but it was not uniquely powerful in the system or in this issue-area.[51] No single state dominated ODS production and consumption. Indeed, by the late 1970s, the EC had surpassed the United States as the world's largest producer and consumer of CFCs.[52] No single state dominated the ozone negotiations. From 1977–1984 the United States and EC argued to a stalemate of inaction. In 1985 the EC prevented the adoption of control measures and the formal listing of CFCs as an ODS in the Vienna Convention while the United States obtained a structured plan for new talks aimed at controls. In Montreal in 1987, a U.S.-led coalition obtained CFC controls and a review process but the EC prevented anything more than a 50 percent reduction over thirteen years, regulations it could meet largely through CFC-aerosol controls. In the 1990, 1992, 1995, and 1997 agreements, complicated and intersecting alliances won, lost and traded concessions on control measures for six different sets of chemicals with no single actor emerging as dominant.

Market Power Hypotheses

Hypothesis H3a appears to be of less immediate importance to ozone as it is to fish stocks and other CPRs. However, changes in demand for particular ODS, and attempts to manipulate this demand, did play important roles in the regime's development. Knowledge by large CFC makers and their governments that they could develop alternatives and control a new market altered their perceptions of the value of CFC controls. Increasing understanding by developing countries of the costs associated with a rapid CFC phaseout and the opportunities available in controlling the market for CFCs and their alternatives also altered their negotiating position. For example, beginning in 1992 developing countries resisted further controls, creating and protecting larger international market shares for their CFC industries. In 1994 and 1995 they sought to overturn regime rules (which many were already openly violating) that prohibited their trading raw CFCs during the grace periods.

The ozone case strongly supports hypothesis H3b. Large current or potential consumers altered perceived values of the CPR by threatening its existence. In short, existing or potential ODS production capacity and the willingness to exercise it conferred clear bargaining power. This power was exploited most obviously by the European Community (supported by Japan and the USSR) in 1985 to prevent ODS controls and in 1987 to get a 50 percent control target that they could meet largely through easy aerosol controls; by the USSR in 1987 to get future production capacity placed in its 1986 baseline; by large developing countries in 1990, 1992, 1993, and 1996 to get the Multilateral Fund, technology transfer language, larger Fund replenishment, and exemptions and extensions from methyl bromide and HCFCs controls; and by the United States to prevent significant new HCFC regulations in 1995 and 1997.[53]

In addition, changes in relative market power, in this case ODS production capacity, produced changes in interests and bargaining power. Developing countries gained obvious bargaining power as production in OECD countries diminished. Some have sought to become significant exporters of ODS as OECD production declines. Moreover, after several years, Russian and Polish concerns for the "special situation of countries with economies in transition" finally gained attention, at the same time that their production exceeded regime rules and black market CFCs arrived in the United States and Western Europe.[54]

Although not directly supportive of the hypothesis, the importance of market power is underscored by continued attempts to maintain and expand it. That is, distributive bargaining over how to divide (the CPR of) ODS production has been central to the ozone negotiations. Control proposals often reflected clear economic interests such as: internationalizing existing domestic policy (e.g., the U.S. and EC on CFCs in 1983–1987; U.S. on methyl bromide in 1994–1997); trying to create CFC control schedules that would cartelize production of ODS alternatives (the U.S. and EC in 1989–1992),[55] and tilting global standards and market dynamics toward specific ODS alternatives produced by domestic industry (e.g., Italy on halons in 1994 and 1995; Germany and Nordic countries on refrigeration in 1992–1995; the U.S. on HCFCs in 1992–1995).

Ozone as a CPR and the Methods and Mechanisms of Effective Management

Although facing new challenges, the ozone regime should be considered a success to date. This would be difficult if the exigencies of CPRs had been ignored. In this way, ozone institutions may represent valuable models from which to begin planning for the management of other CPRs. Two items stand out.

First, effective ozone layer management requires mechanisms that alter the incentive structure of actors from those normally present and destructive in CPRs. Approaching institution building from the public goods perspective or neoliberal institutionalism is not sufficient. Discouraging or making up for the costs of free riders is not sufficient. Rather, steps must be taken to limit conflict over consumption and to accentuate the political and economic advantages of exploiting alternative resources. The core problem is creating new interests, including new market forces, to dissuade actors from using CFCs and to provide them with sufficient incentives to support the switch to alternatives. The use it or lose it dynamic of CPRs must be addressed. The Multilateral Fund, Assessment Panels, provisions for technology transfer, control schedules, trading provisions, and other regime components were designed at least in part to do this. How well they perform in the future will provide clues for improving the design of CPR institutions.

Second, the ozone regime developed the flexibility needed to respond to changes in perceptions, interests, and bargaining dynamics that occur in CPRs in response to changes in actual and perceived resource consumption. Static rule-sets cannot respond to the changes associated with CPRs, including variations in consumption patterns that alter issue dynamics. At Vienna in 1985 and Montreal in 1987, regime proponents insisted that control opponents accept a flexible review system as payment for relatively weak sets of binding controls. The combination of Assessment Panels, the Open-Ended Working Group, the ability to adjust as well as formally amend certain binding regime rules, annual Meetings of the Parties, and a strong precautionary principle have served the ozone regime well.

Notes

1. Representative comments on its importance individually and as a precedent include: Sharon Roan, *Ozone Crisis: The 15 Year Evolution of a Sudden Global Emergency* (New York: John Wiley & Sons, 1989), pp. 255–56; Mostafa Tolba, "The Ozone Agreement and Beyond," *Environmental Conservation* vol. 14 (1989), pp. 287–90; Oran Young and Gail Osherenko, *Polar Politics: Creating International Environmental Regimes* (Ithaca, NY: Cornell University Press, 1993), p. 339; Peter Morrisette, "The Montreal Protocol: Lessons for Formulating Policies for Global Warming," *Policy Studies Journal* vol. 19 (1991), pp. 152–61; Al Gore, *Earth in the Balance* (New York: Plume, 1992), pp. 352–53; Richard Benedick, *Ozone Diplomacy: New Directions in Safeguarding the Planet* (Cambridge: Harvard University Press, 1991), pp. 1–3, 204–11; UNEP, *Action on Ozone* (Nairobi: UNEP), p. 1; and Elizabeth Cook, "Marking a Milestone in Ozone Protection: Learning From the CFC Phase-out" (Washington: World Resources Institute Report, January 1996). For more examples and evaluations of such claims with regard to climate change see David Leonard Downie, "Road Map or False Trail: Evaluating the Precedence of the Ozone Regime as Model and Strategy for Global Climate Change," *International Environmental Affairs* vol. 7 (1995), pp. 321–45.

2. See, for example, Peter Sand, *Lessons Learned in Global Environmental Governance* (Washington: World Resources Institute, 1990); Peter Haas, "Banning Chlorofluorocarbons: Epistemic Community Efforts to Protect Stratospheric Ozone," *International Organization* vol. 46 (1992), pp. 187–224; Peter Haas, "Stratospheric Ozone: Regime Formation in Stages," in Oran Young and Gail Osherenko, eds., *Polar Politics: Creating International Environmental Regimes* (Ithaca, NY: Cornell University Press, 1993); Kenneth Oye and James Maxwell, "Self-Interest and Environmental Management," *Journal of Theoretical Politics* vol. 6 (1994), pp. 599–630; Edward Parson, "Protecting the Ozone Layer," in Peter Haas, Robert Keohane and Marc Levy, eds., *Institutions for the Earth: Sources of Effective International Environmental Protection* (Cambridge: MIT Press, 1993); Karen Litfin, *Ozone Discourses: Science and Politics in Global Environmental Cooperation* (New York: Columbia University Press, 1994); David Leonard Downie, "UNEP and the Montreal Protocol: New Roles for International Organizations in Regime Creation and Change," in Robert Bartlett, ed., *International Organizations & Environmental Policy* (Westport: Greenwood Press, 1995); David Leonard Downie, *Understanding International Environmental Regimes: Lessons of the Ozone Regime* (Chapel Hill: Ph.D. Thesis, University of North Carolina, 1996); and Elizabeth DeSombre and Joanne Kauffman, "Montreal Protocol Multilateral Fund: Partial Success Story," in Robert Keohane and Marc Levy, eds., *Institutions for Environmental Aid: Pitfalls and Promise* (Cambridge: MIT Press, 1996).

3. See, for example, Benedick, *Ozone Diplomacy;* Haas, "Banning Chlorofluorocarbons" and "Stratospheric Ozone: Regime Formation in Stages"; Parson, "Protecting the Ozone Layer"; Litfin, *Ozone Discourses;* Peter Morrisette, "The Evolutionary

Policy Response to Stratospheric Ozone Depletion," *Natural Resource Journal* vol. 29 (1989), pp. 793–820; and Ian Rowlands, "Ozone Layer Depletion and Global Warming: New Sources for Environmental Disputes," *Peace and Change* vol. 16 (1991), pp. 260–84.

4. I define regimes as sets of integrated principles, norms, rules, and procedures that actors create or accept to regulate and coordinate action in particular issue-areas of international relations. Principles are beliefs of fact, causation, and rectitude. Norms are standards of behavior. Rules are specific prescriptions or proscriptions for action. Procedures are prevailing practices, including those for making and implementing collective choice. These components can be structured through formal agreements, international organizations, and accepted norms of international behavior. This definition is a modified version of that found in Stephen Krasner, *International Regimes* (Ithaca, NY: Cornell University Press, 1983). Compare also to the influential definitions and discussions in John Ruggie, "International Responses to Technology: Concepts and Trends," *International Organization* vol. 29 (1975), pp. 557–83; Ernst Haas, "On Systems and International Regimes," *World Politics* vol. 27 (1975), pp. 147–74; Robert Keohane and Joseph Nye, Jr., *Power and Interdependence: World Politics in Transition* (Boston: Little Brown and Company, 1977); Oran Young, "International Regimes: Problems of Concept Formation," *International Organization* vol. 32 (1980), pp. 331–56; Jack Donnelly, "International Human Rights: A Regime Analysis," *International Organization* vol. 40 (1986), pp. 599–642; and Stephan Haggard and Beth Simmons, "Theories of International Regimes," *International Organization* vol. 41 (1987), pp. 491–517.

5. See, respectively, *Vienna Convention for the Protection of the Ozone Layer*, 1985; *Montreal Protocol on Substances that Deplete the Ozone Layer*, 1987; "Report of the First Meeting of the Parties to the Montreal Protocol on Substances that Deplete the Ozone Layer," Helsinki, May 2–5, 1989, United Nations document UNEP/OzL. Pro.1/5; "Report of the Second Meeting of the Parties to the Montreal Protocol on Substances that Deplete the Ozone Layer," London, June 27–29, 1990, United Nations document UNEP/OzL.Pro.2/3; "Report of the Third Meeting of the Parties to the Montreal Protocol on Substances that Deplete the Ozone Layer," Nairobi, June 19–21, 1991, United Nations document UNEP/OzL.Pro.3/11; "Report of the Fourth Meeting of the Parties to the Montreal Protocol on Substances that Deplete the Ozone Layer," Copenhagen, November 23–25, 1992, United Nations document UNEP/OzL.Pro.4/15; "Report of the Fifth Meeting of the Parties to the Montreal Protocol on Substances that Deplete the Ozone Layer," Bangkok, November 17–19, 1993, United Nations document UNEP/OzL.Pro.5/12; "Report of the Sixth Meeting of the Parties to the Montreal Protocol on Substances that Deplete the Ozone Layer," United Nations document UNEP/OzL.Pro.6/7; "Report of the Seventh Meeting of the Parties to the Montreal Protocol on Substances that Deplete the Ozone Layer," Vienna, December 5–7, 1995, United Nations document UNEP/

OzL.Pro.7/12; "Report of the Eighth Meeting of the Parties to the Montreal Protocol on Substances that Deplete the Ozone Layer," San Jose, November 25–27, 1996, United Nations document UNEP/OzL.Pro.8/12; and "Report of the Ninth Meeting of the Parties to the Montreal Protocol on Substances that Deplete the Ozone Layer," Montreal, September 15–17, 1997, United Nations document UNEP/OzL.Pro.9/12.

6. Recent and representative examples include: WMO et al., *Scientific Assessment of Stratospheric Ozone: 1994* (Geneva: WMO for WMO, UNEP, NASA, NOAA, U.K. DOE, 1995); UNEP Environmental Effects Panel, *Environmental Effects of Ozone Depletion: 1994 Assessment* (Nairobi: UNEP, 1994); TEAP, *1994 Report of the Technology and Economic Assessment Panel* (Nairobi: UNEP, 1995); and TEAP Halons Committee, *1993 Report of the Halons Technical Options Committee* (Nairobi: UNEP, 1993).

7. See, for example, "Report of the Eighteenth Meeting of the Executive Committee of the Multilateral Fund for the Implementation of the Montreal Protocol," Vienna, November 22–24, 1995, United Nations document UNEP/OzL.Pro/Excom/ 18/75; To date, the best analysis of the institution is DeSombre and Kauffman, "Montreal Protocol Multilateral Fund."

8. One of the most interesting and important examples of this process occurred during 1995, 1996, and 1997 in discussions with Belarus, Poland, Ukraine, and especially the Russian Federation (conclusion based on my personal experience, discussions with regime participants and reviews of committee documents). See also, UNEP/OzL.Pro.7/12, UNEP/OzL.Pro.8/12, UNEP/OzL.Pro.9/12, and "Report of the Implementation Committee under the Non-Compliance Procedure for the Montreal Protocol on the Work of its Twelfth Meeting," Vienna, December 27–1, 1995, United Nations document UNEP/OzL.Pro/ImpCom/12/3.

9. For authoritative reviews of the impact of ozone depletion, see Environmental Effects Panel, *Environmental Effects*, and World Health Organization (WHO), *Environmental Health Criteria 160: Ultraviolet Radiation* (Geneva: WHO, 1994). For a comprehensive review of ozone-depletion science, including evidence of increasing ozone depletion, see WMO et al., *Scientific Assessment of Stratospheric Ozone: 1994*.

10. See, for example, WMO et al., *Scientific Assessment of Stratospheric Ozone: 1991* (Geneva: WMO, 1991); WMO et al. *Scientific Assessment of Stratospheric Ozone: 1994*; and Rumen D. Bojkov, *The Changing Ozone Layer* (Geneva: WMO and UNEP, 1995).

11. Perhaps the best secondary source detailing CFC production, use and replacement is Arjun Makhijani and Kevin Gurney, *Mending the Ozone Hole: Science, Technology and Politics* (Cambridge: MIT Press, 1995); See also Cynthia Pollock Shea, *Protecting Life on Earth: Steps to Save the Ozone Layer* (Washington: Worldwatch Institute, Worldwatch Paper 87, 1988) and Seth Cagin and Philip Dray, *Between Earth and the Sky: How CFCs Changed Our World and Endangered the Ozone Layer* (New York: Pantheon, 1993). More comprehensive and authoritative reviews are provided by TEAP assessment panels and four volumes by UNEP IE/PAC (Industry and Environment Programme Activity Centre): *Aerosols, Sterilants, Carbon Tetrachloride and Miscellaneous*

Uses; Foams; Refrigerants; and *Solvents, Coatings and Adhesives* (Paris: UNEP IE/PAC, 1992).

12. Halons, used in fire control, and methyl bromide, used primarily as an agricultural fumigant, release bromine, a more potent ozone destroyer than chlorine, into the stratosphere.

13. Mario Molina and F. Sherwood Rowland, "Stratospheric Sink for Chlorofluoromethanes: Chlorine Atomic Catalyzed Destruction of Ozone," *Nature* vol. 249 (June 28, 1974), pp. 810–12. See also J. Lovelock, R. Maggs and R. Wade, "Halogenated Hydrocarbons over the Atlantic," *Nature* vol. 241 (January 19, 1973), pp. 194–96; Richard Stolarski and Ralph Cicerone, "Stratospheric Chlorine: A Possible Sink for Ozone," *Canadian Journal of Chemistry* vol. 52 (1974), pp. 1610–15; and R. Cicerone, R. Stolarski and S. Walters, "Stratospheric Ozone Destruction by Man-Made Chloro-fluorocarbons," *Science* vol. 185 (September 27, 1974), pp. 1165–68.

14. A variety of discussions provide historical detail on the development of national ozone layer protection policies. Lydia Dotto and Harold Schiff, *The Ozone War* (New York: Doubleday, 1978) follows the issue's early path through the complex scientific and regulatory battles that preceded the US CFC-aerosol ban. Works providing insights into later developments within the United States include: Cagin and Dray, *Between Earth and the Sky*; Paul Brodeur, "Annals of Chemistry: In the Face of Doubt," *The New Yorker*, June 9, 1986, pp. 70–87; Roan, *Ozone Crisis*; Benedick, *Ozone Diplomacy*; and Litfin, *Ozone Discourses*. Markus Jachtenfuchs, "The European Community and the Protection of the Ozone Layer," *Journal of Common Market Studies* vol. 28 (1990), pp. 261–77, and James Maxwell and Sanford Weiner, "Green Consciousness or Dollar Diplomacy? Britain's Response to the Threat of Ozone Depletion," *International Environmental Affairs* vol. 5 (Winter 1993), pp. 19–41, examine developments within the EC and UK, respectively. David Leonard Downie, "Comparative Public Policy of Ozone Layer Protection," *Political Science* vol. 45 (1993), pp. 186–97, and Detlef Sprinz and Tapani Vaahtoranta, "The interest-based explanation of international environmental policy," *International Organization* vol. 48 (Winter 1994), pp. 77–106, provide elements of comparative studies.

15. Benedick, *Ozone Diplomacy*; Litfin, *Ozone Discourses*; and Downie, *Understanding International Environmental Regimes*, are among the best studies that attempt broad histories of the international negotiations and related developments. See also: Morrisette, "The Evolution Policy Response to Stratospheric Ozone Depletion"; Haas, "Stratospheric Ozone: Regime Formation in Stages"; Ian H. Rowlands, "The Fourth Meeting of the Parties to the Montreal Protocol: Report and Reflection," *Environment* vol. 35 (July/Aug. 1993), pp. 25–34; and DeSombre and Kauffman, "Montreal Protocol Multilateral Fund."

16. UNEP/OzL.Pro.2/3.

17. UNEP/OzL.Pro.4/15 and Rowlands, "The Fourth Meeting of the Parties to the Montreal Protocol."

18. UNEP/OzL.Pro.5/12, Decision V/9.

19. See UNEP/OzL.Pro.7/12 and "Parties to Montreal Protocol Agree to Phase Out Methyl Bromide By 2010," *International Environmental Reporter*, Dec. 13, 1995, pp. 935–36.

20. See UNEP/OzL.Pro.7/12; WMO et al., *Scientific Assessment of Stratospheric Ozone: 1994*, p. xiii; and UNEP/OzL.Pro.8/12, para. 23.

21. "Status of Ratification . . . ," United Nations document UNEP/OzL.Rat. webversion, <http://www.unep.ch/ozone/reports.htm>.

22. UNEP/OzL.Pro.7/12, p. 33, Decision VII/18, para 2 and UNEP/OzL.Pro/ ImpCom/12/3, para 16.

23. UNEP/OzL.Pro.7/12, pp. 31–36, Decisions VII/15–19.

24. "The 1994 Science, Environmental Effects, and Technology and Economic Assessments: Synthesis Report," United Nations document UNEP/OzL.Pro/WG.1/ 11/3, paras. ES.7 and 14; and Worldwatch Institute, *Vital Signs 1995* (New York: Norton, 1995), pp. 62–63. For Russia, see UNEP/OzL.Pro/ImpCom/12/3.

25. TEAP Halons Committee, *1993 Report of the Halons Technical Options Committee*, pp. 1–4 and interview with K. M. Sarma, Coordinator, Secretariat of the Vienna Convention and Montreal Protocol, United Nations Environment Programme, Vienna, 3–7 December 1995. Use of these very effective fire-control chemicals will continue via recycling through national and international "halon banks."

26. WMO et al., *Scientific Assessment of Stratospheric Ozone: 1994*, UNEP/OzL. Pro.7/12, para. 19, and UNEP/OzL.Pro.8/12, para. 23. In addition, national delegates generally agree that the regime's major institutions, although subject to significant criticism, operate within acceptable limits (e.g., UNEP/OzL.Pro.7/12, paras. 19–55, 58, 70–74, 80–81, and personal observations and discussions during more than 20 regime meetings during the last six years). For example, during 1995, the Executive Committee of the Multilateral Fund approved $211 million worth of projects, 511 individual projects and activities which, when completed, would eliminate 24,000 tons of ODS (UNEP/OzL.Pro.7/1, paras. 45–48). The Assessment Panels continue to provide timely information (UNEP/OzL.Pro.7/12, paras. 19–34, 58). The review mechanisms have allowed Parties to consistently strengthen regime rules and procedures (compare *Vienna Convention*, *Montreal Protocol*, UNEP/OzL.Pro.2/3, UNEP/ OzL.Pro.4/15, UNEP/OzL.Pro.6/7, UNEP/OzL.Pro.7/12, UNEP/OzL.Pro.8/12, and UNEP/OzL.Pro.9/12).

27. See, for example, John Austin, Neal Butchart, and Keith Shine, "Possibility of an Arctic Ozone Hole in a Doubled-CO_2 Climate," *Nature* vol. 360 (November 19, 1992), pp. 221–25; WMO et al., *Scientific Assessment of Stratospheric Ozone: 1994*; UNEP/OzL.Pro.8/12, para. 24.

28. Short of the use of military or economic coercion to prevent ODS production.

29. For discussion of how "concern," "capacity," and the "contractual environment" can impact international environmental policy see Peter Haas, Robert Keohane

and Marc Levy, *Institutions for the Earth: Sources of Effective International Environmental Protection* (Cambridge: MIT Press, 1993).

30. Benedick, *Ozone Diplomacy.*

31. This can be seen in recent debates concerning increasing the size of the Multilateral Fund, establishing exceptions to controls on HCFCs and methyl bromide, and interpreting provisions in the Protocol designed to limit exports of CFCs from developing country Parties during the grace period (e.g., UNEP/OzL.5/12, UNEP/OzL.6/7, UNEP/OzL.7/12, UNEP/OzL.8/12, UNEP/OzL.9/12, and personal observations during ozone negotiations in 1992–1997).

32. For example, CFC production in developed countries froze at 1986 levels and was eliminated in 1995. The baseline "freeze" year for developing countries for CFCs is 1996 and phase out is 2010. Developed countries will freeze HCFCs in 1996, face a 65 percent HCFC reduction by 2010, a 90 percent reduction by 2020 and elimination in 2030. Developing countries will not freeze HCFC production until 2016 (at 2015 levels) and face no interim HCFC reductions before they must phase out production in 2040.

33. For preliminary analysis of the Chinese case, see David Downie and Arvin Wu, "China's dual Ozone Strategy," Unpublished manuscript, School of International and Public Affairs, Columbia University, 1996. During the last three years, many delegates to ozone meetings have told me that without the regulatory extensions and Fund these gains would have been impossible. At the same time, however, without the fund and the extensions, most large developing countries would not have joined the regime.

34. 1986 data is important as that year represents the baseline-freeze year for CFC production in developed country-Parties.

35. "Report of the Secretariat on Information Provided by the Parties in Accordance with Articles 4, 7, and 9 of the Montreal Protocol and the Report of the Implementation Committee," United Nations document UNEP/OzL.Pro.7/6, p. 17.

36. Ibid.

37. Ibid, p. 42.

38. Ibid, p. 45.

39. Ibid, p. 19.

40. Ibid, pp. 44 and 49.

41. See, for example, James Tyson, "Why China Says Ozone Must Take Back Seat in Drive to Prosperity," *Christian Science Monitor*, March 23, 1989; author's interview with K. M. Sarma, Coordinator, Secretariat of the Vienna Convention and Montreal Protocol, Nairobi, May 3, 1993; and personal observations during ozone negotiations, 1994–97.

42. Personal observations during ozone negotiations, 1994–97.

43. See, for example, Maxwell and Weiner, "Green Consciousness or Dollar Diplomacy?"; Oye and Maxwell, "Self-Interest and Environmental Management";

Downie, *Understanding International Environmental Regimes*; "Firms Intensify Race to Find Substitutes for Chemicals Linked to Ozone Depletion," *Wall Street Journal*, September 27, 1988; and "Chemical Giants May Be Winners in Ozone Fight," *Wall Street Journal*, June 29, 1990.

44. For example, despite repeated attempts by developing countries, the language in the regime regarding technology transfer from developed to developing countries is, in my opinion, still vague and ineffectual. OECD countries consistently resisted any effort they saw as threatening intellectual property rights or setting a precedent of uncompensated sharing of commercial products and associated technology. OECD countries have also refused to meet specific funding levels demanded by the G-77 and China. Each agreement of the Fund has been part of a large compromise involving control measures, regime operations and the size and operation of the Multilateral Fund.

45. This conclusion is based on personal observations and conversations during the last six years of ozone negotiations. Also compare summaries of the debate in UNEP/OzL.Pro.5/12, UNEP/OzL.Pro.6/7, UNEP/OzL.Pro.7/12, UNEP/OzL. Pro.8/12, and UNEP/OzL.Pro.9/12.

46. For example, in Vienna the agreement by developed countries to eliminate methyl bromide by 2010 was weakened by a decision to investigate creating an "essential agricultural use exemption" outside the usual and rigorous essential use review process. The agreements by developing countries failed to meet the 'developed country schedule plus ten years' phase-out language in the 1990 London Amendment. If this had been maintained, CFC and halon production would be phased out by 2006 not 2010, HCFCs would still be eliminated by 2040 but with extensive and deep interim reductions, and methyl bromide production would be eliminated by 2020 not frozen in 2002.

47. UNEP/OzL.Pro.7/6.

48. UNEP/OzL.Pro/ImpCom/12/3.

49. These include the United States, UK and France (personal observations and conversations during ozone negotiations).

50. Some of the secondary literature emphasizes that the United States was the largest producer and consumer of CFCs and thus dominated or should have dominated the discussion (e.g., Roan, *Ozone Crisis* and at times Benedick, *Ozone Diplomacy* and Haas, "Stratospheric Ozone: Regime Creation in Stages"). This is simply incorrect. For a broader discussion, see Downie, *Understanding International Environmental Regimes*, chapter 7.

51. The USSR participated in all negotiations and "bipolarity" and "hegemony" conflict. EU states negotiated as a bloc and both they and the Japanese had become near economic contemporaries of the United States by the mid-1980s when Parties negotiated the Vienna Convention and Montreal Protocol.

52. Jachtenfuchs, "The European Community and the Protection of the Ozone

Layer," p. 263. In 1986 the United States produced approximately 311,000,000 ODP weighted tons of the CFCs controlled in the 1987 Protocol and consumed about 306,000,000 tons. In 1986, France, West Germany, Italy, and the UK alone produced approximately 350,000,000 tons. Japan produced and consumed approximately 120,000,000 ODP tons (UNEP/OzL.Pro.7/6).

53. These conclusions based on personal conversations and observations. See also Benedick, *Ozone Diplomacy*, for analysis of 1985, 1987, and 1990 negotiations.

54. UNEP/OzL.Pro.7/12.

55. See Oye and Maxwell, "Self Interest and Environmental Management"; and Downie, *Understanding International Environmental Regimes*, especially chapter 10.

6 Asymmetrical Rivalry in Common Pool Resources and European Responses to Acid Rain

BARBARA CONNOLLY

Introduction

The problem of European acid rain poses an intriguing challenge to conventional wisdom about collective action dilemmas. In part, the acid rain case underscores this volume's main proposition: while the literature on collective action offers innumerable examples of problems conceived as public goods whose supply is jeopardized by free ridership,[1] the vast majority of politically problematic international environmental problems do not fit neatly in the public goods category, and are in some respects better understood as common pool resources (CPRs). European acid rain does exhibit some political characteristics of CPRs. Unlike public goods, common pool resources are subject to rivalry in consumption in addition to supply-side problems. The supply and maintenance of a CPR will become objects of distributional conflict, but so will consumption of the resource itself. Free ridership becomes doubly dangerous, because actors can not only shirk in the provision of a common pool resource, but their threats to overconsume a CPR can threaten the very existence of the resource.

The European acid rain case also throws a second curve at collective action theorists. In contrast to much writing on public goods and common pool resources that tends to assume symmetry among actors,[2] the acid rain issue highlights the frequent possibility that the same problem can present itself with different faces to different actors, causing bargaining dynamics to vary substantially among them. In the example of acid rain, some European states find themselves in more of a public goods situation because their geography or ecosystem characteristics enable them to escape effects of acidifying compounds, whereas others who do suffer those effects from their own and neighboring states' emissions clearly recognize themselves to be in a CPR problem.[3] Levels of free ridership and positions toward international regulation of acid rain vary systematically among European states because of these asymmetrical positions. Thanks to its relatively long history, the European acid rain case also demonstrates how states' knowledge and perceptions of how they are affected by acid rain have changed over time, transforming, for some, a public goods problem into a CPR problem. Studying the variance in bargaining positions and outcomes of cooperative attempts both among states and across time yields insight into how the structure of a given collective action problem[4] influences obstacles to and possibilities for cooperation.

The acid rain case shows that essentially realist arguments on the problems of collective action in a CPR situation, as embodied in the hypotheses of the introductory chapter, do hold up but only to a certain point. For instance, regulation of acid rain in Europe is indeed underprovided, if we consider the optimal point of regulation to be the point at which ecosystem damage is prevented in most parts of Europe.[5] Underprovision of ecosystem protection results from free ridership among states who are able to externalize a large part of the costs of acid emissions. Also consistent with realist expectations, free riders do come out ahead on the bargaining front—they pay less for emissions abatement, and nonetheless enjoy benefits from other states' emissions reductions.

However, the introductory hypotheses do not explain everything in this case. Two puzzles stand out: first, despite some free riding, acid rain regulation across Europe is much more stringent today than it was twenty years ago. The tragedy of the commons has certainly been stalled, if not entirely averted. Substantial emissions reductions are largely attributable to changes in states' perceptions of their interests over time, and specifically to their growing recognition of both the CPR aspects of acid rain and the partly *private costs* of acid emissions. Heightened perceptions of the internal costs from free riding dampened many states' incentives to free ride and facilitated European emissions reduction over time. While the initial hypotheses offer insight into how static perceptions of a collective good generate particular incentive structures, they do not illuminate causes of dynamic variation in states' interests, or how states perceive public and private costs of international environmental problems.

Second, while we expect free riders to exert bargaining leverage over CPR management, in fact free riders win fewer concessions in this case than we might think, and victims of free riding exert unexpected influence. These puzzles demand that we consider actor asymmetries within collective action dilemmas. Asymmetries of positioning mean that not all free riders within the acid rain issue wield the threat to overconsume a CPR, nor are all states equally affected by those who do possess such a threat. For example, international agreements within the European-wide regime on acid rain, Long-Range Transboundary Air Pollution (LRTAP), permit southern Europe to increase acid emissions—seemingly a concession to their free riding. Given the geographical position of these states, however, their increases pose few ecological dangers for neighboring countries—they have no real power to destroy. In contrast, free riding by another group of states does exacerbate rivalry over atmospheric quality for some though not all of their neighbors, generating complaints that the UK, Spain, Belgium, Denmark, and France continue to do less abatement than deemed optimal for Europe or for the victims of their emissions. Still, the acid rain controls of these countries are much more stringent today than two decades ago, and all are subject to costly European Union air quality directives—evidence that the power to impose costs on neighbors has been a less lucrative source of bargaining power than the free-rider hypotheses lead us to expect.

The bargaining outcomes of European acid rain suggest that the image of the free rider as able to extort concessions approaching the total value of the environmental good is an exaggerated notion for many apparent CPRs, because the asymmetries of positioning among actors that commonly come into play can diminish free riders' bargaining power. States such as China or India really may hold the power to destroy the ozone layer and may (as David Downie suggests) prove able to extort concessions from other states who perceive themselves strongly affected by ozone depletion. However, in many other CPR cases, including Beth DeSombre's fisheries examples and Richard Matthew's international waters examples in this volume, states differ in how much they are affected by rivalry.[6] Downstream countries hold no bargaining power in water distribution issues over upstream countries, free riding not-withstanding. Free ridership confers bargaining power where the free rider can impose costs on other beneficiaries capable of delivering concessions, but this condition varies considerably among commons issues and among actors within the same issue—as suggested by Ronald Mitchell's typology of benefi-ciaries in this volume.

The last piece of the bargaining puzzle, the unexpected influence of vic-tim states in advancing acid rain regulation, offers cautious optimism about the role of international regimes in managing commons issues. In European negotiations on acid rain, small states whose sensitive ecosystems and geo-graphic position make them the victims of negative externalities from im-ported acid emissions, such as Sweden, Norway, the Netherlands, and Fin-land, have exerted influence over outcomes far disproportionate to any visible power resource. The influence of these victim states, natural advocates of international acid rain controls as a means of eliminating damages imposed on them by neighboring states' emissions, does *not* lie in manipulation of market power. Rather, small victim states pushed for creation of a nonthreatening international regime, initially containing no substantive obligations for emis-sions control and focused primarily on knowledge-generation. Over time, the Long-Range Transboundary Air Pollution regime created increasingly harmonious incentives for European acid rain controls by creating awareness among key actors not only that acid rain was a CPR problem for a large ma-jority of states but also that a significant share of the costs of CPR exploitation were borne internally by previously reluctant states. While LRTAP has played a critical role in European acid rain management, the underlying physical structure of the problem made this a lucky issue; in other environmental problems knowledge creation may not always lead to more benign incentive structures.

Introduction to European Acid Rain and LRTAP

The issue of acid rain provides a classic example of the problems of col-lective action. Implicated in the disappearance of fish populations in large numbers of lakes in Norway and Sweden, damage to vast stretches of forest in Central Europe, and further damages to European buildings and monuments, acid rain gained prominence on the European environmental agenda through the 1970s and 1980s. Acid rain abatement measures have been the subject of ongoing negotiations and international commitments since the late 1970s.

The most important international agreements on European acid rain have
been arrived at within LRTAP, the Convention on Long-Range Transboundary Air Pollution negotiated within the UN Economic Commission for Europe, and within the European Union in a package of directives regulating air
pollution among member states.

Acid precipitation occurs when sulfur dioxide (SO_2), nitrogen oxides
(NO_x), and ammonia (NH_3), emitted during the burning of fossil fuels primarily by power plants, industrial processes, vehicles and commercial or resi-
dential heating units, and from agricultural practices mix with moisture in the
air, forming sulfuric and nitric acids. When these compounds reach the
ground, they cause acidification of water and soils. Dry deposition can similarly cause acidification. Soil acidification causes the leaching out of nutrients
such as potassium, calcium, and magnesium, thereby reducing soil productivity. Acidification also leads to increased concentrations of aluminum and
other toxic metals in soils, ground water, and surface waters. Although some
scientific controversy remains, a growing consensus links the decline and
death of fish stocks to the acidification of lakes, and widespread instances of
forest decline to soil acidification together with ambient air pollution. Discoveries of lake acidification, forest death, and other damages in many parts of
Europe have prompted actions to control acid rain.

Acid deposition does not necessarily cause immediate damages. In fact, it
is the cumulative load of acids over time that jeopardizes ecosystems. Lakes
and soils have varying amounts of natural buffering capacity that enable them
to tolerate deposition of acids without discernible impact over a certain period of time. However, once the accumulated load of acids exhausts the neu-
tralizing capacity of soils and lakes, damaging effects can appear very quickly
from further acid deposition.[7] This characteristic of acidification has important implications for states' incentives to abate pollution, because states have
very different levels of vulnerability to acid deposition. Scandinavian states,
for example, suffer from very serious acidification problems because of the
limited buffering capacity of local ecosystems. Ecosystems in other states, for
example, in Southern Europe, exhibit much greater tolerance for air pollution without acidification damage.

Starting in the late 1960s, scientists began to link the phenomenon of
acidification with long-range, transboundary transport of air pollutants. In
1968, Swedish scientist Svante Odén identified a long-term trend toward increasing acidity of rainfall in Scandinavia. Moreover, he showed that the area
of Europe with especially acid precipitation had expanded over time, from the

circle of Benelux countries in the late 1950s to a much wider group including most of Germany, northern France, the Eastern British Isles, and southern Scandinavia by the late 1960s.[8] The discovery that finally ignited international action to combat acid rain was Odén's claim that acidification was caused by transboundary pollution. According to Odén, the acidification of Swedish lakes was caused by the long-range transport of sulfur emitted in Britain and Central Europe.[9] Ironically, the tall smokestacks that were widely used in earlier efforts to control local air pollution and mitigate health damage in Europe by dispersing air pollutants at their source are directly responsible for long-range transport of air pollutants.

Acid rain first reached the international political agenda in 1972 as a result of a Scandinavian campaign. As host of the 1972 UN Conference on the Human Environment, Sweden used that occasion to bring international attention to its discovery of serious acidification damage in Scandinavia. Sweden claimed that the increasing acidity of its rainfall was due to the burning of fossil fuels in neighboring countries. That same year, Norway initiated a large research program on the effects of acid precipitation, leading to the discovery of substantial lake acidification and fish kill in southern Norway. In order to resolve international controversy over the possible long-range transport of acid pollution, the Organization for Economic Cooperation and Development (OECD) had begun a study just prior to the Stockholm conference to determine the causes and effects of sulfur emissions and to measure and study the effects of long-range transport of air pollution.

Swedish claims about the long-range transport of air pollution garnered convincing evidence from OECD computer models, completed in 1977, that showed that Norway, Sweden, Finland, Austria, and Switzerland all imported more pollution from abroad than they received from domestic sources.[10] As further research demonstrated, once sulfur dioxide is released into the atmosphere, it can remain there for 1–6 days on average, traveling as much as several hundred kilometers overnight in strong wind. Hence it is possible for pollutants to be deposited as far as 1,000 kilometers away from their source.[11] Evidence of long-range transport of air pollutants soon impelled the Netherlands and Finland to join Sweden and Norway in calling for international controls on transboundary sulfur pollution.[12]

From the 1972 conference on, the issue gathered political momentum, aided in part by the flowering of détente. At the 1975 Helsinki Conference on Security and Cooperation in Europe (CSCE), the Soviet Union had proposed a high-level East-West meeting in the interest of furthering détente. Though the Soviets' principal interest was in high politics rather than in environmental policy, they suggested that the meeting might focus on either environment, energy, or transport issues, seeking to extend détente beyond the realm of security politics while deemphasizing human rights issues. The UN ECE, left with final selection, decided on environment as the best candidate for the upcoming conference. The Soviet initiative thereby enabled Norway and Sweden to seize on an international issue of great importance to them, namely the long-range transport of air pollution. The UN ECE set to work on a legally binding international convention on air pollution. Signed in 1979, the convention on Long Range Transboundary Air Pollution became the first multilateral agreement on air pollution as well as the first environmental accord involving all nations of Eastern and Western Europe and North America.[13]

The LRTAP convention did not set specific pollution reduction goals or emission limits. It did, however, establish a framework for negotiating and implementing further substantive protocols. The framework convention obligated signatories to "endeavor to limit and, as far as possible, gradually reduce and prevent air pollution including long-range transboundary air pollution." Signatories committed to "develop without undue delay policies and strategies which shall serve as a means of combating the discharge of air pollutants . . ." In addition, the convention provided for the exchange of information on emissions and abatement policy, scientific evidence, and pollution control technology, as well as for collaborative research programs.[14] The parties agreed to form an Executive Body, composed of high-level officials from each of the participating states, in order to govern LRTAP's implementation and oversee future negotiations. A separate protocol established permanent funding for the cooperative monitoring system for transboundary air pollution known as EMEP (short for the Cooperative Programme for the Monitoring and Evaluation of the Long-Range Transmission of Air Pollutants in Europe).

Since 1979, four substantive protocols have been signed under LRTAP's auspices: the 1985 Sulfur Dioxide Protocol, which reduced SO_2 emissions by 30 percent from 1980 levels by 1993, the 1987 Nitrogen Oxides Protocol, which froze No_x emissions at 1987 levels, the 1991 Volatile Organic Compounds protocol, and the 1994 second-generation Sulfur Protocol. A fifth protocol on heavy metals and persistent organic pollutants was agreed to in early 1998 and currently awaits signing. This analysis focuses mainly on the two sulfur-related protocols.

As early as 1979, Scandinavian countries were already pressing for a convention with binding reduction commitments, but opposition from the UK and West Germany, among others, prevented such an agreement. However, in 1982 Germany discovered widespread forest death, and dramatically reversed its position on international abatement. France also reversed prior opposition to international acid rain controls in 1984, when massive expansion of its nuclear energy program coincidentally lead to costless SO_2 emission reductions. By 1984 then, a so-called 30-percent club made up of Austria, Finland, Sweden, Switzerland, France, West Germany, Canada, Norway, Denmark, and the Netherlands were already pushing for a protocol mandating 30 percent flat-rate reductions of SO_2 emissions. The Soviet Union signed on, and the Helsinki Protocol was concluded in 1985. Some states refused to sign, most notably the UK, Spain, and Poland.[15]

One of the most interesting aspects of LRTAP negotiations is the way the approach to acid rain controls has evolved over time, from the flat-rate, across-the-board reductions embodied in the original SO_2 and NO_x protocols, to an approach called critical loads. By 1993, Sweden, Norway, Finland, Germany, and the Netherlands had banded together demanding greater reductions in sulfur emissions by the turn of the century, and LRTAP delegates had agreed to base the new protocol on critical loads for the first time. The critical loads approach takes into account countries' differing contributions to acidification in neighboring states as well as differing levels of vulnerability to acidification, and prescribes substantially different abatement targets for each state in an effort to minimize the overall cost of protecting ecosystems across Europe. By the time negotiations of the second sulfur protocol got underway, most European states were pursuing reduction plans significantly exceeding the 30 percent reductions in of the Helsinki Protocol—some mainly for domestic environmental reasons, some because of unrelated changes in energy policy, and a few because of European Community legislation. The Second Sulfur Protocol, finalized in 1994, did in fact include much higher reductions than the earlier Helsinki Protocol, and also called for differentiated reductions among signatories. However, several states including the UK, Belgium, Denmark, France, Ireland, Spain, and Italy pulled back from scientifically determined emissions reductions and instead committed to more lenient targets.

Subsequently, I will argue that the LRTAP regime proved remarkably effective in contributing to progressively stronger regulations on acidifying compounds by providing a forum in which evolving knowledge transformed states' conception of the national interest over time. To be clear about the causal mechanisms involved in this transformation, however, I emphasize that the LRTAP convention and protocols are all essentially voluntary commitments written into international law. Rather than binding signatories into measures they would prefer not to undertake, each of these legal instruments at best reflect the acid rain controls that signatories were already planning to implement at a particular moment in time.[16] The key feature of LRTAP, then, is not that the regime generated international acid rain controls that outpaced national controls, but rather that it fostered dramatic evolution in national interests over time.

While the LRTAP protocols enjoyed the widest participation among European states, a parallel track of acid rain controls implemented within the European Community (EC) adopted more stringent abatement measures for member states. In 1982 Germany, who had previously resisted acid rain controls, discovered massive *Waldsterben*, or forest death, in the Black Forest and hence launched an expensive program of national reductions in sulfur and nitrogen emissions. Subsequently, Germany allied itself with Sweden and Norway in seeking European-wide air pollution controls, and initiated negotiations within the European Community on reductions of sulfur and nitrogen emissions. What followed was the EC's Large Combustion Plant Directive (LCPD), finalized in 1988, which binds member states to meet stringent nitrogen and sulfur emissions standards for large power plants. Precisely because the LCPD did push certain states to implement pollution control measures beyond existing national policies, negotiations over the directive were prolonged and contentious. Between 1987 and 1990, the EC also passed a series of directives aimed at reducing nitrogen oxides emissions from vehicles.

The relatively long history of acid politics in Europe combined with a substantial negotiations record of international agreements demonstrates how perceptions of the acid deposition problem have changed over time and among states, and how increasing recognition both of the CPR characteristics of the problem and of private costs incurred has changed the political dynamics of the issue. The remainder of this chapter takes up five analytical questions. First, I consider the extent to which physical attributes of European acid deposition approximate standard definitions of a public good or common pool resource, and establish how perceptions of the issue vary among states. Second, I evaluate the prevalence and overall effects of free riding in this issue. Third, I ask how asymmetrical rivalry differentiates states in their bargaining behavior and particularly their propensity to free ride. Fourth, I consider the intertemporal dynamics of acid politics, asking about the impact of changing knowledge and interests on states' behavior and on the overall evolution of acid rain controls. Fifth, I question the extent to which free ridership translates into

genuine bargaining power in international negotiations over acid rain management, and consider other important sources of negotiating leverage in this
case. I conclude with suggestions about how this case relates to other instances
of international environmental management and to theories of international
cooperation more generally.

Atmospheric Pollution: Public Good or Common Pool Resource?

As Barkin and Shambaugh point out in the introduction, clean air,
though often cited as an example of a public good, does not generally meet
the definitional criteria of public goods. Public goods are both nonrival and
nonexcludable, meaning that one agent's consumption of a unit of the good
does not detract from the benefit others can obtain from that unit, and that
once the good is provided it is difficult if not impossible to exclude individuals from subsequent benefits.[17] Clean air generally does appear nonexcludable,[18] but unlike a public good, it can be subject to rivalry. Because the real
obstacle to consuming fresh air is the ability of the atmosphere to absorb pollution without ecosystem damage, and because the atmosphere's capacity to
act as a pollution sink is in fact finite, it may improve our understanding of the
issue to think of air pollution as a common-pool resource problem. The more
pollution certain states dump into the atmosphere, the less capacity to absorb
new pollution without sustaining ecosystem damage remains for other states.
Clean air is thus subject to a particular kind of congestion effect, termed quality rivalry by Ronald Mitchell. Consumption of a unit of clean air interferes
with the quality of units obtained by others.[19]

Acid rain fits uneasily into the above categorization. The criterion of
nonexcludability is met in all cases, because it is impossible (or at least extremely costly) to prevent any state from emitting acidifying compounds into
the atmosphere ("consuming the atmospheric sink"), where they can be
transported long distances and potentially cause damage where they land. In
contrast, the rivalry criterion varies; while some states suffer from atmospheric quality rivalry induced by acid rain, others do not. By implication, acid
rain looks like a CPR problem from the perspective of some states, but a public goods problem from the perspective of others. This variability carries important repercussions for states' bargaining positions.

For the most prominent victims of European acid rain, notably Sweden
and Norway, as well as Austria, Switzerland, the Netherlands, and Finland,
other states' emissions of acidifying compounds seriously impinge on their

ability to emit similar pollutants without sustaining domestic ecosystem damage. For example, in 1985, fully 93 percent of Norway's SO_2 depositions came from foreign rather than domestic sources; comparable figures were 87 percent for both Sweden and the Netherlands, 92 percent for Austria, 90 percent for Switzerland, and 81 percent for Finland.[20] For all of these states but especially the Nordic countries, the natural sensitivity of domestic lakes, soils, and forests exacerbates the effect of imported depositions. For these states, air pollution is clearly a common-pool resource problem; other states' consumption of the atmospheric sink through emissions of acidifying compounds leave the above group suffering from acid rain damage despite drastic reductions in their own emissions. Both foreign and domestic consumption of the atmospheric sink through acid emissions results in further degradation of domestic ecosystems within this group of states—a quality rivalry effect, from their position. Not surprisingly, these victim states (Norway and Sweden, subsequently joined by Finland, Austria, Switzerland, the Netherlands, and Germany[21]) became the principal motivators of acid rain abatement within LRTAP.[22]

Remember, however, that natural ecosystem vulnerability to acidifying compounds varies considerably from one region to the next, meaning that states face different degrees of quality rivalry in the use of atmospheric sinks. In stark contrast to the Nordic countries, Ireland, Portugal, Greece, and Spain, among others, exhibit a low degree of ecological vulnerability to acid rain.[23] These states have the capacity to absorb a much higher level of depositions, either from foreign or domestic sources, without incurring acidification. Because of their geographic position and prevailing wind patterns, their emissions of SO_2 and NO_x also have little impact on states with much higher levels of ecological vulnerability. For states such as Ireland, Portugal, Greece, and Spain, then, air pollution does take on the nonrival attribute of public goods; their consumption of the atmospheric sink does not detract from others' or their own ability to deposit further acidifying compounds without ecosystem damage. Not coincidentally, all of these countries refused to sign the 1985 Sulfur Protocol; of these, only Spain signed the 1988 NO_x Protocol.

Picture European states' experiences of the acid rain problem as points on a continuum between a public good and a CPR, where the degree of quality rivalry varies. Exposure to quality rivalry derives more precisely from two factors in tandem, which tend to covary in the groups above, but not in all cases. These two factors are the extent to which states suffer (and recognize) private costs from acid deposition, and the extent to which their acid depositions are imported from neighboring countries rather than produced domestically.

In order to experience the quality rivalry that generates CPR dynamics in the acid rain case, states must both import a substantial share of total acid depositions from abroad and also recognize significant domestic costs from those depositions. A state that produces most of its total acid depositions domestically, as opposed to importing them, may experience a private bad in acidification, but has no inherent incentive to push for international regulation of acid depositions. In contrast, the victim of substantial acid imports and domestic damages has an obvious incentive to prefer international regulation. Keep in mind, however, that certain states can experience a high level of acid depositions without incurring—or recognizing—domestic damage. These states either do not experience quality rivalry or do not perceive that they are doing so. Consequently, they will likely be unwilling to contribute to international management of an acid rain problem.

Because of their importance in the politics of European acid rain, two additional groups of states merit consideration. The first of these occupies a position similar to southern Europe, in that they escape quality rivalry from acid emissions and thus experience the issue more as a public good. The United Kingdom through the late 1980s,[24] the Soviet Union (and subsequently Russia), France, and Italy all either enjoy relative immunity from domestic acidification damages or fail to recognize accruing damage. For the UK and Russia, foreign contributions to acid deposition remain strikingly low in comparison to other countries. France and Italy receive somewhat more acid imports, but acidification damage has not been an object of significant public concern in either country. From their structural positions, these countries would likely behave the same way as Southern Europe, by refusing to contribute to international management of acid rain.

A final group of states sits in a more ambiguous position closer to the middle of the public goods/CPR continuum. Through the 1980s, much of East Central Europe (Poland, Czechoslovakia,[25] and Hungary) shared with West Germany[26] a significant but not always recognized or acknowledged vulnerability to acid emissions from foreign as well as domestic sources. In 1985, for example, these countries imported between 53 and 61 percent of total SO_2 depositions from abroad—notably less than Scandinavia, but still a significant share. Acid deposition during this time was also causing real damage, from the massive forest death publicized in Germany in the early 1980s to the health effects resulting from high ambient air pollution, forest damage, and corrosion to buildings that remained officially unacknowledged under Communist regimes in East Central Europe but increasingly evident. The most interesting feature of this group should be the evolution of their bargaining positions over time. *Prior to perceiving domestic acidification damage*, these states ought to behave similarly to the Southern tier by free riding on the abatement efforts of the Northern group. *With recognition of domestic damage*, however, these states find themselves in an international CPR and gain some incentive to support European abatement efforts.

The preceding categorization of states' positions with respect to acid rain raises an empirical question about the extent to which states confronting a CPR problem will demonstrate the same tendencies toward free ridership as states enjoying a public good. Garrett Hardin's famous "tragedy of the commons" portrays free riding as endemic in common pool resource situations.[27] Evidence from the acid rain case tempers those conclusions. The following two sections consider the problem of free ridership in general, and then show how states' willingness to participate in international abatement varies as a function of their recognition of the "CPR-ness" of the acid rain problem, and of the acidification costs borne within the state.

Bargaining Behavior and Free Ridership

While states vary as to whether or not air pollution produces quality rivalry in this case, the temptation to free ride is a nearly universal problem because of the transboundary nature of acid rain. The optimal outcome for most states, except those with highly sensitive ecosystems or whose depositions come mostly from domestic sources, would be to shirk on costly abatement measures while other European states all participate in international emissions reduction agreements, thereby providing joint gains in air quality. Britain, the largest emitter of SO_2 in Western Europe through the 1980s, was tagged "Dirty Man of Europe" for its free ridership by refusing to sign on to the 1985 Sulfur Protocol, despite Britain's substantial contribution to sulfur depositions in countries that *did* participate in the protocol, such as Denmark, the Netherlands, and Norway.[28] Poland and Spain also refused to sign the 1985 Sulfur Protocol, their positions among the top-ten emitters of sulfur in Europe notwithstanding.

The diplomatic history of European acid rain strongly indicates that states' bargaining positions on international environmental regulation are much more sensitive to domestic ecological vulnerability than to responsibility for causing pollution problems in neighboring states.[29] In other words, recognition that European acid rain is a CPR problem without the attendant discovery of private costs is not sufficient to motivate states to abate emissions of acidifying compounds. Free ridership is still a popular policy, and consequently, acid rain controls remain underprovided, at least when viewed from the perspective of environmentalists and selected states.[30]

One indicator that acid rain controls suffer from underprovision is that as recently as 1993, air pollution experts estimated that 35 percent of Europe's ecosystems were suffering sulfur deposition above the threshold of ecological tolerance.[31] Moreover, the reduction plans that states had in place at that time for the year 2000, which would result in a decline of sulfur emissions by 39 percent over 1980 levels, would still leave 22 percent of European ecosystems experiencing deposition above critical loads, at levels leading to acidification damage.[32] While overall European abatement of sulphur emissions during the 1980s and early 1990s represented a marked improvement in ecosystem protection over the status quo at the beginning of that period, many regions remained significantly underprotected, especially in the Czech Republic, Slovakia, Finland, Norway, Poland, Sweden, and the UK.[33]

Even the Second Sulfur Protocol concluded in 1994 did not solve the problem of free riding. Environmentalists criticized negotiators from the UK, Belgium, Denmark, France, Ireland, and Spain for pulling back from the stringent targets for emissions reductions set scientifically as part of a uniform goal to narrow the gap between current sulphur depositions and critical loads. As one environmentalist argued, "some countries, namely Finland, Sweden, Norway, Germany, and Austria, are doing all the reducing under current reduction plans, while the others are largely free riding on the reduced deposition benefits created by them."[34] Environmentalists' disgust for the political haggling of the protocol process was justified in certain respects, as even the chair of LRTAP's executive body noted that the protocol's stated goal of reducing the gap between 1990 depositions and critical loads by at least 60 percent by the year 2000 would not be reached until around 2015, given many states' unwillingness to commit themselves to the original goal.[35] Negotiations of the Second Sulfur Protocol disappointed hopes that scientifically established targets would guide states in their emissions reductions, confirming instead the existing trend within LRTAP whereby states' international commitments trailed existing national emissions reduction plans.[36]

Asymmetrical Rivalry

Since states' bargaining positions within LRTAP negotiations *at any single point in time*[37] boil down to the level of abatement they are willing to undertake domestically, those positions can be predicted fairly easily on the basis of how much states find themselves on the victim side of a CPR problem.[38] As indicated above, we can measure the "CPR-ness" of the acid rain problem for individual states by measuring how much of a states' total depositions are imported from abroad, together with perceptions of national damage. These data shows that European states experience very different levels of quality rivalry induced by acid rain, leading to systematic differences in bargaining behavior.

In 1985, when the first Sulfur Protocol was concluded, five states imported greater than 80 percent of their total sulfur dioxide deposition: Norway, Austria, Switzerland, Sweden, and Finland. By contrast, the UK and Spain imported only 15 and 21 percent of their SO_2 depositions, respectively, while the USSR, GDR, Italy, and Portugal imported less than 50 percent of their SO_2 depositions.[39] Particularly for the UK and Spain, and to a lesser extent for the other four states, if acid rain were to become a problem at all (as it later did in the UK) it would be a mostly *private* bad, perhaps generating incentives for abatement domestically but not for international action. Already these two categories of states, the major importers of air pollution and the group that is spared such transboundary effects, correlate closely with those that led the drive for a European protocol on sulfur emissions versus those that refused to participate in the protocol (including the UK, Spain, and Portugal), or that signed on but implemented only the minimum emission controls (including the USSR, GDR, Italy). Table 6:1 provides a snapshot of emissions transport positions in 1985.

Transport data alone does not fully predict states' positions, however. For example, Greece imported 68 percent of its total SO_2 deposition in 1985, but still did not sign the Sulfur Protocol. West Germany, while not a top importer of SO_2 deposition, was nonetheless a driving force behind the protocol. The missing explanatory factor is the discovery of private costs from acidification. Evidence from the acid rain case bears out the initial hypothesis that "the more the cost of free riding is internalized by the actor in question, the weaker the incentive to free ride."[40] The Scandinavian countries were the first to discover domestic acidification damage in the early 1970s, primarily in lakes and fish stocks. Discoveries of forest damage spread through central Europe in the 1980s. Southern Europe in general has very low ecological sensitivity to acid depositions, so Greece's imports of SO_2 have not caused the kind of ecosystem damage found in regions such as Scandinavia and central Europe. West Germany, in contrast, began to discover massive forest damage (only partly attributable to acidification) in the early 1980s, and immediately

Table 6:1
TRANSPORT OF SULFUR EMISSIONS 1985
COUNTRIES RANKED BY PERCENT
IMPORTED AND EXPORTED SO2 DEPOSITION

Country	Imported SO$_2$ Deposition (%)	Country	Exported SO$_2$ Emissions (%)
Norway	93%	USSR	14%
Austria	92	Spain	26
Switzerland	90	Greece	35
Netherlands	87	Portugal	38
Sweden	87	Ireland	41
Finland	81	Italy	42
Denmark	75	Norway	42
Belgium	74	UK	42
Greece	68	Sweden	44
Yugoslavia	62	Romania	46
FRG	61	Yugoslavia	47
Romania	60	Finland	48
Ireland	59	France	48
Bulgaria	58	Poland	52
Czechoslovakia	57	Bulgaria	54
Poland	56	Switzerland	57
France	55	Germany	62
Hungary	53	GDR	69
Portugal	46	Austria	69
Italy	41	Czechoslovakia	70
GDR	34	Hungary	71
USSR	28	Netherlands	78
Spain	21	Denmark	79
UK	15	Belgium	83

Source: Detlef Sprinz, "The Impact of International and Domestic Factors on the Regulation of Acid Rain in Europe: Preliminary Findings," *Journal of Environment and Development* vol. 2 (1993), p. 51.

thereafter the government sold the German public on the most expensive acid rain abatement program in Europe as a means of averting forest death.

Table 6:2 provides a quick and rough glance at the level of perceived acidification damages in European states, including when and where those

Table 6:2
NATIONAL DAMAGES FROM ACID DEPOSITION

State	Perceived National Damages[1]	What/When
Sweden	High	Acidification of lakes, groundwater/early 1970s; extensive forest damage in S, SW/mid-1980s
Norway	High	Lake acidification, fish kill/early 1970s
Netherlands	High	Widespread lake acidification in SE, extensive forest damage/mid-1980s
FRG	High	Pervasive forest death/early 1980s
UK	High	Forest damage/late 1980s
Scotland	Significant	Lake acidification/early 1980s
Wales	Significant	Streams, rivers, lakes/early 1980s
Czechoslovakia	High but state secret prior to late 1980s	Very serious health effects in northern Bohemia due to high ambient air pollution/early 1980s; pervasive forest damage/late 1980s water pollution from fertilizers, sewage/mid-1980s
Poland	High; secret before 1980s Solidarity movement	Very serious health effects, especially in Silesia, due to high ambient air pollution/mid-1980s; acid smogs and corrosion of buildings, structures in Krakow/late 1970s; some forest damage, especially in Silesia/mid-1980s
Finland	Significant but little studied	Lake acidification/mid-1980s, forest damage in S, SW but no systematic forest surveys conducted
Austria	Significant	Forest damage/mid-1980s
Switzerland	Significant	Forest damage/mid-1980s
GDR	Significant but secret prior to 1989	Forest damage, soil acidification/mid-1980s
Hungary	Significant	Urban smogs, high concentrations of local air and water pollution; soil acidification/mid-1980s
Soviet Union/ Russian Federation	Low-significant (mostly unstudied)	Forest damage in European Russia/mid-1980s
Belgium[2]	Low (mostly unstudied)	

Table 6:2 (*continued*)

State	Perceived National Damages[1]	What/When
France[3]	Low public concern	Limited forest damage/mid-1980s
Greece	Low (main concern is smog)	Damage to historic buildings and monuments, local air pollution late1970s/early 1980s
Ireland	Low (main concern is smog)	Urban acid smog
Italy	Low (mostly unstudied)	Some reports of lake acidification, forest damage, corrosion of historical buildings and monuments
Luxembourg	Low	Some forest damage/mid-1980s
Portugal	Low (mostly unstudied)	
Spain	Low (mostly unstudied)	

Sources: Among sources consulted on damages were: John McCormick, *Acid Earth* (London: Earthscan Publications Ltd., 1989).

1. Any coding of the level of perceived damages is necessarily subjective; however, the coding used here derives from judgments drawn by John McCormick in *Acid Earth*.

2. Belgium's dramatic reduction in sulphur emissions in the early 1980s (more than 42% from 1980 to 1984) resulted mostly from a shift from oil and coal to nuclear energy.

3. France also achieved substantial reductions of sulphur dioxide emissions (55% from 1980 to 1983) as a fortunate side-effect of a large expansion in reliance on nuclear power, a shift that did not derive from environmental concerns.

damages began to be recognized. The dynamic element of how these perceptions evolve over time turns out to be critically important for international abatement efforts, but before turning to dynamics I focus on a static analysis of the importance of national damages. In general, the states that recognized high levels of domestic acidification damage, along with several states that discovered somewhat lower but still significant domestic damage, have been leaders of acid rain abatement, both domestically and internationally. Sweden, Norway, the Netherlands, and West Germany, all with relatively high domestic damages, both strongly supported and substantially overcomplied with the terms of the 1985 Sulfur Protocol, calling for 30 percent reductions in emissions from 1980 levels by 1993. Finland, Austria, and Switzerland, all with significant damages, did the same. By the 1994 negotiations of the Second Sulfur Protocol, these seven states were all pushing for uniform adherence to the much more stringent gap closure targets set in accordance with the critical loads approach.

In stark contrast, many of the states with little domestic damage, or little awareness of damage, refused even to sign the 1985 Sulfur Protocol, notably Greece, Ireland, Portugal, and Spain. In 1994, Greece and Portugal found themselves in the fortunate position of being allowed to increase sulfur emissions through the year 2000 under the critical loads approach, while Ireland and Spain sought to duck the reduction targets demanded of them by the new approach.[41] A few apparent anomalies within the group with low damages are easily explained: the Soviet Union, Belgium, France, and Italy all signed the 1985 protocol, but none for environmental reasons. The Soviet Union had pursued East-West negotiations of an environmental treaty largely for the value of extending détente outside the realms of security and human rights, and did the bare minimum to comply with the 1985 protocol. Belgium and France participated in the 1985 protocol because it cost them nothing, both having recently increased reliance on nuclear power and as a fortunate side effect reduced SO_2 emissions. When the gap closure targets of the second-generation 1994 protocol demanded deeper reductions than these states had already taken for reasons of energy policy, Belgium, France, and Italy all pulled back from the optimized targets and offered somewhat more lenient commitments.[42]

Because of the tendency for the share of imported depositions to covary with domestic damages, it is somewhat difficult empirically to disentangle their individual effects. Empirical shortcomings notwithstanding, I argue that states' willingness to contribute to international management of acid rain, and by extension to other CPRs, hinges on the *combination* of experiencing CPR rivalry and substantial private costs, rather than on either factor individually. Table 6:3 captures the predicted behavior of states with respect to their willingness to undertake costly abatement and their desire to implement controls internationally as a function of these two factors in tandem. This table helps to illuminate the behavior of the UK, in addition to other states discussed above.

The UK's free-riding in international agreements, as embodied in its failure to sign the first Sulfur Protocol, its negotiations of reduced obligations under the European Community's Large Combustion Plant Directive, and its

Table 6:3
"CPR–NESS" OF ACID RAIN FOR INDIVIDUAL STATES
AND EXPECTED ABATEMENT PREFERENCES

| | | Percent Imported Emissions | | |
		Low	Medium	High	
National Damages	Low	USSR, Spain, UK through late 1980s	France, Portugal Poland before 1980 FRG before 1982 Italy, Greece, Ireland	Belgium	No action
	Medium	GDR	Hungary	Switzerland, Austria, Finland	
	High	UK after late 1980s	Czechoslovakia, Poland after 1980, FRG after 1982	Norway, Sweden, Netherlands	Stringent controls

National action   International action

insistence on lower reduction targets than demanded by the critical loads approach in the Second Sulfur Protocol, has generated vehement opposition by environmental groups. Yet the UK experiences quite considerable acid rain damage, both to forests and freshwater. Environmentalists have pointed to the irony that Britain has inflicted most of this damage on itself. The following section chronicles the consequences of Britain's discovery of this damage, but the important point here is that because most of the country's SO_2 depositions come from domestic sources, Britain has no real environmental incentive to bind itself to *international* acid rain controls. It should not be surprising then, that despite Britain's new awareness of acidification damage at home, its negotiating position within LRTAP and the EU continues to annoy other states that remain afflicted by British emissions.

As the above evidence suggests, the more interesting cases of states' bargaining behavior are not the states on the outer edges of the CPR-public good continuum, but rather those states somewhere in the middle whose perceptions of the nature of the acid rain problem change over time. With those changes in perceptions come significant alterations in their international bargaining positions on acid rain abatement. Hence the next section considers prominent cases of these "swing voters," and examines why states' perceptions of the acid rain problem have changed over time.

"Swing Votes": Evolving Knowledge and Changes in Bargaining Behavior

Despite the limitations mentioned above, acid rain abatement policies are much more developed today than they were twenty years ago. Today most countries recognize acid rain as a regional, interdependent problem resulting from long-range transport of air pollution, whereas twenty years ago only the Scandinavians supported the notion that acid rain was a problem at all. Evolving knowledge about the effects of pollution and the vulnerability of diverse ecosystems caused major changes in the political dynamics of international negotiations on acid rain controls. Perhaps the real contribution of the LRTAP regime, then, has been the creation and dissemination of new knowledge that led to broadening recognition of the CPR characteristics of the acid rain problem.[43] Several states that originally believed emissions of acidifying compounds would not cause environmental degradation, or in other words that use of the atmospheric sink was nonrival, later discovered evidence both of long-range transport of air pollutants and of damage to their own ecosystems, transforming a public goods problem into a CPR problem.

The two most influential states to change positions on acid rain controls as a result of discovering domestic acidification damage were Germany and Britain. West Germany's discovery of *Waldsterben* in 1982 led them to reverse their opposition to substantive cuts in SO_2 and NO_x emissions.[44] The forest damage provided dramatic evidence of the limited capacity of domestic soils to provide a buffer against acidification. Vehement public concern following exposure of *Waldsterben* together with the expensive abatement measures adopted domestically led the German government to become a driving force behind subsequent LRTAP protocols as well as acid rain legislation within the European Union. Indeed, Germany's conversion was probably the single most important factor that made the 1985 Sulfur Protocol possible, and it was Germany's determination that it would not bear the comparative disadvantage of stringent acid rain legislation alone in the European Community that caused it to push so hard for an EC directive to level the playing field.

Although the acid rain case provides little empirical evidence one way or another to test initial hypotheses about the role of market power in CPR management regimes, the Large Combustion Plant Directive (LCPD) may be one instance in which market power played a role. The LCPD grew not out of environmental concerns but rather out of Germany's determination not to be disadvantaged within the Common Market after having implemented an expensive domestic abatement program. Modeled after German domestic legislation, the LCPD sets limitations of SO_2, NO_x, and dust for large new combustion plants licensed after 1987, along with targets for SO_2 and NO_x reductions from existing large combustion plants.

Most important for my analysis of the political dynamics of acid rain is the fact that several member states including the UK, Italy, Greece, and Ireland initially opposed this directive, as did Spain and Portugal when they joined the EC in 1986, all out of concern for the unacceptably high costs of abatement and possible restrictions on economic development.[45] The bargain that made this directive possible was that states would be allowed to adopt non-uniform reductions, with Ireland, Portugal, and Greece allowed to increase emissions through 2003 while Italy, Spain, and the UK received more lenient targets than the remaining member states. Despite the concessions, the LCPD obligated these initially resistant states to tougher abatement efforts than they had already undertaken at that time. The ability of greener member states and particularly Germany to push emissions agreements within the broader context of establishing necessary conditions for the Common Market seems to have provided an important source of bargaining leverage.

Britain, a real latecomer to acid rain controls as evidenced by its continuing reluctance in negotiations over the LCPD, dramatically reversed course in the late 1980s. Whereas in the early stages of LRTAP, British negotiators had been preoccupied with resisting international controls and denying British responsibility for Scandinavian acid rain, by 1993 Britain was voluntarily pursuing SO_2 reductions of 70 percent from 1980 levels.[46] The turnabout came, in part, from British research on critical loads, adopted as a new methodology for protocol-setting within LRTAP during the late 1980s. As British scientists proceeded with mapping critical loads, they discovered large areas of highly vulnerable ecosystems in Scotland and Wales, among other areas. While other factors, most notably privatization of the Central Electricity Generating Board, also contributed to a reduction in British sulfur emissions, the discovery of ecosystem vulnerability transformed British perceptions of the acid rain problem for the first time from a primarily foreign problem to a domestic problem as well.[47] However, for Britain, as is increasingly true for Germany since reunification, the acidification problem is generated mostly by domestic sources—a fact that could considerably dampen enthusiasm for international commitments.

For many more states, the research and monitoring programs sponsored by LRTAP and the OECD created recognition that acid rain was a common pool resource problem. Because OECD computer models were able to accurately monitor the transport of SO_2 and NO_x emissions from their source to deposition, European states became aware of long-range transport of air pollution. Collaborative research programs within LRTAP developed consistent methodologies to measure acidification damage to national forests, buildings and materials, and lakes. The mapping of critical loads led to further recognition of sites of ecological vulnerability, and of economically efficient means for reaching critical loads through pan-European policies. Even though international abatement measures did not outpace already planned domestic policies, collaborative research and monitoring efforts did lead to major changes in the way in which the acid rain problem was defined, and in the stake held by several states in international management of acid rain.

The shift to a critical loads approach for protocol-setting provides the strongest evidence of relatively broad European recognition that acid rain is a regional commons issue. Critical loads, defined as "the highest load that will not cause chemical changes leading to long-term harmful effects on the most sensitive ecological ecosystems,"[48] capture the concept of an atmospheric sink. The idea is that ecosystems can absorb a certain level of acidifying compounds without any damage, but once the critical loads threshold is crossed, damage mounts rapidly.

The critical loads approach marks a real improvement, from an ecological perspective, over the previous flat-rate reductions. Because countries—indeed, regions within countries—possess very different critical loads, or different levels of ecosystem vulnerability, the flat-rate reductions of the first SO_2 and NO_x protocols made little sense environmentally. The critical loads approach takes into consideration varying ecosensitivity, varying costs of emissions reductions, and wind patterns that account for pollution transport. Under the critical loads approach, states would set abatement policy interdependently rather than individually, adopting markedly uneven levels of abatement. Basing further emissions reductions on critical loads would protect ecosystems on a European scale in the most cost-efficient way. Economic efficiency, however, is not always politically popular, and in practice significant shirking of the abatement targets established with critical loads methodology has appeared among states beset by high economic costs. During negotiations of the 1994 Second Sulfur Protocol, the UK, Belgium, Denmark, France, Ireland, and Spain all pressed for weaker reduction targets than that specified by the overall target of negotiations—to reduce the gap between 1980 emission levels and the levels needed to attain critical loads by 50 percent.[49]

Barkin and Shambaugh hypothesize in the introduction that variation in shadows of the future among the consumers of a CPR will affect bargaining positions, and the likelihood of successful CPR management. I found no evidence that states formulated positions on acid rain abatement policies on the basis of explicit or implicit comparisons of future and current values of ecosystem protection. Indeed, once states became aware that acidification damage was occurring, virtually all of them launched abatement efforts, suggesting uniformly long shadows. However, the argument above lays out a related and more general claim about how changes in perceptions of the costs of CPR exploitation explains negotiating positions. States' recognition of the degree to which European acid rain is in fact a commons problem has increased significantly over time, along with growing knowledge about the long-range transport of air pollutants. That recognition combined with discoveries of the private costs of acidification, which occurred at different times for individual states in Europe, appears to explain both states' evolving positions toward support of international acid rain controls and the timing of those positions.

Leaders, Free Riders, and Bargaining Power

Is it true, as Barkin and Shambaugh suggest,[50] that free riders can extort concessions in environmental negotiations through threats to overconsume CPRs, and that the problem posed by rivalry of consumption in a CPR makes the role of a free rider uniquely powerful? If so, the ongoing danger of free ridership in the management of CPRs means that benevolent hegemons cannot effectively guarantee CPR maintenance, even if a hegemon were willing and able to absorb the cost of maintaining the resource. By implication, where CPR dynamics are at work, we should observe that free riders get better terms in international environmental negotiations than leaders in CPR management, and that coercive hegemonic solutions are more likely than in public goods problems. However, observed outcomes in the acid rain case differ substantially from these projections.

The free riders in the acid rain case were primarily those states that did not recognize domestic damage to ecosystems and perceived themselves able to externalize negative effects of pollution, including most of southern and eastern Europe. Germany also resisted international abatement measures before the discovery of forest death, and Britain continued to be everyone's favorite scapegoat for its intransigence throughout the 1980s. What concessions, if any, did these free riders gain?

The 1988 EC Large Combustion Plant Directive and the 1994 Second Sulfur Protocol both provide some evidence that free ridership does bring bargaining power in a CPR situation. For example, the UK and Spain, the largest SO_2 polluters within the European Community, were both allowed to make smaller percentage cuts in their SO_2 emissions under the LCP Directive than most other member states—60 percent for the UK and 50 percent for Spain from 1980 levels by the year 2003, as compared with 70 percent for Germany, France, Italy, Denmark, Belgium, and the Netherlands. Under the Second Sulfur Protocol, states in southern Europe—particularly Greece and Portugal—were permitted to increase their emissions of SO_2 from 1980 levels through the year 2000. Additionally, "parties in transition"—Russia and Eastern Europe—were permitted extended deadlines of 2005 or 2010 to meet their obligations under the protocol.

It is not surprising that under necessarily weak international law instruments, free riders would obtain less stringent obligations than other states, or that large polluters such as the UK, Spain, and (before 1982) even Germany should exercise veto power over international abatement measures. Indeed, the extended deadlines and looser targets given to laggard states may in some respects resemble concessions won by developing countries in the Montreal Protocol, described in David Downie's chapter. Still, the limited concessions extended in acid rain negotiations did not provide laggards with any additional benefit beyond existing national policies, nor were any financial concessions provided as they were in the ozone case. The free riders of acid rain do not hold the power to destroy European ecosystems as a whole, though many of them do impose significant damages on at least several neighboring states. Nor have they succeeded in converting a more limited power to destroy into particularly large concessions.

What is much more surprising in this case is the extent to which small victim states—the victims of free ridership—have managed to influence international outcomes over time in acid rain abatement. The leaders in pressing for the creation of LRTAP, subsequent protocols, and European Community legislation were the states incurring the highest costs from acid rain that also recognized themselves to be in a CPR problem. Germany's role as a leader on acid rain controls after the discovery of domestic damage was perhaps to be expected—after all, Germany is typically one of the dominant players in European Union policy making. More surprising is the leadership role of small states. Marc Levy claims that Norway and Sweden reduced emissions for environmental reasons, but would have done so even without

LRTAP.[51] In other words, they would have done so despite the likelihood of free ridership by other states, even though the high level of foreign responsibility for their acid rain problem meant that domestic measures alone stood no chance of eliminating acidification.

In light of conventional wisdom on collective action problems, these states present real puzzles. First, why would they undertake substantial and costly domestic abatement programs given the fact that virtually all of their acidification problem resulted from uncontrollable imported emissions, and given the likelihood that the foreign culprits would continue to free ride? The Scandinavians appear to have hoped that the demonstration value of abatement programs would outweigh what would otherwise be futile expenditures. Second, why should the leadership efforts of small, apparently powerless states turn out to be so effective, particularly when much larger states initially resisted internationalization of the acid rain problem? Conventional wisdom has it that hegemonic states positioned to appropriate large benefits from international regulation will provide leadership. Certainly the Scandinavians stood to reap large benefits from international abatement programs, but they are evidently *not* hegemons. Contrary to more conventional theories of influence, in this case small victim states, not hegemons, are able to exert leadership by using international institutions as a forum for knowledge creation and dissemination which then changed interests of larger, more pivotal states.

This dynamic suggests a conclusion that runs counter to the "use it or lose it" imperative Barkin and Shambaugh attribute to CPR beneficiaries, as exemplified by actors sharing an international oil field.[52] Instead, the conclusion emerging from the acid rain case is that recognition of scarcity, or the finite ability of domestic ecosystems to absorb air pollutants without resulting in acidification, facilitated rather than impaired cooperation. It was precisely the recognition of domestic damages that led countries to take abatement measures, and follow up with international agreements. At the same time, the "CPR-ness" of acid rain also proved critical, because any state whose domestic depositions result heavily from domestic emissions (such as the UK or Spain) has no need to become entrapped in international regulation to deal with acidification problems. The tremendous increase in European acid rain controls over the past two decades is in many ways remarkable. While distributional conflict over the depth of each countries' reduction targets undeniably remains, that conflict now takes place at a much higher overall level of emissions abatement than before LRTAP's creation.

Conclusion: CPRs and Theories of International Cooperation

One influential explanation for what makes cooperation possible in collective action problems is the theory of hegemonic stability. Hegemons provide public goods either benevolently, because they benefit disproportionately from the existence of the public good and are thus willing to absorb the costs of free ridership, or because they are able to use their power to coerce beneficiaries into paying a reasonable share for the good's provision. The acid rain case suggests that perhaps an important distinction between public goods and CPRs is that the benevolent hegemonic solution is inapplicable to CPR problems. While a hegemon can surely provide a public good such as nuclear deterrence, it is not possible for a single state to provide clean air. It is certainly true that individual states who adopt stringent abatement measures often provide external benefits for neighboring states that therefore import less pollution. Still, the collective good of clean air cannot be provided without the participation of most members of the commons.

The acid rain case offers hope that such cooperation is not only necessary, but possible. In the same vein as Elinor Ostrom's work on small scale CPRs, which shows how self-organization is a viable alternative to state-imposed cooperation or privatization,[53] the experience of acid rain suggests that cooperation on collective action problems in the absence of hegemony is in fact more common than we tend to believe. Moreover, the improvement of acid rain controls does not seem to have resulted merely because LRTAP reduced the transaction costs of negotiating and enforcing an agreement, or because of the expectation of ongoing interaction among those affected by acid rain. Indeed, the most important factor contributing to tougher abatement measures seems to be states' changing understanding of the nature of the acid rain problem, of their interdependence, and of the private costs attributable to the varied capacity of diverse ecosystems to act as a buffer against acidification. Similar processes of knowledge generation may well facilitate cooperative CPR management in other issues, but it is worth stressing that not all such information-gathering efforts will uncover underlying interest structures that induce higher levels of cooperation.

The acid rain case, which displays characteristics both of public goods and CPRs depending on which state is concerned in which time period, may provide a relevant model for other international environmental problems—particularly those where states differ in the extent to which they experience rivalry in consumption. Many international environmental problems display asymmetrical rivalries similar to those in acid rain, as when upstream actors externalize the effects of water pollution or overconsumption onto their downstream counterparts. If the acid rain case holds generalizeable implications, they would be that we might expect actors' preferences on cooperation to vary systematically as a function of these positions. This observation should redirect lines of analytical inquiry away from whether an environmental problem is purely a public good or a CPR problem, and toward how individual states perceive the nature of the issue, and how those perceptions guide their bargaining behavior.

Notes

1. A classic statement of the public goods problem is Charles Kindleberger, *The World in Depression* (Berkeley: University of California Press, 1973).

2. For example, see Garrett Hardin, "The Tragedy of the Commons," *Science*, vol. 162 (1968), pp. 1243–48; Mancur Olson, *The Logic of Collective Action* (Cambridge: Harvard University Press, 1965); Elinor Ostrom, *Governing the Commons: The Evolution of Institutions for Collective Action* (Cambridge: Cambridge University Press, 1990); Duncan Snidal, "Public Goods, Property Rights, and Political Organization," *International Studies Quarterly* (Dec. 1979); Michael Taylor, *The Possibility of Cooperation* (Cambridge: Cambridge University Press, 1987). For a noteworthy discussion on various forms of asymmetry in collective action problems, see Russell Hardin, *Collective Action* (Baltimore: Resources for the Future, 1982), pp. 67–89.

3. In more formal terms, the former group does not experience quality rivalry in consumption of the atmospheric sink, whereas the latter group does. Rivalry in consumption is the feature that distinguishes CPRs from public goods, whereas both types of goods share the feature of nonexcludability. Technically speaking, acid rain emerges as a negative externality of states' nonexcludable use of the atmospheric sink, primarily for the burning of fossil fuels.

4. Because the asymmetries of actors' positions frequently make it impossible to label a collective good as definitively a public good or a CPR, I use the term *collective action* problem to encompass both possibilities.

5. For a provocative criticism of the collective action literature hinging on the claim that free riding is much less common than theorists assume and that our observance of free riding mistakenly derives from overvaluation of the perceived public benefits of goods such as clean air, see Donald P. Green and Ian Shapiro, *Pathologies of Rational Choice Theory* (New Haven: Yale University Press, 1994), pp. 72–97. This critique raises the important and difficult question of how to determine a valid benchmark for optimal provision of collective goods.

6. Matthew refers to these differential positions as a "structural CPR" problem, although more accurately the problem appears as a CPR to downstream actors because the consumption of international waters by upstream actors diminishes their own ability to consume, but *not* to upstream actors, who instead appear to enjoy a public good provided by nature.

7. Gregory S. Wetstone and Armin Rosencranz, *Acid Rain in Europe and North America: National Responses to an International Problem* (Washington, D.C.: Environmental Law Institute, 1983), p. 28.

8. Wetstone and Rosencranz, pp. 25–26.

9. Svante Odén, "The Acidification of Air and Precipitation and Its Consequences in the Natural Environment," *Ecology Committee Bulletin*, No. 1 (Stockholm: National Science Research Council, 1968).

10. Wetstone and Rosencranz, p. 19.

11. Wetstone and Rosencranz, p. 15.

12. Joseph Alcamo, Roderick Shaw, and Leen Hordijk, eds., *The RAINS Model of Acidification: Science and Strategies in Europe* (Dordrecht: Kluwer Academic Publishers, 1990), p. 47.

13. Armin Rosencranz, "The ECE Convention of 1979 on Long Range Transboundary Air Pollution," *Zeitschrift für Umweltpolitik* (December 1981), p. 511.

14. Amy A. Fraenkel, "The Convention on Long-Range Transboundary Air Pollution: meeting the Challenge of International Cooperation," *Harvard International Law Journal*, vol. 30 (1989), p. 456.

15. For a longer history of negotiations of the first and second sulfur protocols, see Barbara M. Connolly, *Organizational Choices for International Cooperation: East-West European Cooperation on Regional Environmental Problems*, Ph.D. Dissertation, U.C. Berkeley, 1997, pp. 256–83.

16. Indeed, Chayes and Chayes remind us not to expect more from international law instruments in noting that "The most basic principle of international law is that states cannot legally bound except with their own consent. So, in the first instance, the state need not enter into a treaty that does not conform to its interests." Abram Chayes and Antonia Handler Chayes, "On Compliance," *International Organization*, vol. 47 (1993), p. 179.

17. Though terminology differs, these definitions are standard in the public choice literature. For one discussion of definitions, see Richard Cornes and Todd Sandler, *The Theory of Externalities, Public Goods, and Club Goods* (Cambridge: Cambridge University Press, 1986), pp. 6–7.

18. In fact, collective goods are very rarely fully nonexcludable. Hardin, for example, points out that private good substitutes for the collective good of clean air could be provided through the installation of private air-cleaning systems in homes and cars, thereby creating excludability mechanims. The creation of exludability mechanisms is often how collective action dilemmas are resolved. See Russell Hardin, *Collective Action* (Baltimore: Resources for the Future, 1982), pp. 72–75.

19. For a primer on congestion effects, as well as collective goods issues more generally, see Barry B. Hughes, *Continuity and Change in World Politics* (Upper Saddle River, NJ: Prentice Hall, 1997), pp. 166–76.

20. Detlef Sprinz, "The Impact of International and Domestic Factors on the Regulation of Acid Rain in Europe: Preliminary Findings," *Journal of Environment and Development* vol. 2 (1993), p. 51.

21. As discussed later, Germany's support of acid rain controls derived more from growing knowledge of domestic damages than from the victim status shared by the group of states discussed here.

22. For an excellent negotiating history of LRTAP and its protocols, see Marc A. Levy, "European Acid Rain: The Power of Tote-Board Diplomacy," in Peter M. Haas,

Robert O. Keohane and Marc A. Levy, eds., *Institutions for the Earth* (Cambridge, MA: MIT Press, 1993), pp. 75–132.

23. For a model that predicts countries' positions on abatement policies as a function of ecological vulnerability and abatement costs, see Detlef Sprinz and Tapani Vaahtoranta, "International Environmental Policy," in *International Organization* vol. 48 (1994), pp. 77–105.

24. The UK's position changed dramatically in the late 1980s, as documented in the following section on "Swing Votes." With increasing recognization of domestic damages resulting from acid rain, the UK's perceptions of the acid rain issue underwent a shift from public good to private bad—domestic damages, in other words, were documented and found to be largely "made in Britain."

25. Now the Czech Republic and Slovakia.

26. Prior to the reunification of Germany only; because of the character of GDR emissions, reunification led increasingly to a private bad dynamic in Germany where the large majority of acid depositions derived from domestic sources.

27. Garrett Hardin, "The Tragedy of the Commons," *Science*, vol. 162 (1968), pp. 1243–48.

28. Friends of the Earth, "From 'Dirty Man' to 'Drittsekk': UK Acid Rain Policy" (London: Friends of the Earth, November 1993): 11–12.

29. For example, Detlef Sprinz's research concludes that states' levels of exported SO_2 and NO_x emissions poorly predict their position on international regulation, whereas a high level of depositions originating mainly from abroad is much more likely to impel states to participate in international abatement measures. See Detlef Sprinz, "The Impact of International and Domestic Factors on the Regulation of Acid Rain in Europe: Preliminary Findings," *Journal of Environment and Development* vol. 2 (1993).

30. As Green and Shapiro underscore, it surely is not fully accurate to take environmentalists' judgment of the optimal provision of acid rain controls as an indicator of the value accorded to avoidance of acidification damage by European citizens or states as a whole. However, this optimal level of provision is notoriously difficult to establish. (See Donald P. Green and Ian Shapiro, *Pathologies of Rational Choice Theory* [New Haven: Yale University Press, 1994], pp. 72–97). What I have done, therefore, is simply to provide a transparent benchmark used by environmentalists and selected states to argue that fee riding is occurring and does result in suboptimal provision of abatement efforts.

31. "European Ecosystems Will Suffer Unless Energy Changes Are Made, Says WWF," *The Bureau of National Affairs International Environment Daily* (March 1, 1993).

32. Markus Amann, Imrich Bertok, Janusz Cofala, Ger Klaassen, and Wolfgang Schöpp, "Strategies for Reducing Sulfur Dioxide Emissions in Europe," background paper prepared for the UN/ECE Task Force on Integrated Assessment Modelling, June 3–5, 1992, Bilthoven, the Netherlands.

33. Jim Sweet, "Who's Afraid of Acid Rain?" *Energy Economist* (Nov. 1993).

34. Jim Sweet, "Who's Afraid of Acid Rain?" *Energy Economist* (Nov. 1993).

35. "New Sulphur Protocol May Not Meet Acid Rain Targets," *AEGIS* (May 1994), p. 6.

36. Levy characterizes both the 1985 Sulfur Protocol and the 1988 NO_x Protocol as "least common denominator" protocols, arguing, "In neither case did any party sign intending to use the protocol as a guide to revisions in its domestic emission reduction policies. In fact, there is no evidence that any state (with the possible exception of the Soviet Union) signed any protocol without first determining that already-planned policies would bring it into compliance more or less automatically." Even the 1994 Sulfur Protocol, which significantly increases SO_2 abatement beyond the original 1985 protocol, does not move beyond currently planned reductions. See Marc A. Levy, "International Cooperation to Combat Acid Rain," *Green Globe Yearbook 1995* (Oxford: Oxford University Press, 1995), pp. 4, 9.

37. Over time, however, domestic interests change considerably, and consequently bargaining positions change as well.

38. Important exceptions to this rule will be discussed later in this section: namely France, Belgium, the Soviet Union and its East European allies.

39. For more complete transport data, see Detlef Sprinz, "The Impact of International and Domestic Factors on the Regulation of Acid Rain in Europe: Preliminary Findings," *Journal of Environment and Development* vol. 2 (1993), p. 51.

40. Barkin and Shambaugh, "Introduction."

41. Marc A. Levy, "International Cooperation to Combat Acid Rain," *Green Globe Yearbook 1995* (Oxford: Oxford University Press, 1995).

42. "UK Does the Dirty at Geneva," *Power Europe* (Nov. 5, 1993).

43. Marc Levy argues that LRTAP's effectiveness derives in large measure from collaborative research programs that have led to the development of knowledge about acidification damage in countries that would not otherwise have discovered it, thus transforming their preferences for abatement policies. Levy identifies four countries— Austria, Finland, Netherlands, and Switzerland—who gained knowledge about domestic acidification damage as a direct result of LRTAP. See Marc A. Levy, "European Acid Rain: The Power of Tote-Board Diplomacy," in Peter M. Haas, Robert O. Keohane and Marc A. Levy, eds., *Institutions for the Earth: Sources of Effective International Environmental Protection* (Cambridge, MA: MIT Press, 1993): 76, 119.

44. Boehmer-Christiansen and Skea argue that it is too simplistic to explain the German policy reversal on acid rain abatement solely as a response to *Waldsterben*. In fact, they claim that for political purposes, the severity of the forest death was exaggerated at first, and wholly attributed to air pollution when in fact its causes are more diverse. *Waldsterben* was thus partly the public relations campaign to promote expensive, technology-forcing policies already planned by the German government. See Sonja Boehmer-Christiansen and Jim Skea, *Acid Politics: Environmental and Energy Policies in Britain and Germany* (London: Belhaven Press, 1991): 190; also Sonja Boehmer-

Christiansen, "Anglo-German Contrasts in Environmental Policy-Making and their Impacts in the Case of Acid Rain Abatement," *International Environmental Affairs* vol. 4, (1992): 295–322.

45. Sonja Boehmer-Christiansen and Jim Skea, *Acid Politics: Environmental and Energy Policies in Britain and Germany* (London: Belhaven Press, 1991), pp. 234–46.

46. Marc A. Levy, "International Cooperation to Combat Acid Rain," *Green Globe Yearbook 1995* (Oxford: Oxford University Press, 1995), p. 10.

47. Ibid.

48. Jan Nilsson, ed., *Critical Loads for Sulphur and Nitrogen: Report from a Nordic Working Group* (Solna: The National Swedish Environment Protection Board, 1986).

49. Levy, "International Cooperation to Combat Acid Rain," 8.

50. Barkin and Shambaugh, hypotheses 2a-c.

51. Levy, "European Acid Rain: The Power of Tote-Board Diplomacy," in Peter M. Haas, Robert O. Keohane and Marc A. Levy, eds., *Institutions for the Earth: Sources of Effective International Environmental Protection* (Cambridge, MA: MIT Press, 1993).

52. The point of the oil field example is that since consumption of oil is rival in an international oil field, there are strong incentives to extract the remaining oil as quickly as possible. Expectations of future benefits from the CPR diminish to near zero, which exacerbates distributional conflict over allocation of oil resources among members of the commons.

53. Elinor Ostrom, *Governing the Commons: The Evolution of Institutions for Collective Action* (Cambridge: Cambridge University Press, 1990).

7 Scarcity and Security: A Common-Pool Resource Perspective

RICHARD A. MATTHEW

Introduction

In the past thirty-five years, as contemporary forms of environmentalism have moved to a more central position in the theory and practice of world politics, the relationship between scarcity and security has received considerable attention. In this chapter, I use a common pool resource (CPR) model to evaluate this relationship. The link between competition over limited resources and conflict is not a new problem, but the rate at which certain key resources are becoming scarce has given it an unprecedented magnitude and urgency. Since the 1970s, concerns about interstate crises and wars resulting from competition over CPRs like oil and water have been particularly widespread. For example, many analysts have argued that the Gulf War was motivated as much by a desire to protect access to Middle Eastern oil supplies as to redress Iraq's violation of Kuwaiti sovereignty. Perhaps more alarming, a 1995 UN report claimed that "eighty countries with 40 percent of the world's population already have water shortages that could cripple agriculture and

155

industry."[1] The potential for violence, especially in the Middle East and parts of Africa where water supplies are heavily overused, appears high. Recently, depleting fish stocks also have emerged as a growing source of interstate tension. Gareth Porter notes that in 1994, thirty conflicts over fishing grounds were reported, "including several in which force was used."[2] Lester Brown contends that the world is facing a rapidly worsening food shortage;[3] soon the poorest states in the world may have few options other than to fight for survival.

In this chapter I apply the three sets of hypotheses presented in the Introduction to the problem of scarcity-related security issues. The argument I develop is a deductive one based on the implications of the common pool resource (CPR) model for a conventional understanding of national security focusing on military threats to core values. The model is illustrated with cases that are well known in the field of "environmental security." My objective is to present a model that indicates the conditions under which competition over CPRs may become relevant to the security community. I do not suggest that this model predicts conflict—too many variables will determine actual outcomes. But models do not need to be able to predict specific outcomes to be useful—indicating ways in which the likelihood of conflict can be reduced or identifying areas in which scarcity is likely to play a causal role can be useful for improving our understanding of world politics and developing more effective security policies.

I begin with a brief discussion of recent debates over the relationship between scarcity and security, highlighting several concerns that have been raised in regard to current research. I then demonstrate the utility of evaluating these issues using a CPR model. By carefully restricting the terms "scarcity" and "security," it is possible to develop a model with a high degree of explanatory power, although it is limited in terms of the number of cases to which it is appropriate. To illustrate this point, I work out some of the implications of this model using a variety of examples. I conclude that (1) this model is extremely useful for clarifying the security implications of certain forms of scarcity and (2) it is particularly helpful in identifying the requirements of an effective policy response in these cases.

Background to Environmental Security

In an address delivered at Stanford University on April 9, 1996, Secretary of State Warren Christopher stated:

The environment has a profound impact on our national interests in two ways: First, environmental forces transcend borders and oceans to threaten directly the health, prosperity and jobs of American citizens. Second, addressing natural resource issues is frequently critical to achieving political and economic stability, and to pursuing our strategic goals around the world.[4]

The claim that there is an important relationship between environmental forces and national interests is not a new one. Indeed, in general terms, the complex relationships between social and ecological systems have been studied for millennia. But it is only in the past few years that environmental change has been viewed as a national security problem. This particular strand of research, debate, and policy making began in the late 1970s when scholars such as Richard Ullman and Lester Brown suggested that, in light of our growing awareness of the impact of environmental degradation on human welfare, we needed to rethink the concept of security.[5] Although their proposals received little attention at first, mounting evidence of environmental problems intersected with the end of the Cold War to motivate the security community to take their advice seriously. The past decade has witnessed a flurry of research, discussion, and policy initiatives loosely united by the concept of "environmental security."[6]

Debate over this concept has been vigorous and far-reaching. As is the case with many debates over fundamental terms such as "security," scholars, activists, and policy makers have entered the fray armed with a wide array of normative biases and political agendas. Nonetheless, two broad areas of disagreement capture a significant amount of the controversy.

The first concerns the scope of the concept. In very simple terms, some thinkers (such as Thomas Homer-Dixon, Shin-wha Lee, Marc Levy, and myself) have sought to consider the implications of environmental change for traditional security affairs.[7] I refer to these thinkers as "environmental security minimalists." Others, however (including Lester Brown, Norman Myers, and Gareth Porter) have sought to reshape how we think about security.[8] I refer to these writers as "environmental security maximalists."

Maximalist writers explicitly seek to use the politically charged vocabulary of security as the basis for an ecological worldview. They attempt to sever the close connection between security and the state, and advocate linking security more directly to the individual. In this way they hope to underscore the importance of an undeniable truth: ecological systems are not aligned with state-based social systems. Hence, state-centric thinking does not provide a satisfactory basis for addressing many of the insecurities associated with environmental change that individuals experience.

Minimalists contend that it is premature and hence misleading to attempt to redefine security in strictly environmental terms. Premature because the specific ways in which various forms of environmental change affect human security are not always clear and vary enormously from place to place; misleading because many threats to human security—such as warfare and crime—are at best tenuously related to environmental change and do not depend on it. Thus, while "rethinking security" in fundamental ways is an intriguing and useful exercise, more can be achieved in the short-term by focusing on the ways in which environmental change may be relevant to the traditional national security community. A more narrowly focused approach does not undermine the larger project; it does, however, facilitate dialogue and provide a basis for policy making today. Not all scholars, however, agree with this.

A second area of scholarly dispute focuses on problems associated with characterizing any environmental issues as national security issues. The most forceful critique of this entire project was published by Daniel Deudney in 1990. According to Deudney, environmental degradation is an unconventional threat that rarely leads to interstate war, military tools are not of much value in addressing environmental issues, and the military penchant for secrecy and "we versus they" thinking is antithetical to the interdependent nature of most environmental problems, which require information sharing and cooperation to be resolved.[9] In a slightly different scale, subsequent writers such as Marc Levy have attacked research done under the label "environmental security" for being sloppy and uninteresting.[10] Levy's point is that scholars have not yet succeeded in demonstrating that many environmental issues are really national security issues. In trying to make this connection, scholars have situated environmental factors in such a broad context of threat and violence that their salience is difficult to assess. Instead of being highlighted, they are lost in a cluttered background of diverse social, economic, and political variables. They may affect these, but the extent to which they do is hard to estimate.

The intellectual landscape is a complicated one, and each perspective merits careful consideration. Fears of the militarization of environmentalism (Deudney) should not be dismissed too quickly; concerns about the scant results of recent research programs (Levy) raise important methodological issues;

and attempts to reorient how we think about the relationship between social and ecological systems contribute to the development of a global ecological sensibility. Nonetheless, it is useful to engage the traditional security community in discussions of (1) how in fulfilling its mandate its activities—training, weapons testing and war fighting—can cause or amplify environmental degradation; (2) how military and intelligence assets might be used to support environmental policies; (3) how certain forms of environmental scarcity can threaten national interests in ways that might be prevented or will have to be addressed with traditional security tools—force and diplomacy; and (4) how environmental concerns might be included in conflict resolution processes. This chapter focuses on item (3).

Insofar as environmental scarcity is concerned, three positions have been suggested. Peter Gleick has argued that scarcity does generate interstate conflict; he relates conflict in the Middle East, for example, to conflict over scarce fresh water.[11] Deudney has criticized this position on the grounds that resource wars are unlikely in an era of economic interdependence and technological innovation—that is, states can usually obtain what they need through trade, develop substitutes for it or devise other technological solutions.[12] These are more rational and cost-effective strategies than war. In many ways, Homer-Dixon's work begins to reconcile these opposing views by suggesting that scarcity is most likely to cause or exacerbate intrastate violence in developing countries, which lack economic or technological capacity. This may in turn lead to regional instability, thus becoming a security issue for both North and South.[13]

Homer-Dixon's argument is compelling, but his particular approach to studying the impact of scarcity in Third World states has tended to enmesh environmental variables with social ones so well that the former are at times difficult to evaluate. This leads to policies that focus on state-building or restructuring activities as much as, if not more than, schemes to manage environmental goods.

It is very likely that many cases of scarcity have to do with both overuse of the good itself and the way in which the good is made available to those who need it, but it is difficult to determine whether these are best viewed as scarcity-related security problems or state-building problems in which scarcity plays some role and national security may be threatened. In such cases, managing the good may not eliminate or even reduce the violence, although it may be essential to any long-term solution.

But in other cases, scarcity may be the key issue. A model of these cases can be developed by focusing on common pool resource-type scarcity. The advantage of this approach is that it rules out scarcity that results primarily or largely from inefficient or unjust domestic systems. It is relevant to fewer cases, but the significance of the environmental variable is clearer.

A CPR Model of the Scarcity-Security Link

Scarcity

Environmental scarcity is an elusive concept. From a strictly scientific perspective, many environmental goods are not becoming scarce. There is, for example, more than enough fresh water almost everywhere to provide everyone on the planet with the four to six liters a day each requires to survive. On these terms, very few people experience water scarcity. Social scientists, however, argue that this way of thinking about scarcity is not analytically interesting. Political behavior is affected by water supplies long before they fall to the level of four to six liters per person. By including the vast amounts of water used for agricultural and industrial purposes, social scientists conventionally define scarcity as less than 2,740 liters per person per day. On this basis, water scarcity is widespread through much of the developing world. Natural scientists counter that even if one rejects a survival measurement, since water use varies enormously from place to place, establishing a threshold quantity is misleading. And so the debate continues.

It is clearly very difficult to generate a number that defines scarcity for water or many other environmental goods. But it is not unreasonable to suggest that many people in the world do not have access to enough good-quality water to fulfill their various objectives. Scarcity, then, is not simply a scientific measurement, but also a subjective and socioeconomic phenomenon. A good is scarce when people cannot obtain as much of it as they think they need. In an effort to integrate the natural and societal dimensions of scarcity, Homer-Dixon defines it as follows:

> There are three types of environmental scarcity: (1) supply-induced scarcity is caused by the degradation and depletion of an environmental resource, for example, the erosion of cropland; (2) demand-induced scarcity results from population growth or increased per capita consumption of a resource, either of which increase the demand for the resource; (3) structural scarcity arises from an unequal social distribution of a resource that concentrates it in the hands of relatively few people while the remaining population suffers from serious shortages.[14]

Homer-Dixon's definition considers scarcity in terms of quantity, rate of consumption, and access. It is especially useful insofar as it relates scarcity to domestic politics. The many case studies his project has generated indicate clearly the complex interactions between social and ecological variables. The problem with this is that the political and economic weaknesses evident in many developing states (in comparison to their Northern counterparts) make it difficult to distinguish between the role of scarcity and other variables in causing national security problems. Consequently, the solution sets invariably include state-building together with better environmental management. In many, perhaps most, cases, the two are intimately linked. But it is also useful to focus on those cases in which scarcity is the principal problem, and in which addressing it will enhance security, more or less regardless of domestic political factors. The CPR model considers only these cases and seeks to identify ways in which they may be resolved.

In contrast to Homer-Dixon, the common pool resource approach focuses on environmental goods that have two properties: nonexclusivity and rivalness. Domestic systems will affect the rate of depletion, but the artificial scarcities that they create are not all relevant to this model, which focuses on scarcity in an international context. This focus makes it easier to theorize an unmediated relationship between environmental change and security affairs. From a CPR perspective, scarcity means that one state (rather than some individuals) does not have the access to an environmental good that it desires. Using states as the unit of analysis makes it possible to identify two situations in which environmental goods can be considered CPRs. First, any goods in the global commons that can be diminished are CPRs for all states, such as fisheries. Environmental goods located in the global commons that can be depleted but cannot be privatized will be called "pure CPRs." Second, certain goods are CPRs for some states but not others. For example, for a downstream riparian state, water is a CPR: the state cannot exclude other states from using the water, but their use of it may affect its access to or enjoyment of this good. The upstream riparian state, however, often does not experience water as a CPR: sovereignty gives it a right to use the water as private property.[15] It has the right to exclude other states from enjoying this good. In the following pages I will argue that "structural CPRs," that is, goods that are experienced as CPRs by some but not all states, are especially relevant to national security.[16]

Security

The term *security* is used by scholars in very different ways. For the purpose of this chapter, I adopt a very limited (and conventional) understanding:

Security concerns the preservation and satisfaction of the core values of a state. At a minimum, these include a state's territory, population, and way of life—that is, the values, beliefs, institutions, and practices it regards as essential. A state's security community is mandated to address threats and vulnerabilities on these terms.

Insofar as this understanding of security is concerned, a CPR could become a security issue if state A's core values depend on access to it and state A is vulnerable insofar as the behavior of state B could or does threaten this access. Today, goods such as water and oil have this potential; goods such as krill and tuna do not, although competition over these may exacerbate security tensions. This is a streamlined definition. State A's situation may, in fact, depend on the behavior of many other states. For example, state A's access to water may depend on how several other states exploit a given riparian system.

To be useful, any model of the relationship between CPR-type scarcity and national security must provide the basis for answers to two questions: (1) Under what conditions is this type of threat likely? (2) What could be done to manage these conditions in order to generate a cooperative rather than conflictual outcome?

Before presenting such a model, however, it is useful to flesh out the range of potential conflictual outcomes, as responses are likely to vary according to the perceived or real severity of a threat. The range of security threats to core values includes, in order of severity:

- war
- crisis (important values at stake, limited information and short time frame to respond, threat of war is high)
- heightened tension (worsening of the strategic context or security dilemma; threat of force typical)
- domestic stress (international scarcity places stress on domestic institutions due to immigrant crowding, narrowing of policy options, deterioration of domestic welfare, civil war)

At first blush, this might seem excessively complicated, but one of the problems in the literature has been a failure to carefully define the dependent variable: security. Because of this, claims that national security is threatened by environmental change often are greeted with skepticism. The above framework specifies the range of outcomes that define security problems and allows for these outcomes to be prioritized.

CPR Scarcity and Security Model

The basic relationship to be investigated can be modeled as in Table 7:1. This is a deductive model the limitations of which should be made clear.

First, the outcomes (IV) are limited to those that fit squarely within the conventional understanding of security. The policy objective is to avoid or deescalate these outcomes. It is, of course, conceivable that scarcity might lead to cooperative outcomes more often than to security problems. This is not denied by the model which, however, is limited to the latter. Moreover, it is likely that other variables will be significant in determining the way in which a state responds to scarcity. The focus here, however, is on cases in which scarcity might be said to play a key role in shaping the outcome.

Second, these outcomes are presented as the result of a specific type of scarcity—the depletion of a CPR (III). Not all environmental goods are CPRs (e.g., sunlight is not), and not all forms of scarcity are CPR-type forms (Homer-Dixon's structural scarcity is not always this type). But, as noted earlier, there are pure and structural forms of CPR-type scarcity.

Third, CPR scarcity is in turn presented as the outcome of three problems (II): overuse of a good due to discounting the future heavily; collective management problems due to a willingness to free ride; and/or market failure insofar as the market is unable to provide dependent parties with the good or

Table 7:1
CPR SCARCITY AND SECURITY MODEL

I (Indirect Sources of Scarcity)	II (Direct Sources of Scarcity)	III (Independent Variable)	IV (Dependent Variable)
Domestic variables	Time horizons		War Crisis
International context	Free riders	Scarcity	Heightened tension
Nature of good (CPR)	Market power		Domestic stress
		Intervening variables: economic crisis weak institutions social tensions militarized context	

develop substitutes for it. Other direct causes of scarcity may exist, but they are not considered in this model.

Finally, the above three problems are likely to be shaped by broader domestic and international conditions (indirect causes) as well as by the nature of the good itself (I). For example, the willingness to discount the future heavily is likely to reflect domestic pressures, the international context in which the state operates, and the value of the good.

This model suggests two general strategies for states. First, a state experiencing a CPR-induced security problem can focus on the three direct sources of scarcity. It might, for example, use force or economic incentives to encourage other states to reduce discount rates or cooperate. Or it might employ market power by expanding trade or creating incentives for technological innovation. Developing an effective policy will depend to some extent on whether it is facing a pure or structural CPR problem. All things being equal, the latter are likely to be more difficult to resolve peacefully because the incentives to manage the good collectively vary enormously depending on position. In such cases, the model predicts that deterrent or preemptive military action is more likely if market solutions are not viable. In contrast, pure CPR problems—in which the incentives to manage the good collectively are less varied—are more likely, all things being equal, to be resolved through some sort of regime.

Second, a state can choose to focus on altering the broader domestic and international socioeconomic contexts within which the more direct causes of scarcity arise. In general, this is a desirable long-term goal, but will be a difficult course of action for policy makers seeking immediate results.

Illustrations of the Model

Water in the Middle East: Structural CPR Scarcity and Security

According to Peter Gleick, "Where water is scarce, competition for limited supplies can lead nations to see access to water as a matter of national security. History is replete with examples of competition and disputes over shared fresh water resources."[17] In the Middle East, three river systems provide good examples of structural CPRs: the Nile, Jordan, and Euphrates.[18]

Downstream Egypt depends on the Nile for 97 percent of its water; the Nile is fed by tributaries that flow into it from the Sudan, Ethiopia, and elsewhere in central Africa. Both the Sudan and Ethiopia have an interest in drawing water from the tributaries that cross their countries in ways that might affect Egypt adversely but would strengthen their own economies.

From their perspectives, these waters are not CPRs, but sovereign holdings of a valuable environmental good. Per capita income in both countries is low; drought and famine have been frequent and devastating. Large-scale irrigation projects are attractive to both countries. On the surface, it would appear that both have reasons to discount the future and free ride.

Downstream, Egypt has no other comparable source of water—it is unable to use the market to find an alternative or affect the preferences of its neighbors. But with two-thirds the population of Ethiopia and the Sudan, Egypt's economy is three times the size of the other two combined. It is able to use its status as a regional great power to compel Ethiopia and the Sudan to limit their use of the Nile's tributaries. To avoid severe scarcity, Egypt has used its military might and international role as a regional stabilizing agent to control its neighbors. The threat of force deters them from overusing the water on which Egypt's national interests depend. In 1995, for example, President Hosni Mubarak warned the Sudan "that any interference with the river would not be tolerated, a warning that was noted well beyond Sudan's borders."[19]

According to the model, the Nile situation creates heightened tensions—the stakes are high and Egypt has signaled a willingness to intervene militarily to protect its national interests. Scarcity is real, but the negative impact of scarcity has been shifted to the upstream states. The one regime negotiated to resolve the situation, a 1959 agreement between Egypt and Sudan, clearly reflects the superior power of Egypt, which is guaranteed three times as much water as Sudan is.

Under these conditions a long-term and more equitable resource management scheme appears unlikely, although such a scheme might be possible through modifying existing water practices. As long as Egypt dominates the region, it will compel other states to respect its preferences. However, eight other states depend on the Nile—the possibility of a crisis or war is real and is likely to increase if (1) the regional distribution of power shifts to strengthen an upstream state, or (2) the experience of scarcity continues to worsen for any or all parties. In the former case, Egypt could initiate a preemptive strike. In the latter case, any of the other countries might draw more water and risk a confrontation because of limited alternatives. Such a strategy would be rational given the hope that international intervention to stabilize the region would result in a more equitable distribution of water.

Whenever a policy of deterrence is possible, it is likely that it will be employed to address structural CPR problems, even though it is a tenuous solution. When power is distributed more equitably in a region or when the downstream state is relatively weak, the bargaining leverage of the upstream state is far greater. In those cases, however, cooperation is also unlikely.

The Euphrates provides an example of this second scenario. Its waters are a CPR problem for downstream Syria and Iraq, which depend on them and which are relatively weak (at least at the moment) in comparison to upstream Turkey. This situation is even more volatile than that of the Nile—unlike Sudan and Ethiopia, Iraq and Syria could be denied water. Thus, "In 1974, Iraq threatened to bomb the al-Thawra dam in Syria; it massed troops along the border, alleging that the flow of water to Iraq had been reduced by the dam."[20] Tensions escalated in 1990 when Turkey "interrupted the flow of the Euphrates for a month to fill [a] reservoir."[21] That same year, "Turkish President Turgut Ozal threatened to restrict water flow to Syria to force it to withdraw support for Kurdish rebels."[22] Today, Turkey is "embarked on a vast irrigation project . . . If completed, this scheme could reduce Syria's and Iraq's share of the Euphrates by 40 percent and 60 percent respectively . . . But the two countries, no friends to each other, can only protest."[23]

Unless, like Egypt, they enjoy a clear power advantage, downstream states faced with structural CPR scarcity have little bargaining leverage, and war or crisis are likely outcomes. In this example, Turkey is able to claim and defend a sovereign right to the waters of the Euphrates—its incentives to reduce consumption or participate in a collective management scheme are not very great. Indeed, Turkey has undertaken large-scale water projects without international financing in order to protect its sovereign claim—most international lending agencies require the agreement of all riparian states to major water projects. Syria and Iraq can attempt either bribery or coercion, but without much hope of success. Iraq is relatively better off in that it has oil to trade and access to the Tigris, but at present its capacity to exploit these is limited. Consequently, the potential for a worsening security problem is high.

The case that has received the greatest attention in recent years concerns the Jordan River Basin. Four parched countries (Lebanon, Syria, Jordan, and Israel) depend on a declining pool of water, a significant amount of which is contained in the Jordan River Basin. Demand for water has been growing steadily. In the hostile environment that has existed since 1948, "dispute over the Jordan River is an integral part of the ongoing conflict."[24]

According to the general CPR model, cooperation is most likely when discount rates are similar, the incentive to free ride is low, and market forces can be mobilized to shape interests. In this case of structural CPR scarcity, the international context of Arab-Israeli hostility ensured, however, that cooperation would be difficult. For Israel, water scarcity was a matter of national security; thus it is not surprising that war figured prominently in its solution set. In 1967, Israel occupied most of the headwaters of the Jordan River Basin, transforming itself into a de facto upstream state with far greater bargaining leverage. Although the situation in this part of the Middle East is too complex to be reduced to a single-variable analysis, it seems plausible that recent peace agreements have been facilitated by the increase in Israel's bargaining chips.

Once again, however, traditional security tools appear as a tenuous solution to structural CPR scarcity. Discount rates for all parties are high. Miriam Lowi notes that in 1991 Israel alone used 2,100–2,200 million cubic meters (mcm) of water "while the total renewable fresh water supply was about 1950 mcm."[25] Demand is expected to reach "2,800–2,900 mcm between the years 2015 and 2020. However, supply projections for Israel . . . do not exceed 2,060 mcm."[26] Recent negotiations with Jordan and the Palestinians have included water management, but a variety of forces endlessly conspire to upset the implementation of agreements—collective management is desirable, but defection is always possible. Market forces can and probably will help to lower demand and increase supply, but the gains may not be sufficient. Consequently, Jordan water is likely to remain a contentious security issue, with the threat or use of force ever in the shadows.

What is interesting about this case is that it demonstrates how, for structural CPRs, a change in strategic position (here from downstream to upstream state) can alter the bargaining situation. Achieving this change, however, required an interstate war. Moreover, the long-term prospects for peace are not great regardless of who has bargaining leverage because there is simply not enough water to satisfy demand. Altering discount rates, overcoming the free rider problem, and using market power could, however, mitigate security problems.

These three cases support the following conclusion: the collective management problems associated with CPRs are magnified in the case of structural CPRs and therefore the security outcome is likely to tend toward the upper end of the spectrum—heightened tension, crisis, or war. In these cases, military power is likely to play a prominent role. This is one reason why environmental security maximalists often point to the sovereign state as a fundamental obstacle to environmental rescue—as long as some states can describe environmental goods that are essential to other states as private property, cooperation is rendered extremely difficult. CPR analysis helps clarify this problem but it does not provide grounds for optimism. It does, however, suggest that economic inducements to upstream states or the use or threat of force will be rational policy options. Obviously the involvement of third parties and the capacity of states to link issues could, as regime theory suggests, enable some form of collective management.

Finally, it is not insignificant that the three cases I have used concern water scarcity in the Middle East. Deudney has argued that interstate resource wars are unlikely; Levy has argued that most environmental problems cannot be usefully described as threats to U.S. national interests. Both authors are correct: scarcity is most likely to become a national security issue when it occurs in the South and involves a valuable and irreplaceable good such as water.

The Global Commons: Pure CPR Scarcity and Security

As the case of ozone depletion amply illustrates, the depletion of pure CPRs may threaten national interests. But as Levy has argued, this rarely happens and when it does it may be best to treat the issue as low politics.[27] The language of economics suggests cooperative solutions; the language of security, as Deudney has noted, suggests win-lose situations. Pure CPRs are, of course, quite common. What is less common is that they merit the attention of the traditional security community. Their impact tends to be felt at the lower end of the security spectrum; their universality inclines them to cooperative solutions. Nonetheless, pure CPR scarcity is increasingly being implicated in security affairs.

The 1995 conflict between Canada and Spain over exploitation of the Northwest Atlantic fishery provides a good example of a pure CPR scarcity problem.[28] The background to this dispute is long and complex, but needs to be sketched briefly. The 1982 United Nations Convention on the Law of the Sea (UNCLOS) was negotiated in part to address the problem of overfishing. It endorsed a 200-mile exclusive economic zone (EEZ) for coastal states—the idea was that by privatizing portions of the global commons, they could be better protected. Since that time, however, the plight of most of the world's fisheries has deteriorated steadily. New technologies and increased demand have led to heavy overfishing worldwide, and because fish stocks move in and out of EEZs, privatization has failed to generate sustainable practices. To the contrary, the world's fishing nations have exhibited classic tragedy of the commons behavior—taking as much as they can for fear that if they do not, others will.

The Grand Banks fishery off the coast of Newfoundland provides a good example of this. Parts of it, known as the Nose and Tail, are not contained within Canada's EEZ, and have been plundered by European fishing fleets. To resolve this problem, the Northwest Atlantic Fisheries Organization (NAFO) was established in 1979 to negotiate fishing quotas. The European Union, however, has used its right to opt out of these quotas, which it regards as unjust, and some member states have adopted the practice of fishing under the flags of non-NAFO states to avoid both NAFO and EU limits. After filing numerous protests, Canada resolved to take unilateral actions to protect the Nose and Tail, passing the Coastal Fisheries Protection Act (CFPA) in 1994, which gave Canadian officials the authority to enforce NAFO quotas on all ships.

While many ships left the area, Spain chose to regard Canada's law as a domestic justification for piracy. On March 9, 1995, Canada chased and captured the Spanish ship *Estai*. Spain responded by sending a naval patrol boat to protect its fishing ships. Canada refused to back down and went after the *Pescamero Uno*, cutting its nets. Tension mounted, the world watched with a certain amount of amusement, shots were exchanged, arrests made, and fines imposed. On April 15th, as Canada prepared to arrest several more Spanish ships, an agreement was reached involving new quotas for the EU and stricter enforcement measures.

Insofar as the model is concerned, this might appear to be a minor security issue, but seizing a ship in international waters is a serious incident, and the stakes—enjoyment of a vital CPR—are high and likely to rise in the years ahead. According to the UN, most of the world's 200 fisheries are being exploited beyond sustainable limits. For many states, fish are an essential but declining source of nutrition; the world fishing catch peaked in 1989 and has been declining steadily since then. The Canada-Spain dispute is neither an isolated incident, nor one that should be ignored. In this case, however, both parties have an interest in low discount rates and cooperative management, although to encourage recognition of this by Spain and the EU required the use of force by Canada. The fact that decades of negotiation produced unsatisfactory results until the issue become a matter of national security does not bode well for the future of collective management of pure CPRs. However, unlike structural CPRs, the prospects for a long-term negotiated settlement are greater because sovereignty does not create as high an incentive for one or more states to resist collective management.

Conclusions

Today, water, oil, and fisheries are the CPRs that can be related to national security most clearly. Stratospheric ozone and the global climate might also fall into this category. However, pushing them in this direction may be counterproductive. For example, Levy has argued persuasively that, in the case of ozone depletion, "we probably saved more lives by treating the stratosphere as low politics than we would have by treating it as high politics."[29] Some studies suggest, however, that the problem has yet to be satisfactorily resolved—ozone depletion could reemerge on the global agenda, this time as a security problem. Global climate change, although strongly endorsed by the scientific community, does not yet have the urgency generally associated with security issues, at least as I have defined them. This is not to suggest that it could not be considered a security problem: in fact, Levy argues that

> Climate change is a problem . . . like the problem of containing the Soviet Union; it requires a grand strategy to guide actions in the face of distant, uncertain threats, and an overarching commitment from high levels of leadership to stay the course through the ebbs and flows of popular sentiment.[30]

But to date, few members of the security community have chosen to strengthen this linkage; it might well be that keeping climate change in the arena of low politics will facilitate multilateral policy making. However, as the example of Canada-Spain suggests, this approach may not bear fruit. Conflicts over emissions that affect the global climate are not unimaginable.

It is also conceivable that other forms of environmental change and scarcity could worsen to the point where they become national security problems and begin to be described as CPRs. For example, some environmentalists and policy makers have suggested that rain forests and biodiversity should be thought of as CPRs, even though they historically have been understood through the lens of state sovereignty as private goods. Global thinking about these goods may follow the trajectory of human rights thinking, which now holds that the state is expected to provide and protect human rights, but when it fails, the international community has a right and an obligation to intervene.

In terms of the model I have presented, then, environmental scarcity can be imagined as operating at three levels. First, scarcity of oil, water, and fisheries are clearly related to conventional security affairs, generating wars, crises, and other forms of interstate tension. Second, problems such as ozone depletion or climate change are not obviously producing the security-relevant outcomes I have identified, but they have the potential to do so. A forward-looking policy approach would appreciate this potential and promote cooperative solutions to mitigate it. Finally, certain forms of scarcity such as deforestation or loss of biodiversity that usually have not been regarded as CPRs in the political realm (although they have been described this way in the UN and scientific communities), might be redescribed as CPRs in the years ahead. Again, a proactive policy would seek to address these problems today, because by the time they become security issues, they may no longer be manageable.

To this end, market power may be an underutilized tool. Had developed countries heeded the early warning signs of the 1970s and invested in alternative sources of energy, the Gulf War might not have occurred. Using market power could alter the logging value of rain forests and provide protection for species threatened by extinction. Small-scale experiments in Latin America with eco-tourism and other ways of using rain forests have indicated that discount rates can be changed by market forces. Even water scarcity might be mitigated by market strategies that gradually make economies less thirsty. Waiting until the level of scarcity mobilizes the security community, however, disables the great potential of the market, which has to be used before a crisis occurs in order to change preferences.

Hindsight is instructive for some problems, but not for all. This chapter has focused on the first set of scarcity problems and its findings do not provide much ground for optimism. In the case of structural CPR scarcity involving water, a good that is vital to the core values of all states, security outcomes tend, and will continue to tend toward the upper end of the spectrum—war, crisis and heightened tensions. This can be explained by considering the relative discount rates, incentives to free ride and market power of upstream versus downstream states, regardless of which are more powerful.

All other things being equal, downstream states are more likely to be concerned about the future and more willing to participate in a collective management scheme than are upstream states. Market power has little impact on these preferences. If the upstream states are more powerful (like Turkey) or even relatively equal (like Israel), they will have a huge incentive to defend the good as private property and to use it to meet domestic demands even if they risk depleting the resource. Downstream states will have to fight (as Israel did to seize control of the Jordan headwaters) or capitulate to other demands to protect what they are allowed (as Syria has done). Conversely, when downstream states are more powerful, they are likely to use force or the threat of force to compel upstream states to behave in accordance with their preferences (as Egypt does vis-à-vis Ethiopia and Sudan).

It is conceivable that third-party involvement might enable more cooperative outcomes. Water-sharing discussions between Israel and the Palestinian Authority have certainly been facilitated by the mediating role and financial resources of the United States. But given UN claims that eighty countries now face serious water shortages, the prospects for cooperation appear slim. It is very likely that water will be a national security issue for much of the world in the years ahead, and that it will lead to tension and conflict.

The prospects for pure CPR scarcity are significantly better. In these cases, decades of UN-style dialogue have created a negotiating environment sympathetic to cooperation. In theory, at least, all states have an interest in the future of the resource and somewhat less incentive to free ride. Of course, these will vary enormously from case to case. In general Third World states are likely to discount the future more heavily and seek to free ride whenever possible because they lack the resources necessary for the alternative positions. It is conceivable, however, that they often will have no choice but to accept the cooperative management schemes negotiated by Northern states. This has already happened in cases such as the Antarctic and stratospheric ozone.

Developed states, however, are prone to try to overconsume in the present and free ride, as the example of Canada-Spain demonstrates. Some degree of force may have to be used to bring states to the bargaining table to work out a more permanent solution than force itself can maintain. Thus, in the final analysis, it is hard to avoid the conclusion that both forms of CPR scarcity do and will lead to the threat or use of force.

The utility of this model is not exhausted by this set of cases. To the contrary, it contains an important message relevant to the other two sets of cases outlined above. Discount rates, free riding, and market failure can lead to forms of environmental scarcity that then cause security problems. When this happens, force is likely to figure in the responses. To avoid this outcome, it would be wise to implement forward-looking policies that might alter discount rates, overcome free riding, and correct market failures before they produce security-relevant scarcity. Levy is right in suggesting that a grand strategy is needed today "in the face of distant, uncertain threats."[31] The world is probably going to experience frequent conflict over water, oil, and food; but it may not have to experience conflict over emissions that cause climate change or the loss of biodiversity. Sadly, there is a sort of catch-22 character to all of this: until an issue becomes a security problem, it does not attract sufficient resources to manage it peacefully; once it has become a security issue, however, cooperative management is extremely difficult. It would be wise for the world to look at the problems water scarcity is causing today and is likely to cause in the future, and remember that water is not the only scarce resource on which human life depends. As Edmund Burke wrote, "Never, no never, did Nature say one thing and Wisdom say another." Unfortunately, the practitioners of world politics are far more Machiavellian than Socratic.

Notes

1. "Severe Water Crisis Ahead for Poorest Nations in Next Two Decades," *The New York Times* (August 10, 1995), p. A13.

2. Gareth Porter, "Environmental Security as a National Security Issue," *Current History* (May 1995), p. 220.

3. Lester Brown, *Who Will Feed China? Wake-up Call for a Small Planet* (New York: W. W. Norton, 1995).

4. Warren Christopher, "American Diplomacy and the Global Environmental Challenges of the Twenty-first Century," Stanford University, April 9, 1996.

5. Lester R. Brown, "Redefining National Security," Worldwatch Paper 14 (1977), and Richard Ullman, "Redefining Security," *International Security* vol. 8 (1983), pp. 129–53.

6. For a brief overview of this activity, see Richard A. Matthew, "Environmental Security and Conflict: An Overview of the Current Debate," *National Security Studies Quarterly* vol. 1 (1995), pp. 1–10. For a more comprehensive overview, see Daniel Deudney and Richard A. Matthew (eds.), *Contested Grounds: Security and Conflict in the New Environmental Politics* (Albany: SUNY Press, 1999).

7. Thomas Homer-Dixon, "On the Threshold: Environmental Changes as Sources of Acute Conflict," *International Security* vol. 16 (1991), pp. 76–116, and "Environmental Scarcities and Violent Conflict: Evidence from Cases," *International Security* vol. 19 (1994), pp. 5–40; Shin-wha Lee, "Not a One-Time Event: Environmental Change, Ethnic Rivalry, and Violent Conflict in the Third World," IAS Paper (April, 1996); Marc A. Levy, "Is the Environment a National Security Issue?" *International Security* vol. 20 (1995), pp. 35–62; and Richard A. Matthew, "Rethinking Environmental Security," in Nils Petter Gleditsch, ed., *Conflict and the Environment* (Dordrecht: Kluwer, 1998), pp. 71–90.

8. Brown, "Redefining National Security"; Norman Myers, *Ultimate Security: The Environmental Basis of Political Stability* (New York: Norton, 1993); Gareth Porter, "Environmental Security as a National Security Issue," *Current History* (May 1995), pp. 218–22.

9. Daniel Deudney, "The Case Against Linking Environmental Degradation and National Security," *Millennium* vol. 19 (1990), pp. 461–76.

10. Marc A. Levy, "Is the Environment a National Security Issue?"

11. Peter H. Gleick, "Environment and Security: The Clear Connection," *Bulletin of the Atomic Scientists* (April 1991), pp. 17–21, and "Water and Conflict," *International Security* vol. 18 (1993), pp. 79–112.

12. Daniel Deudney, "Environment and Security: Muddled Thinking," *Bulletin of the Atomic Scientists* (April 1991), pp. 23–28.

13. See, for example, Matthew Connelly and Paul Kennedy, "Must It Be the West Against the Rest?" *The Atlantic Monthly* vol. 274 (1994), pp. 61–83.

14. Valerie Percival and Thomas Homer-Dixon, "Environmental Scarcity and Violent Conflict: The Case of South Africa" (Washington, DC: American Association for the Advancement of Science and the University of Toronto, Occasional Paper, 1995), pp. 5–6.

15. In this chapter, I will use the terms "upstream states" and "downstream states" to refer to the different perceptions inherent in structural CPRs, regardless of the good at stake.

16. This is a variation of what Homer-Dixon refers to as structural scarcity. It is a more limiting case, however, in that it focuses solely on interstate situations. From the perspective of the downstream state, the good really is scarce given the way property rights have been assigned in the international system. In the domestic cases that Homer-Dixon focuses on, states are failing to do what they are supposed to do according to international law—protect the rights of their citizens. Thus a structural CPR simply accepts the structure of the international system as given and, in this sense, it is not artificial.

17. Peter Gleick, "Water and Conflict: Fresh Water Resources and International Security," *International Security* vol. 18 (1993), p. 79.

18. For further information on these cases, see, among others: J. A. Allan, ed., *Water, Peace and the Middle East* (London: I. B. Tauris, 1996); Elisha Kally, *Water and Peace: Water Resources and the Arab-Israeli Peace Process* (Westport, CT: Praeger, 1993); Steven Spiegel, ed., *Practical Peacemaking in the Middle East*, vol. II: The Environment, Water, Refugees, and Economic Cooperation and Development (New York: Garland, 1995).

19. "Water in the Middle East," *The Economist* (Dec. 23, 1995–Jan. 5, 1996), p. 54. "In 1979, President Anwar Sadat said, 'The only matter that could take Egypt to war again is water.' More recently, Egypt's foreign minister, Boutros Boutros-Ghali. . . , said 'The next war in our region will be over the waters of the Nile, not politics.'" Gleick, "Water and Conflict," p. 86.

20. Gleick, "Water and Conflict," p. 88.

21. Ibid., p. 89.

22. Ibid., p. 89.

23. Ibid., p. 54.

24. Ibid., p. 85.

25. Miriam Lowi, "Bridging the Divide: Transboundary Resource Disputes and the Case of West Bank Water," *International Security* vol. 18 (1993), p. 119.

26. Ibid, p. 119.

27. Levy, "Is the Environment a National Security Issue?" p. 51.

28. Information for this case comes largely from Allen L. Springer, "Unilateral Action in Defense of Environmental Interests: An Assessment," ISA Paper (March 1996).

29. Levy, "Is the Environment a National Security Issue?," p. 51.

30. Ibid., p. 54.

31. Ibid., p. 54.

8 Conclusions: Common Pool Resources and International Environmental Negotiation

J. SAMUEL BARKIN

AND

GEORGE E. SHAMBAUGH

Introduction

Does the logic of common pool resources (CPRs) help us in understanding the dynamics of international environmental politics? The evidence from the case studies in this volume suggests that it does. Whatever the technical nature of an international environmental issue, the evidence suggests that it is likely to show the political characteristics of a common pool resource, and can fruitfully be analyzed as such. This has important ramifications for the management of environmental issues internationally. In particular, it means that institutions created to manage the global commons must be designed and maintained in a way that takes the politics of the distribution of the limited benefits of environmental amenities into account.

Before discussing these ramifications in more detail, this chapter will review the empirical findings in the case studies, and gauge the level of support they provide for the various hypotheses deduced in the introduction. There are two parts to this undertaking. The first is to review the hypotheses individually and discuss the degree to which they are supported by the case material. Almost all of the hypotheses help to explain at least some of the cases, and some of the hypotheses can be found at work in almost all of the cases. The logic of common pool resources, thus, highlights one set of dynamics in the politics of international environmental issues. To fully explain international environmental management, however, one must take scientific and normative, as well as political, inputs into account. Consequently, the second part of our review of the case studies looks at how the political dynamics of common pool resources interact with other inputs into international environmental management. Three particular sorts of inputs will be analyzed: institutional structures, changes in the knowledge base, and changes in actors' definitions of their own interests. This chapter will then conclude with some thoughts on directions for further research in the analysis of the political dynamics of common pool resources and the management of international environmental issues.

The Case Studies and Their Implications

The first chapter of this volume presents a set of logically deduced hypotheses on common pool resources and international environmental politics, while the second develops the argument that CPR issues should be both more prevalent and more problematic internationally than domestically. This section reviews those hypotheses in light of the findings of our empirical chapters. The case studies suggest that changes in shadows of the future, in the role of the free rider, and in market power in CPR situations do affect the strategic policy preferences of actors and the political dynamics of cooperation and conflict in international environmental management.

Time Horizons and the Likelihood of Cooperation

The first set of hypotheses emphasizes the importance of time horizons on the likelihood of cooperation. In chapter 2, Ronald Mitchell argues that because actors value different environmental amenities in completely different ways, the lengths of shadows of the future with respect to these amenities can vary dramatically. In particular, actors that value environmental amenities for their existence value are likely to have almost infinitely long shadows of the future, while shadows of the future for amenities valued for their consumptive benefits are likely to be significantly shorter. The discussion of time horizons began with the proposition, common in the literature on cooperation under anarchy, that lengthening the shadow of the future for all actors equally will increase the likelihood of cooperation. The question then is, How often is this an issue in international environmental relations? The cases suggest that it can be an important factor, but is not necessarily a common occurrence. More specifically, examples of this sort of dynamic are found in two of the five empirical chapters, Christopher Joyner's study of the Convention on the Conservation of Antarctic Marine Living Resources and Richard Matthew's study of the security ramifications of CPR issues. In Joyner's case, the effectiveness of sanctuaries for fur seals and whales in the Southern Oceans was greatly facilitated by an across the board change in attitudes toward marine mammals, from consumptive amenities to existence amenities. This was reflected by an increase in each participant's shadow of the future to lengths approaching infinity, in turn facilitating cooperation among them. In contrast, in Matthew's study of relations over water rights, negotiations were more prone to conflict when the shadows of the future of all of the actors involved were short. These two cases thus do suggest that lengthening shadows of the future equivalently all around will facilitate solutions, but it is not clear how this can be easily translated into practical policy options, except for policies that encourage the perception of CPRs as existence amenities.

> H1a: If consumers recognize different shadows of the future, or if potential agreements affect these shadows differently, then the consumer(s) with the shorter shadow of the future should have greater bargaining power than those with longer shadows.

This hypothesis is a core proposition of this project; it is the primary mechanism through which the strategic dynamics created by common pool resources in an international setting generate political conflict. Four of five of the case studies bore out this hypothesis, which suggests strongly that it is a predominant feature of the dynamics of CPR politics in international environmental management. In chapter 3, on the regulation of tuna fisheries, Elizabeth DeSombre addresses this point directly, by indicating the ways in which states with shorter shadows of the future were able to gain explicit exceptions from quotas in exchange for agreement to remain formally within the regulatory structures. The most extreme case of this phenomenon was the ICCAT, the convention that regulates Atlantic tuna fisheries, where exceptions were specifically designed for individual states. Similarly, in chapter 4, Chris Joyner describes the unanimity decision rule of CCALMR, which greatly reduces the effectiveness of the regime in managing the resources in its charge but was the only way to keep states with traditionally shorter shadows of the future for these resources, particularly Japan and the Soviet Union, within the regime.

In chapter 5 on the Montreal Protocol negotiations, David Downie shows how the greater bargaining power of countries with shorter shadows of the future, most notably China and India, resulted both in exemption from the rules of the ozone regime for over a decade and in financial rewards for cooperation. Both the exemptions and the financing were rationalized formally as exceptions for less-developed countries, but Downie argues that the realities of the negotiations suggest that a CPR dynamic, rather than an aid dynamic, was at work. In chapter 6, Barbara Connolly's study of LRTAP and the politics of transboundary airborne pollution in Europe, it is very difficult to isolate differentials in shadows of the future. The countries that one would expect to have the shorter shadows of the future tend also to be the countries that are either upwind or least sensitive to the effects of acid rain, so their behavior in gaining concessions within the LRTAP framework is overdetermined. This case is thus better examined through the lens of free-rider arguments than that of shadow of the future arguments.

Finally, in chapter 7, Richard Matthew discusses the differential bargaining power caused by differences in shadows of the future. He argues that even in "pure CPR" situations, which should be less likely than structural CPRs to generate security issues, cases can be found that display this dynamic very distinctly. For example, the origins of the Spanish-Canadian dispute over turbot lie in the decision mechanism of NAFO, the body that is supposed to regulate catches of the fish. NAFO rules clearly allow countries to exclude themselves from specific quotas, because without such an exclusion clause states with short shadows of the future for North Atlantic fish, notably Spain, would simply not have acceded to a regulatory regime in the first place. It was the habitual use by the EU, largely at Spanish instigation, of the exclusion clause that led directly to the Spanish-Canadian confrontation.

H1b: Over time, an actor with a shorter shadow of the future should increase its bargaining leverage over an actor with a longer shadow if it threatens to delay an agreement or to overconsume at any point during the negotiations.

H1c: A country with a short enough shadow of the future can wield a credible threat to destroy a CPR, and thus may be able to extract concessions from other potential CPR beneficiaries up to the total future value of the resource.

These two hypotheses are being considered here together because they both gain empirical support from the same cases. Support for both hypotheses was not as universal as was true for H1a, primarily because the scenario in which they would apply, one in which an actor has the ability either to significantly draw out and delay negotiations, or to actually destroy the environmental amenity in question, does not appear in all cases. In those cases where actors possessed such abilities, though, they were able to extract major concessions as a result.

David Downie argues, for example, that the increasing proportion of ozone-depleting substances consumed in developing countries, particularly China and India, is giving those countries greater leverage in ongoing negotiations on the issue. Their ability to extract concessions is increasing over time and in proportion to their ability to credibly threaten to do harm to the ozone layer. The longer they continue to use ozone-depleting chemicals, the greater their leverage will become. Similarly, Chris Joyner argues that whatever the ability of CCALMR to successfully manage fishing stocks in the southern oceans today, the potential ability of China and India to overconsume the stocks to the point of extinction gives them a source of leverage over future negotiations.

Finally, Beth DeSombre's study provides an example in which the concessions demanded and received over time by countries with shorter shadows of the future came to approximate the total value of collective management so closely that the management regime itself became largely irrelevant. This in fact happened with both the Atlantic and the Pacific tuna regimes. She also suggests one way in which states can counter the bargaining advantage that results from comparatively short shadows of the future. Given that states with relatively short shadows of the future can use that differential as a source of leverage in multilateral negotiations, she argues that actors who are at a bargaining disadvantage due to their relatively long shadows of the future will often avoid multilateral negotiations and seek to resolve their problems through unilateral actions. She finds that Latin American countries had relatively longer shadows of the future regarding the preservation of tuna than U.S. factory vessels fishing off their coasts. Rather than negotiate in a multilateral forum where they would be at a comparative disadvantage, and despite the imposition of sanctions by the United States, the Latin American countries chose to preserve their stocks through the unilateral enforcement of fishing restrictions within self-declared exclusive economic zones. Similarly, the United States acted unilaterally to enforce dolphin-safe tuna-fishing techniques when it became clear that significant progress was unlikely in multilateral fora.

The Free-Rider Problem

The second set of hypotheses emphasizes the role of the free rider in the use and management of international environmental amenities. The ability of a free rider to inflict costs on others by diminishing the amount of a CPR available to them gives any state that is willing to free ride a potential source of political leverage.

> H2a: Once resource limits are recognized, free riders should be able to gain concessions in environmental negotiations that approach the costs (economic, social, and political) that they can impose by overconsuming the CPR.

As with H1a, this hypothesis forms a core proposition of this project. It is the deductive starting point for our arguments on the role of free riders in international environmental negotiations. As was true of H1a, it is broadly supported by the cases, with examples to be found in each of the five empirical chapters. Beth DeSombre describes how the concessions offered to free riders in order to keep them within existing fisheries management regimes led to ineffective quotas that failed to maintain tuna stocks in both the Pacific and the Atlantic fisheries. Furthermore, in the Atlantic case free riders outside of the regime made the agreed quotas meaningless. Similarly, as described by Chris Joyner, free riders were allowed free reign in CCAMLR. In this case such behavior was sanctioned formally by the rules of the Convention; national vetoes in this context amount to a license to free ride at will. When, however, the largest of the free riders, the Soviet Union, ceased most of its harvesting activities, pressure increased on the other substantial free rider, Japan, to cooperate. Once free ridership as a whole had for exogenous reasons become less important, Japan's de facto ability to extract concessions from the other participants in the regime declined as well.

David Downie describes an ongoing process whereby the major free riders on the ozone regime, most notably China and India, continue to gain new concessions from the agreement as the costs that they can impose by consuming ODS increase. These concessions include lengthening the grace periods on new additions to the protocol, and may well include greater transfers of resources in the future. As the free riders come to dominate global production of ODS, these concessions may well continue to become ever greater. Barbara Connolly's study suggests, on the other hand, that the free riders on the LRTAP regime are able to gain fewer concessions, as they are able to impose fewer costs on the regime. The signatories that fail to comply fully with the regime, primarily in Southern Europe, are able to gain significant concessions, in the form of transfer payments and a blind eye turned to their free riding. They are unable to gain the same level of formal concessions as the free riders on the ozone regime largely because they do not possess the same ability to impose costs. They can weaken the regime by polluting, but not by enough to completely undercut the efforts of those that do not free ride.

Finally, both of Richard Matthew's sets of cases show an interesting variation on this hypothesis. In both, free riders are able to gain significant concessions. In the turbot case, the concession to the EU was similar to that granted to free riders in CCAMLR, a formal mechanism for exemption from quotas. In the examples involving distributional conflict over river water resources, the free riding is even more direct; upstream states may simply take what they want. In both cases, though, other major users of the resource became willing at a certain point to escalate the conflict beyond the scope of environmental negotiation, and to turn it into a more traditional security dispute. This suggests that when the costs that free riders impose become greater than the costs to other users of gaining compliance through coercive means, conflict escalation becomes a real possibility. This is one of the primary mechanisms through which environmental politics can translate to traditional security issues.

H2b: Benevolent hegemonic solutions in environmental negotiations will not necessarily facilitate collective management of environmental problems because the hegemon cannot guarantee that the CPR will be maintained.

Benevolent hegemonic solutions did not succeed in solving any of the international environmental problems studied here. We will focus here, though, only on those cases where benevolent hegemony was tried and failed. This happened in three of the cases, the protection of dolphins from tuna fishers, the management of the Southern Oceans, and the protection of the ozone layer. In each case a state attempted through leadership and example to undertake to protect an environmental amenity, and failed to do so appreciably. In the dolphin case, the United States passed laws requiring its own tuna fleet to use dolphin-safe methods, and encouraged others to follow suit. This effort failed, succeeding only in reducing the American fishery's market share by increasing its costs. Similarly, the effort by most of the world's major powers to create a whale sanctuary in the Antarctic will likely continue to fail unless and until some coercive pressure is brought to bear on Japan to cease whaling there. And finally, a decade of policy leadership by the United States in reducing ODS emissions from the mid-1970s through the mid-1980s failed to protect the ozone, as only a few states followed their lead for most of that period.

> H2c: Since free riders can undermine benevolent hegemonic solutions in CPR situations, coercive hegemony will be the preferred form of unilateral management of CPRs.

In two of the cases where benevolent hegemony failed, coercive hegemony succeeded. It succeeded as well in most of the cases used to demonstrate the link between CPRs and international security. In the dolphin case, the United States followed up its failed attempt at benevolent leadership with trade restrictions on tuna caught in dolphin-unfriendly ways, and this attempt at coercive hegemony succeeded. In the ozone case there is no clear case of coercive hegemony in action, and the success of the Montreal Protocol round of negotiations cannot be explained without taking increased knowledge into account. Yet the negotiations took place under an implicit threat of American coercive hegemony should they fail. Gauging the precise impact of this implicit threat is probably impossible, yet it may well have had a significant effect. Finally, in Richard Matthew's cases coercive hegemony was tried wherever it was possible. Both Egypt and Israel resorted to clear military threats to coerce upstream states so as to gain the lion's share of water resources from their respective river systems, and Canada made clear its intention to prevent Spanish overfishing by force. These cases suggest that coercive hegemony as a tool for international environmental management is resorted to relatively often, and that it can work effectively.

> H2d: The more the cost of free riding is internalized by the actor in question, the weaker its incentive to free ride.

The proportion of the costs of free riding internalized by the actor in question can increase in two ways, through a change in knowledge regarding the distribution of the costs of its actions, and through a change in the contractual environment within which the free riding takes place. There was one case of each discussed in this volume. Barbara Connolly tells us that as some of the larger European powers, particularly first Germany and then the United Kingdom, discovered the extent of the damage they themselves were suffering from acid rain, their attitudes toward and bargaining stances within LRTAP changed radically. In other words, they ceased free riding when they discovered that this behavior was hurting themselves as much as anyone else. And in the various attempts to manage tuna fisheries discussed by Beth DeSombre the creation of EEZs did have a slightly beneficial effect on fisheries management. The effect was only slight, though, because the highly migratory behavior of tuna means that the privatization of coastal waters out to 200 miles leads to only a marginal increase in the internalization of the costs of free riding.

It is worth noting here that valuing environmental amenities for their existence benefits has an effect similar to internalizing the costs of free riding. If an actor values the existence of an amenity for its own sake, then that actor is highly unlikely to free ride by consuming any of the resource, because it would be directly reducing the benefit it gains from the resource. This observation is born out by the cases. Since these actors are least likely to free ride, they might be expected to be more prone to act hegemonically, where feasible. Thus perhaps paradoxically, the countries that value the amenity for its existence rather than consumptive benefits may be most likely to forego cooperative mechanisms for preserving it.

Market Power

Market power represents one means of affecting the incentives of potential free riders to alter their behavior. Altering the current or future value of a resource can alter the shadow of the future and the incentives of actors to free ride on CPR management agreements.

> H3a: If an actor can decrease the elasticity of demand for a CPR or increase the potential future value of the resource, then it should decrease the incentive for competitive exploitation and increase the likelihood of CPR management.

There was no direct evidence in the case studies to support or refute this hypothesis. Actors did not attempt to encourage environmental management by directly altering elasticities of demand, or by increasing the future value of resources, in this basket of cases. This may suggest that such strategies are not common, but might be considered as strategic alternatives in the future. In two cases, though, environmental management was improved by simple decreases in the demand for the amenity in question. CCAMLR's success in managing finfish stocks improved notably when the general level of demand decreased with the demise of the Soviet fleet. And the management of ozone depleting substances was made much easier when practical replacements for the chemicals in question became available. This sort of demand management would thus appear to have significant potential as a mechanism for decreasing the severity of common pool dynamics in international environmental politics.

> H3b: Large consumers, or countries with large consumer markets, should be able to gain bargaining power by using their markets to alter the value of CPR extraction for others. This leverage should increase as the number of alternate markets decreases and more consumers join the process.

Market power had a major effect in promoting international environmental management in two of the cases in this volume, the protection of dolphins from tuna fishers and the management of ozone-depleting substances. In another case, the management of tuna fisheries, market power was tried and failed. Beth DeSombre's chapter explicitly compares the success of market power in the dolphin case with its failure in the tuna case, and ascribes the difference to two factors. The first is that there was far more widespread support within the United States in the former case, making the official use of market power more credible. The second difference was that the attempt to use market power to create a tuna regime had much greater redistributional effects than the use of market power to promote dolphin-safe fishing techniques. It thus generated a much greater degree of opposition from the target states. This suggests that market power can be an effective tool, but more effective when it is backed by widespread popular support, and when the management regime that the market power is supporting is not seen by others as simply an attempt at the redistribution, rather than the conservation, of environmental amenities. Market power is also discussed in a broader sense by Barbara Connolly, who identifies an implicit use by some of the larger Western European countries, particularly Germany, of their economic weight in an attempt to convince their European Community partners to limit emissions of sulfuric acid.

Summary

The case studies suggest that international environmental politics can be fruitfully studied through the logic of common pool resources. The findings support our hypotheses, derived from the general literature on international

Table 8:1
HYPOTHESES TESTING

	Chapters				
Hypotheses	**3**	**4**	**5**	**6**	**7**
H1a	Yes	Yes	Yes	N/A	Yes
H1b	Yes	Yes	Yes	N/A	N/A
H1c	Yes	Yes	Yes	N/A	N/A
H2a	Yes	Yes	Yes	Yes	Yes
H2b	Yes	Yes	Yes	N/A	N/A
H2c	Yes	N/A	N/A	N/A	Yes
H2d	Yes	N/A	N/A	Yes	N/A
H3a	N/A	N/A	N/A	N/A	N/A
H3b	Yes	N/A	Yes	Yes	N/A

cooperation, while demonstrating some of the unique political dynamics of CPR negotiation and management. In particular, the cases strongly supported our two core hypotheses, that consumers with relatively short shadows of the future will have greater bargaining power than those with relatively longer shadows, and that free riders can gain concessions in international environmental management regimes that approach the costs they are willing to impose by overconsuming the CPR. The other hypotheses were supported in smaller numbers of cases, but were with few exceptions supported where they applied. The cases also suggested that Mitchell's categorization of environmental amenities by the kind of benefit they provide is useful in analyzing the political dynamics of international attempts to manage these amenities. The results can be summarized as in Table 8:1, with "yes" indicating support for the hypothesis and "N/A" indicating that the hypothesis did not apply to the case.

CPRs in the Broader Context

The previous section has shown that the hypotheses derived in the introduction are useful: Understanding international environmental politics as common-pool resource issues helps both in explaining the dynamics of international negotiations on these issues, and in predicting the effectiveness and longevity of the resulting agreements to manage and protect the environment on an international and global scale. Yet these hypotheses are clearly not by themselves sufficient for a complete understanding of the political dynamics of international environmental management and institutions. This section will look at some of the other factors most often discussed in the literature on international environmental politics, and describe inductively what our cases have to say about them, and the ways in which these factors and our hypotheses interrelate. In particular, three broad categories of factors will be discussed: the independent effects of international institutions, the effects of knowledge creation and change, and the effects of changes in patterns of perceived interest. Institutions are important in international politics as influences on and mediators of interstate relations. The effects of changes in knowledge are particularly important in international environmental politics because the knowledge base changes much more quickly than in most other areas of international relations. And finally, national interests are a key variable the study of foreign policy, but one that is often left implicit in the study of international environmental politics.

Institutions

There is a considerable literature on both the creation and effectiveness of institutions and regimes in international environmental management. The research in this volume bears on both of these aspects of international environmental institutions. With respect to the creation of institutions, for example, it suggests that where significant differentials in shadows of the future exist among states party to a negotiation, a consensus-building approach will lead to constraints on behavior weaker than those preferred by the average of those states. This is because states with relatively short shadows of the future with respect to a particular environmental good, and which therefore are less enthusiastic than other states about the creation of constraints on their ability to access the good, can exploit this differential as a means to secure bargaining concessions that make the regime weaker than it otherwise would be. CPR analysis also looks at circumstances in which market power can be brought to bear effectively in the creation of institutions that reflect a particular state's preferences. With respect to the question of institutional effectiveness, the research suggests that in order to discourage free riding, institutions must be designed with incentive mechanisms, either positive or negative, that accurately reflect the interests of those most likely to free ride.[1]

While the approach used in this volume highlights how institutions might be used to manage CPR issues effectively, it must be emphasized that institutions cannot solve CPR problems by themselves. The fact that free riders can always threaten to exploit an environmental good means that the potential for CPR problems to develop will always exist, regardless of the effectiveness of institutional mechanisms established to manage their use. This means that participants in the environmental management situations discussed in this volume must be monitored in perpetuity because the free-rider problem can always threaten to undermine the management regime and re-create the problem.

One particular aspect of international environmental institutions that is not derived from our hypotheses, but that was a consistent empirical phenomenon in our case studies and thus merits note here as a subject of future research, might be called institutional stickiness. Once an institution is created, it often continues to exist beyond the point where it no longer continues to fulfill it original function. Changes in management regimes often occur through the evolution of existing institutions rather than through the creation of new ones. And perhaps more important, when a regime to manage a given environmental issue becomes formalized, this often takes place through the expansion of existing institutions, rather than the creation of new ones. The reasons for this phenomenon are unclear. A potential rational systemic argument might look at sunk costs; it may be more cost-efficient to modify existing bureaucracies than create new ones.[2] There may also be bureaucratic explanations. Once an institution is created, it fosters a bureaucracy with both expertise and resources in a given issue-area, resources that it can use to protect its position. That bureaucracy then has a vested interest in ensuring that it can monopolize future attempts at management within its issue-area, so as to protect its existing prerogatives.[3] Other reasons, ranging from the psychological to the consensual, are possible.

Three of the chapters in this volume show evidence of this sort of institutional stickiness. Beth DeSombre tells of two institutions. The IATTC was designed mostly to collect data on Pacific tuna stocks. When the information made clear a need for regulation, this was done through the existing organization. The IATTC has failed to regulate meaningfully for a decade and a half, yet it still exists, while attempts to create new and meaningful regulatory institutions fail. Similarly the ICCAT, designed to regulate the catch of Atlantic tuna, has a history of thirty years of consistent failure, yet continues to exist. Barbara Connolly tells a different kind of story, one of institutional success rather than failure, yet it highlights the phenomenon of institutional stickiness most strongly. The LRTAP Convention was created largely at the instigation of the Scandinavian countries, which do not have the capabilities to enforce acid rain regulations on the larger European countries. Yet once those countries began to see regulation as being in their own interest, they negotiated within the existing framework, rather than creating a new one. Thus the

Scandinavian countries, by creating the institution before it could be effective, were able to have a disproportionate impact on the form of cooperation once it could be effective. Finally, the CCAMLR, as Chris Joyner suggests, continued to be the focus of efforts to manage Antarctic marine living resources even when one or two of the signatory states were using the institutional framework to undermine the goal of conservation shared by a large majority of signatories. Even though free riding by Japan and the Soviet Union might have been better managed within a different institutional design, no serious attempts were made to negotiate alternatives.

Two effects of this pattern of institutional stickiness in international environmental regimes may be noted, one highlighted by the Connolly chapter and the other by the DeSombre and Joyner chapters. The first might be called a first-mover advantage. Because existing institutions are often deferred to in the management of a given environmental amenity, whoever creates the first one to manage that amenity can have a disproportionate influence on the institutional setting within which management happens. For a group of small states like the Scandinavian countries, this can give them influence over the management of an issue of particular national importance potentially greater then they could otherwise achieve, if they have the foresight to create an appropriate institution first. It is worth noting, though, that while a first mover advantage can be used, as in the LRTAP case, to create stronger institutions than might otherwise be the case, a first mover advantage captured by countries with a primary interest in the exploitation rather than the management of a resource can have the opposite effect, of creating weaker institutions than might otherwise be the case. The identification of global warming issues with development issues at Rio may well turn out to be an example of this opposite effect—by institutionalizing a discourse on development as a necessary accompaniment to any discourse on restraining emissions of greenhouse gasses, countries less interested in the latter may have helped postpone it.

The second effect of the pattern of institutional stickiness is the corollary of the first. Since the first institution created to manage a given environmental amenity is likely to remain the primary one, it becomes that much more important to get it right on the first try. Poorly designed institutions can be as sticky as well-designed ones. Therefore, from the point of view of successful management of limited resources, a bad institution may be worse than none at all, because a well-designed institution, once available, can much more easily replace a vacuum than it can a poorly designed but entrenched one.

Knowledge

Changes in knowledge can be crucial in shaping the way in which issues and options for action are defined in international environmental politics. It is the recognition that carrying capacities are limited that generates the incentive to manage common resources internationally, as environmental amenities formerly thought to be nonrival public goods become recognized as rival common pool resources. Examining the relationship between changes in knowledge and the international politics of common pool resources is complicated, though, by the variety of ways in which the concept of knowledge is understood in the study of international relations.

Much of the literature on international environmental politics discusses the effects of changes in knowledge on behavior and outcomes. The general observation that knowledge should affect actions and outcomes in this field is relatively uncontentious. Yet this observation, stated generally, tells us little about what those actions and outcomes might be, for two reasons. The first is that we do not know how knowledge interacts with other inputs in international politics. The second is that there is no consensus in the field about exactly what we should understand knowledge to be, and how we should go about studying it. There are three broad schools of thought in the literature on international environmental politics as to what we should understand knowledge to mean. These can be categorized as the rationalist school,[4] the constructivist school,[5] and the epistemic community school.[6] Each school usefully illustrates aspects of the case studies presented here.

The rationalist school understands knowledge to be empirical and objective; new knowledge comes from science, and consists of things that are objectively true but that we simply did not know before. From the rationalist perspective, new knowledge or information acts as an intervening variable between preexisting interests and outcomes. The effect is unidirectional, from interests to knowledge to strategy. Changes in knowledge affect strategy, but do not effect the interests of the actor in question. This was clearly the case to some extent at least in all of the cases in this volume. New knowledge of the decline in fish stocks motivated efforts to manage fisheries. Knowledge of the mechanics of ozone depletion was a major motivating factor in the negotiation of the Montreal Protocol. And knowledge of the damage caused domestically by acid rain fundamentally altered the cost-benefit analyses of first Germany and then the United Kingdom with respect to reducing sulfur emissions, which led in turn to radical changes in their negotiating stances.

The constructivist school understands knowledge as being at least partially intersubjective, a socially constructed phenomenon. According to this view, empirical observations are open to a number of interpretations, none of which is necessarily objectively more accurate. What constitutes change in knowledge about the international environment, then, is as much a result of changes in social consensus as it is a result of new data. Constructivists argue that neither discourse nor action in international politics generally, and international environmental politics specifically, can be understood without looking at this broader understanding of knowledge as a socially constructed phenomenon. It is, for example, a matter of broad social consensus in the United States that dolphins should be valued for the existence benefits they provide, whereas tuna are important only as a source of consumptive benefits. There is no objective rule to base this judgment on, yet American fisheries policy cannot be understood without it. Similarly, there is a general consensus that environmental change is bad. This is not objectively true, certainly not uniformly. Global warming could well prove a major boon to some parts of the world. Yet there exists a general social consensus that climate change is bad. It is not based on universal and objective data and decision rules, rather it exists because most people, for whatever reason, agree with it.

A third way of interpreting and evaluating the effects of knowledge on international environmental politics is through the study of epistemic communities. These are "networks of professionals with recognized expertise and competence in a particular domain and an authoritative claim to policy-relevant knowledge within that domain or issue-area."[7] As such, epistemic communities are intellectual hybrids of rationalist and constructivist approaches. The authoritative claims to knowledge that the networks of professionals make are based on a claim to a monopoly on rationalist knowledge in a field. Yet the knowledge output of the community is knowledge in a constructivist sense; it is the shared values and interests of the members of the community, as well as or perhaps even rather than the shared 'objective' knowledge, that forms the basis of the community. Thus epistemic communities represent a particular form of intersubjective or social knowledge, one in which the society in question is a group of experts rather than society at large, and in which claims to authoritativeness are based on claims of objectivity. They serve to delimit the options for cooperative behavior with respect to a given issue once it has been broadly accepted, as a result of changes in either objective or social knowledge, that the issue merits a political response. Thus an epistemic community of experts on Antarctic marine living resources, once it decides that an ecosystemic approach is the appropriate one for managing these resources, can affect management by creating a regime based on this approach. The success of the management effort, though, remains hostage to state interests. Epistemic communities differ from broader forms of social knowledge in that they are more able to affect the specific content of institutions, but less able to directly change states' perceptions of their own interests.

Thus each of these three epistemologies of international environmental politics helps to explain outcomes, but in different ways. Rationalist knowledge can lead to proximate changes in individual behavior, as actors take new data into account in calculating how best to achieve their interests. Changes in social knowledge affect both the ways in which problems are posed and the underlying interests that actors seek to fulfill. Finally, the creation of epistemic communities helps to define and shape the options that guide group behavior. Strategies of international environmental management that focus on the creation of knowledge can therefore be very effective even if they do not address the politics of the issues in question, by changing actors' perceptions of the costs and benefits of cooperation. None of the three approaches to knowledge, though, either individually or together, succeed in explaining the case studies in this volume without the intervening variable of international political processes in which states pursue their own perceived interests through the bargaining dynamics associated with common pool resources.

Interests

The final general category of factors affecting international cooperation on environmental issues is that of state interests. Rationalist analysis takes interests as given, and focuses instead on how various costs and benefits affect the policy preferences of actors trying to fulfill these interests. The hypotheses deduced in the introduction follow this pattern, looking at how common pool dynamics affect the strategies of states given a particular set of preferred outcomes. Even outside of the rationalist literature, there is often an implicit assumption that all people share an objective interest in environmental protection, though some people may not yet be aware of this interest. Yet too strict an adherence to the assumption that interests with respect to particular outcomes like environmental protection are fixed restricts our ability to understand the development of an underlying environmental consciousness that has helped to drive the increase in international environmental cooperation in the past two decades.

These sorts of changes in expressed national interests toward a greater environmental consciousness provide the background conditions for a number of the specific political interactions discussed in the case studies in this volume. For example, increased public interest in cetaceans as an existence amenity affected both the strategies for and the outcomes of environmental management in two of the cases, the treatment of whales in the Antarctic and the American attempt to protect dolphins from tuna fishers. In the former case, an agreement designed to manage whales as a resource evolved over time into an agreement that functioned mainly to prevent whaling altogether, a change that cannot be understood without allowing for an exogenous change in interest in whales from consumptive to existence amenities. In the latter, the rate of incidental kills of dolphins in the tuna fishery is not new knowledge, it has been common knowledge for decades. Recent active American attempts to reduce this rate reflect an exogenous increase in concern for dolphins as individuals. Finally, the history of negotiations toward the Montreal Protocol reflects a mixture of new knowledge and change in interests. Evidence of the effects of CFCs on the ozone layer has been around since the mid-1970s, yet until the mid-1980s many governments remained opposed to strong regulations on CFCs. True, levels of knowledge increased in the mid-1980s, but not by enough to explain the radical change in many expressed national interests.

Before proceeding, we must note again the difference between changes in behavior and changes in interest. Changes in behavior can result from the interaction of static interests with new information or with a changed strategic environment. For example, a consistent interest in a healthy ozone layer will lead to greater activity to protect the ozone layer the more information that is received on its depletion. A constant level of interest in dolphins as existence amenities will lead to different levels of action to protect them from tuna fishers depending on the level of threat to dolphins perceived, and on the extent to which actors expect that they can succeed in changing the behavior of tuna fishers. Changes in behavior resulting from the interaction of constant levels of interest with changing information, though, are different from changes in the interests themselves. For example, a change in the valuation of an environmental amenity from consumption to existence benefits can only be explained by a change in individual interests, a change in personal values. Changes in shadows of the future similarly can be the results of shifts in preferences rather than reactions to new information.

Changes in interest can thus have a real impact on international environmental cooperation, since they can cause major changes in behavior even without new information. From the point of view of the international environmental activist, the fact that interests can change without any necessary change in information can be used in two important ways. The first is by exploiting differences in expressed preferences between states as specific institutions and their populations. This can be thought of, to borrow a term from finance, as moral suasion. It can also be thought of as the power to embarrass, and the greater the difference in expressed preferences between government and populace, the greater is the potential for this sort of power. When the population of a country, or even a vocal minority of that population, is more interested in the management of an environmental amenity than its government, popular pressure can be used to change the bargaining position of that government. An outside actor, be it a state or nonstate actor, trying to encourage greater cooperation in the management of an international environmental issue, can do so by finding such differentials in interest and publicizing them, in an attempt to create just such pressure. The clearest example of this phenomenon in the case studies is the success by the Scandinavian countries in embarrassing some of the larger European states into more cooperative bargaining stances in negotiations under the auspices of the LRTAP convention. By counterbalancing the interests of acid-generating industries, this sort of moral suasion had the effect of changing the interests of the state actors as represented at the bargaining table. Our hypotheses focus on behavior at the state level; it is important to recognize, though, that the domestic processes that determine the interests that a state expresses are an important element of that behavior.

The second, and more fundamental, way in which environmentalists at the international level can make use of the fact that interests change is by actively trying to change them. This is often the primary function both of environmental NGOs and of many international organizations and agreements. The Rio Conference, for example, did not succeed in altering the strategic behavior of states in any substantial way. Whether or not it succeeded in changing the way in which people think about environmental management, and thus creating the groundwork for changing states' definitions of their own interests, is not yet known: only time will tell. The important factor to point out, though, is that this sort of consciousness-raising, of changing perceptions of self-interest, can be a very effective way of approaching international environmental problems, particularly for actors without the traditional power resources of international relations. By the same token, achieving these new objectives requires strategic interaction in the context of competition over common pool resources. Understanding the dynamics of this interaction requires that the factors discussed in this volume, such as shadows of the future, free riders, and power resources, be taken into account. There is a tendency, given the current methodological tensions in the field of international relations, for argument over which is the more important or more effective way of affecting behavior toward the international environment. This argument misses the point: both the process of creating interests and the processes of strategic state interaction are equally important, but simply discuss different aspects of the processes of international relations.

Directions for Further Research

This volume suggests two broad directions for future research. The first follows directly from what we have done here. The case studies strongly suggest that the dynamics of common-pool resource politics can help to explain much of what goes on in international environmental relations. Further research into these dynamics and their effects is therefore called for. Beyond the effects of common pool dynamics themselves, the second direction for future research involves the relationship between these dynamics and other factors affecting international environmental politics, such as those discussed above. This volume has focused on negotiations among states to create regimes to manage international environmental problems. All three of the categories of factors discussed above can affect such negotiations in ways that interrelate with but cannot be captured entirely by the formal rationalist approach underlying the analysis in most of this volume.

One particular way in which these factors can affect the outcomes of negotiations over the management of common pool resources is by altering the relative bargaining power and resources of states. The first two sets of hypotheses discussed in the introduction, those concerned with shadows of the future and free riders, suggest ways in which countries that care less about the conservation of environmental amenities can and do gain bargaining advantage over those that care more. The final hypothesis, about market power, identifies one way in which countries that care more can directly affect the value of the amenity in question, thereby gaining some bargaining advantage back. The factors discussed above suggest a number of other, potentially complementary sources of bargaining leverage that can be used to create more effective regimes for managing the environment internationally.

Barbara Connolly's chapter on the history of the regime to control acid rain in Europe suggests that the preemptive creation of institutions can be an effective source of bargaining leverage. The Scandinavian countries, those most interested in a strong management regime, created the LRTAP framework even though they knew that it could not be immediately effective. They then aggressively marketed the framework, helping to ensure that it, rather than a less demanding regime, would become the standard for managing the European acid rain problem. Their active involvement in creating and promoting the institution gave them a degree of leverage over outcomes that they would not otherwise have had.

Several of the chapters suggest that, in the context of international environmental politics, knowledge is indeed power. In particular, states without other sources of bargaining power can invest in the creation of new knowledge, in the hopes that this new knowledge will support the case for environmental management in a given issue area. The best example of this phenomenon in the cases is the use of the LRTAP convention by Scandinavian countries to generate the knowledge that in the end succeeded in creating broad European support for controls on acid rain emissions. The conscious use of knowledge creation and manipulation can thus be an effective source of bargaining power, not necessarily by specific countries as much as specific perspectives on environmental management. The interactions of the power to destroy and the power to know could well prove an interesting study.

Finally, the fact that interests in environmental management exist within as well as among countries can give actors what might simply be referred to as the power to embarrass. When a government's policy is less oriented to environmental management than much of its population would prefer, other actors can take advantage of this difference by advertising the policy to those who think it insufficient. For example, both the Scandinavian governments in the case of acid rain, and NGOs in the case of ozone-depleting substances, actively advertised their cause among Greens in Continental Europe, helping to embarrass the governments of the Continental European countries into a more environmentally friendly stance on the issues than they might otherwise have been disposed to.

Thus actors in international environmental politics have a number of resources that can be used to overcome the bargaining advantage of states with short shadows of the future in negotiating management regimes. These include market power, but also include the ability to manipulate institutional structures and resources, knowledge sources and evaluation, and differences in opinion on environmental management within individual states. Richard Matthew's chapter suggests that in certain sorts of situations traditional power resources, even military ones, might also be brought to bear in countering this bargaining advantage. Determining the relative effectiveness of different bargaining strategies, and the situations in which each might be most fruitful, would not only increase our theoretical understanding of international environmental politics, but would also provide invaluable policy advice to those engaged in creating international environmental regimes.

Notes

1. For a broader discussion of the effectiveness of positive incentive mechanisms in international environmental institutions, see Robert Keohane and Marc Levy, eds., *Institutions for Environmental Aid* (Cambridge, MA: MIT Press, 1996).

2. See, for example, Robert Keohane, *After Hegemony: Cooperation and Discord in the World Political Economy* (Princeton: Princeton University Press, 1984), pp. 102–3.

3. This is closely related to the phenomenon that Graham Allison calls "organizational imperialism," in *Essence of Decision: Explaining the Cuban Missile Crisis* (Boston: Little, Brown, 1971), p. 93. Allison defines the term as the propensity for organizations to define success in terms of the growth of their budgets, personnel, and responsibilities.

4. See, for example, Peter Haas, Robert Keohane, and Marc Levy, eds., *Institutions for the Earth: Sources of Effective International Environmental Protection* (Cambridge, MA: MIT Press, 1993). The preference in that volume seems to be for the term *information* rather than the term *knowledge*, suggesting an accumulation of objective facts rather than a social construct.

5. A good illustration of this approach in the literature on international environmental politics is Karen Litfin, *Ozone Discourses: Science and Politics in Global Environmental Cooperation* (New York: Columbia University Press, 1994). She defines her approach as discursive, but this definition fits neatly within the definition of constructivism used here.

6. The seminal work of this approach is Peter Haas, *Saving the Mediterranean: The Politics of International Environmental Cooperation* (New York: Columbia University Press, 1990).

7. Peter M. Haas, "Introduction: Epistemic Communities and International Policy Coordination." *International Organization* vol. 46 (1992), p. 3.

Contributors

J. Samuel Barkin is Assistant Professor of Political Science at the University of Florida. He has published research on international environmental politics, political economy, and international relations theory in *International Organization*, *Environmental Politics*, *Millennium*, and *German Politics and Society*.

Barbara Connolly is Assistant Professor of Political Science at Tufts University. Her main research and teaching interests are in international cooperation and international environmental politics. She has published several articles and chapters on environmental aid, especially related to nuclear reactor safety and to Eastern Europe, in Keohane and Levy, eds., *Institutions for Environmental Aid*, and in *Environment*.

Elizabeth R. DeSombre is Assistant Professor of Government and Environmental Studies at Colby College. She has published research on fishery and ocean issues, the Montreal Protocol Multilateral Fund, the use of sanctions and aid in international environmental politics, and the environmental impact of the international trading system.

David Leonard Downie is Director of Environmental Policy Studies at the School of International and Public Affairs and Assistant Professor of Political Science and International Affairs at Columbia University. His research and teaching interests focus on environmental politics and international relations, with particular emphasis on the creation, operation, impact, and content of effective international environmental institutions.

Christopher C. Joyner is Professor of International Law in the Department of Government at Georgetown University. He has published extensively on law and politics of the polar south. Recent books include *Antarctica and the Law of the Sea, Eagle over the Ice: The US in the Antarctic*, and *Governing the Frozen Commons: Environmental Protection in the Antarctic*.

Richard A. Matthew is Assistant Professor of International and Environmental Politics in the School of Social Ecology at the University of California at Irvine. He has published numerous articles on environmental issues, ethics in international affairs, and international organization. Forthcoming works include an edited volume entitled *Common Grounds: Security and Conflict in the New Environmental Politics* and *Shared Fate: Ethics, World Politics and Environmentalism*.

Ronald Mitchell is Assistant Professor of Political Science at the University of Oregon. His book *Intentional Oil Pollution at Sea: Environmental Policy and Treaty Compliance* received the Harold and Margaret Sprout Award for 1995 from the International Studies Association for the best book on international environmental issues. He has published articles in *International Organization, Journal of Theoretical Politics, International Studies Quarterly* and *Journal of Environment and Development*.

George E. Shambaugh IV is Assistant Professor of International Affairs and Government at Georgetown University. He is the author of *States, Firms, and Power: Successful Sanctions in US Foreign Policy*, as well as articles, books chapters, and professional papers on international politics, economic statecraft, and the environment.

Index